AMDO

Tso Ngonpo
(Lake Kokonor)

■ Taktser

CHINA

Drichu (Yang

Zachu (Me

Marchu

Pelbar
■

Shothalh

Kongpo
Nyingtri
■

Brahm

Sorrow Mountain

Also by Adelaide Donnelley

Boundary Water

Sorrow Mountain

The Journey of a Tibetan Warrior Nun

Ani Pachen &
Adelaide Donnelley

KODANSHA INTERNATIONAL
New York • Tokyo • London

Kodansha America, Inc.
575 Lexington Avenue, New York, New York 10022, U.S.A.

Kodansha International Ltd.
17-14 Otowa 1-chome, Bunkyo-ku, Tokyo 112-8652, Japan

Published in 2000 by Kodansha America, Inc.

Library of Congress Cataloging-in-Publication Data

Pachen, Ani, 1933–
    Sorrow mountain; the journey of a Tibetan warrior nun/by Ani Pachen, Adelaide
    Donnelley.
        p. cm.
    ISBN 1-56836-294-3
    1. Pachen, Ani, 1933– 2. Political prisoners—China—Tibet—Biography.
3. Buddhist nuns—China—Tibet—Biography. I. Donnelley, Adelaide, 1941–
II. Title.

DS786.P24 2000
951'.5042'092—dc21
[B]   99-046761

Book design by Deirdre C. Amthor

Manufactured in the United States of America on acid-free paper

00 01 02 03 04   RRD/H   10 9 8 7 6 5 4 3 2 1

Contents

Foreword

THE DALAI LAMA

With the communist Chinese takeover of Tibet, everything changed. Our ancient peaceful way of life was turned upside down. Nothing was left unscathed. Not only have the Tibetan people been brutalized in almost every way possible, even the wild animals, the land, the trees, the lakes and rivers have been made to suffer. Even though many Tibetans today agree that change and development in Tibet was long overdue, it is difficult to understand how the Chinese thought they could do this in such a rough, cruel, and inconsiderate way.

In recounting the events of her life here, Ani Pachen tells a story that is typical of Tibet over the last fifty years. The final years of freedom reveal a simple, contented way of life. Her family, like so many others, was guided by values strongly influenced by the Buddha's teachings of compassion, interdependence, and an awareness that nothing lasts forever. Ani Pachen's father, a Khampa chieftain, clearly commanded respect more for his sense of justice and responsibility than for his mere position. Compared with what was to come, in those days of contentment we Tibetans were truly wealthy.

As this story shows, the people of Kham and eastern Tibet were the first to bear the brunt of the creeping Chinese brutality. In the face of ruthless and overwhelming force, even these strong and fiercely proud people were dismayed. Their struggle to defend their country, religion, and culture was met with a crushing response. No family was untouched by suffering and loss.

Ani Pachen herself, like so many Tibetans in this period, was imprisoned for more than twenty years in conditions of unspeakable harshness. And for what? Because she refused to bend to the Chinese will. There are few, if any, countries elsewhere in the world where criminals are subjected to such treatment.

What shines through this otherwise sorry and moving tale are Ani Pachen's unflinching patriotism, her active concern for her fellow countrymen and -women, and her deep-seated desire to retire into solitude to pursue the spiritual life. It is the kind of strength and resilience she embodies that gives me grounds for optimism that ultimately the truth and justice of our cause will triumph.

 Preface

It is now a half century since the Chinese invaded and raped Tibet; forty years since His Holiness the Dalai Lama escaped into exile; ten years since His Holiness won the Nobel Prize for peace. And still the Tibetan tragedy continues.

Not unlike those of the Jewish Holocaust, the Tibetan stories of mindless cruelty, betrayal, loss, and quiet tenderness continue to be told. Need to be told.

There is an old saying that God created man because He loves stories. Herein is one of His most extraordinary ones. It is the true story of a very special princess in a remote area of Tibet whose happiness would abruptly end one day and who would enter decades of darkness, to survive only by the remembered words of her kind teachers: that she is in truth a being of light, and that light is eternally clear and bright.

It is a beautiful, disturbing, and deeply inspiring story, and although it is wildly fantastic, it is not unique in this troubled period of Tibetan history. The long and continuing Chinese occupation of Tibet provides a limitless source of Tibetan tragedy and survival.

Upper Dharamsala is a small hill station village in northern India, an overnight train ride toward the Himalayas from New Delhi, and not far from the Tibetan border farther to the north.

Since 1959 it has been the home of His Holiness the Dalai Lama, the Tibetan government-in-exile and now about fifteen thousand Tibetans, and a handful but growing number of Westerners. It is the heartbeat of the Tibetan cause, and the center of all cultural, religious, and political activities on the Tibetans' behalf.

It is all there because the Dalai Lama is there. He is the center of the Tibetan universe. He is the *axis mundi*. He is the living Mount Meru. He is the sun itself.

During a break from His Holiness's spring teachings a few years ago, I ran into an old Tibetan friend I hadn't seen in some time. He was now editing *Amnye Machen,* a Tibetan literary publication that was breaking new creative territory for Tibetan thinkers, writers, and poets. We talked about their projects for a while with great enthusiasm, and I found myself asking why no serious "literature" that I was aware of had emerged from the Tibetan holocaust. Important religious, philosophical, and ecstatically visionary works to be sure, but no secular narrative works, no great Tibetan novel. I was curious and sad as to why Tibetan writers had been unable thus far to express that side of themselves to themselves—and to the rest of the world—in a book that could be embraced solely on its creative merits, if need be. We agreed a book of this nature would be an enormous help to the Tibetan cause.

My friend suggested a Tibetan nun named Ani Pachen as a strong subject for a potential book. She was a warrior princess from the Kham region who became a leader of the resistance, was captured, tortured, and imprisoned by the Chinese for twenty-one years. She escaped to India, had taken vows as a Buddhist nun, and by chance was living in a nunnery nearby.

Intrigued, I entered the nunnery gate from the busy market streets of McCleod Ganj and was led to her small room. She met me at the door with the generous smile of a serious meditator and the challenging gaze of one who had survived a life too hard lived, beaten but never defeated, an extremely formidable woman. I liked her immediately. That was the beginning of this book.

I thought it might be necessary for a Western writer to become involved, and with wonderful drunk luck we found Daidie Donnelley, who enthusiastically took on the project. She soon became Ani-la's friend, confidante, and co-conspirator. Her writing is a miracle of truth. Daidie has written Ani-la's tale with an almost storybook simplicity that is quietly devastating in its emotional and poetic force—like Ani Pachen herself.

May this book help to dispel the darkness of this darkest night of Tibetan history and be of benefit to all beings everywhere. May the hearts of our Chinese brothers and sisters be opened and may they quickly come to their senses.

Richard Gere
July, 1999

Sorrow Mountain

In the ancient time of King Gesar, Tibet was a place of the gods. But during the reign of the Fifth Dalai Lama, the area stretching from the western region known for its nutmeg trees to the eastern region known for brocade was brought under the administration of the Tibetan government. Since that time, a succession of lay and monk district officials carried out the land's administration in accordance with the Buddhist principles of compassion and justice.

In those days it was customary to have chieftains looking after the welfare of the region's communities. All were men of virtue, honest and widely learned. Skilled in the affairs of their community and courageous in subduing their enemies, their task was to increase their people's prosperity and guard it from mishap. They ruled by the teachings of Buddha, taking affectionate care of their subjects. Under their rule, the land prospered and there was great happiness.

As the years passed, Tibet divided into three provinces: U-Tsang, the province of religion to the west; Amdo, the province of superb horses to the north; and Kham, the province of the black-headed people to the east.

In Kham, settlements in the district of Gonjo developed around the banks of two rivers: the Marchu, flowing from the south toward the west, and the Rechu, flowing from west to east. Both of these rivers had nomad settlements in the highlands and agricultural settlements in the valleys.

In the course of time, hermitages and monasteries were built in silent and solitary places in the foothills of the nearby mountains. They were a source of life. Like the relation of moon and ocean, those connected by karma and prayer were always in harmony.

Prologue

There is a day, one day each year, when light from the rising sun strikes the peak of my childhood monastery in such a way that it looks, for a moment, as if it were lit from within. The very tip of its cone-shaped stupa glows like a torch in the sky. In those few moments, it shines with such radiance that everything stops to pay homage: the winds through the valley die down, the birds cease their song, and the families beginning to work in the fields fall silent. It lasts for only the blink of an eye, then it's gone. But its light, shining so pure, so bright, has stayed with me all these years.

My name is Lemdha Pachen, chieftainess of Lemdha. I was born in 1933, the female Water-Bird Year. Since birth I have lived many lives: lives of privilege and happiness, lives of sorrow and loss. My lamas taught that nothing in this world is permanent. I have seen their teachings come true.

My country was once at the roof of the world, a place where the great spirits lived. Its vast open spaces stretched as far as the eye could see. Wide pastures lay like a blanket of green on the valley floor; crops of wheat, barley, mustard grew in abundance.

Now the forests are gone, the animals killed, and the great teachings scattered to the winds. Once I lived in a house four stories high, but today my room is like the size of my palm. There are days when my stomach aches from the long years in prison, and I lie on my bed in the dark. Holding my Mani beads tight in my hands, I recite from the sacred texts as I did in those times.

And at night, when the wind comes over the top of the nearby hills, there are times when I think I hear the sound of my mother's voice. Later, in the stillness, it slips away, but I answer just the same. It's all right, I say, don't worry. After twenty-one years I am finally free. I'm in India now, near our beloved leader, His Holiness the Dalai Lama. My prayers are answered, I am blessed.

1
Dharamsala

I hear footsteps on the cement floor outside my room. Someone is coming down the walk. Tat-tat, tat-tat. Getting closer.

I see a shadow outside the door. Om Mani Peme Hum. I tighten my stomach against what is to come.

"Lemdha Pachen," a voice calls out. The door swings open.

In the familiar room of ropes, bamboo rods, and iron pails, of bloodied walls and urine-stained floors, they tie my hands behind my back. They hoist me up by my wrists. Once again flame shoots through my shoulder, bile fills my mouth.

I swing, senseless, and the room fades into darkness.

I awake out of breath. Tat-tat-tat. Tat-tat.

Someone is knocking on the door to my room.

I tighten my stomach and wait.

Tat-tat-tat. Tat-tat.

I shrink toward the wall.

"Pachen . . . Ani Pachen . . . are you there?"

I turn my head to listen.

"Ani Pachen-la . . ."

Blessed Jewels, it is Dechen, the nun from next door. I sink back onto my pillow.

I'm in Dharamsala, I remember with relief.

"Ani-la . . ." Dechen's voice is urgent.

"Lo . . . ," I call out. My skin sticks to the bedding as I turn. "What is it?"

"He is coming, Ani-la. . . . He is coming today."

"Today?"

"Yes."

"Praise to the Three Jewels."

"No need to get up," she whispers, "there is time yet."

"Ah lay."

He is coming home at last! My heart speeds up, blending with the tapping of rain on the tin roof above.

I turn and stare at the wall. In places where the graying paint has chipped and fallen away, the plaster is crumbling and worn.

Small beads of moisture rise up through a crack like liquid in an
open wound. My eyes follow the crack to the ceiling where it joins
a welter of lines crossing one over another like scars left by bamboo
rods. In the corner, a dark shape clings to the wall, its legs bent, its
body glistening. I pull the covers over my head. I try not to move.

"*Om Mani Peme Hum.*" So many things in India are still difficult
to accept. Rains beat down day after day, mud grabs hold of my feet,
thick, hot air leaves me gasping for breath, and spiders . . . I cringe as
I think of the creature over my head.

Mama was afraid of spiders. "A spider!" I cried out one day, and
she ran screaming into the house. "I'm only teasing," I called after
her. I couldn't stop laughing, but she wouldn't come out.

Mama. Her face spins slowly around.

In a darkened corner of my mind, a small patch of green appears. I
watch it grow brighter, larger, until a vast green meadow stretches
out at my feet. The meadow is dotted with clusters of flowers and is
treeless, except for a willow or two. To one side, a river winds quietly through; on its bank is a village.

At the far end a house rises taller than the rest. An old house, like
a fortress, whitewashed. On its eastern wall, above slits that once
served as lookouts, there are places where red soil shows through,
gashes from long ago, scars of an ancient attack. And at each corner
of the roof, prayer flags stand like spirit sentinals. Their long, silent
shapes wave slowly in the breeze, unfurling prayers on the breath of
the wind.

Below, to the side of the house, a small group of people sits in the
morning sun. Steam curls from pots of tea at their feet and glistens as
it catches the light. On a bench an old woman with a child in her lap
makes tsampa.

*Folded into my Anya's soft lap, between her large strong arms, I
watch her twisted fingers mixing tea and flour in a small earthen
dish. In a circular motion she scoops it away from the side of the*

dish and squeezes it between her fingers. Scooping, squeezing the
warm, moist dough, she kneads my morning tsampa. Behind her a
fire is crackling, and the smell of hot milk is sweet in the air.

The room begins to lighten. The posters I've hung to cover the cracks
on the walls regain their color. The small yellow bird on the garden
poster emerges from out of the dark green branches. The letters
m-o-t-h-e-r-I-l-o-v-e-y-o-u on the American poster become clear.

He is coming today! I remember and get out of bed.

I straighten my yellow undershirt, wrap an orange underskirt
around my waist, and climb onto the end of my bed, my legs crossed
under me. I take up my Mani beads and begin my morning prayer.

> *Homage to the Buddha, the Dharma, the Sangha,*
> *In whom I take refuge.*
> *May I achieve Buddhahood so I can benefit all living beings.*

On the altar above my bed, pictures of His Holiness the Dalai Lama,
the Lord Buddha, and Padmasambhava sit in a row. I stand and bow
to each. *"Let the essence of your teachings be expressed in my mind,*
my speech, my body."

I raise my hands above my head, kneel until my head touches the
floor, and prostrate three times in front of the altar. *"May the source*
of happiness and well-being be experienced by all."

Six metal bowls on the altar are still filled with yesterday's water. I
empty them into a pitcher and take it outside to pour on a bush at
the bottom of the stairs, chanting, *"This ground anointed with in-*
cense and strewn with flowers . . ." Farther down the path, in a darkened room, I fill the pitcher, *". . . adorned with Mount Kailash, the*
four continents, the sun and moon . . ."

And back in the room, refilling each bowl, *". . . may all beings be*
blessed."

I continue my morning tasks, my tea, my tsampa, and later the
dough for my bread, which I fry in the skillet over my old rusted

burner. Every day the same. Predictable. Known. Small comforts, after years of uncertainity.

"Ani-la! People are gathering! He will soon be here!"
"Ah-lay!"
I leap up and open the trunk at the foot of my bed. A rush of cool air pours out, carrying smells of damp wool, aging silk, sheep skin, incense, tarnished silver. I run my fingers lovingly over the clothes at the top. My only possessions.

I take out a yellow silk blouse, put it under my long brown dress, my chupa, with a pouch of blessed seeds around my neck. Though the day is hot, I pull on a pair of white socks banded in red. "Those are socks for sportsmen," an American tourist once told me. "What does it matter," I said, "they cover my feet."

About to go out, I take an umbrella off the hook in my closet, just in case. And a small tan hat for the sun.

A mirror, set on the table by my bed, catches my reflection as I pass by. For a minute my stomach turns over. In the faded glass, I see a parched landscape. Deep furrows, crisscrossing lines, spreading brown spots, like earth dried out by the summer sun. I pull the skin taut at the corners of my eyes and squint, trying to see some sign of the face that was once there.

"You are my beautiful girl," my father says, stroking my forehead. "The most beautiful girl in Kham." I rest my head on his shoulder and smile.

The foreigners bring me pictures. "There!" they say. "Aren't you beautiful!" "Beautiful?" I say. "All I see is a face full of wrinkles." I wrinkle my face even more, to quiet them.

"Beauty!" I think to myself. What do they know?

I feel a heat rising in my chest and I take my Mani beads from my neck.

"To give protection against anger, practice tolerance and patience . . ." the words of my lama come to my mind . . . *"Develop acceptance of all situations, all people, without judgment, experience them free from limiting thoughts."*

My mind softens, but the heat in my chest remains, its sharp little fingers pull at my heart. *Om Mani Peme Hum,* I say to myself. Forgive my thoughts. Especially today.

A rush of hot air hits me on the landing outside my room. I take a key out of my pouch and lock the door. It gives me a feeling of happiness to watch its dull metal shape turn in the lock. Even after so many years in Dharamsala, my heart still leaps as I turn it myself. I am free, I think. My beauty has faded, my youth has gone. But I'm free.

At the end of the path there is much commotion. A long-horned cow runs wildly through the street. On either side the vendors shout in Hindi, *"Bago, bago! Chalo!"* A stream of children follows behind, throwing stones, laughing, calling. Mud, fruit, vegetables fly in all directions. After they pass, I step over a stream of water still flowing from last night's rain and walk quickly into the street.

The road to the nunnery is lined with Hindu merchants. I lift my chupa, stepping carefully through the darkened slime at my feet, between the faded mats of fruits and vegetables, until I see my favorite vendor, a one-eyed man with a lilting voice. He is crouched, as he always is, behind a high stack of fruit.

I point to a cluster of apples. He nods his head back and forth in a snakelike motion as I take several in my hand, turning each over and over. This one, this, and this, I will take these. Gifts for *him.*

I give the merchant one coin. More, he starts to protest, but I shake my head, and tuck the fruit in my chupa and walk on. The street is full of vendors, beggars, nuns, monks, schoolchildren, foreign tourists. I make my way through the crowded street, bowing here and there to people I know. I tousle the hair of two children and run ahead as they chase me. At the end of a row of buildings I turn onto the main road.

Already people are gathering at either side of the road. Women in bright colored chupas. Men in billowing white shirts. Some crouch down, fingering their Mani beads, some hold sticks of incense, others pile boughs of juniper over earthen pots, preparing to light them. A group of young nuns run ahead of me, carrying yellow silk banners and baskets of flowers. The road, where paved, is covered with large white chalk letters, and overhead prayer flags stretch across on poles and trees.

A half-mile down at the gate to the main temple, monks are wrapping pillars at either side with colored brocades. They set a table with vases of flowers and fruit. Great urns to the side have begun to billow with smoke.

"Ani-la." Someone is calling my name. I turn and see Yeshe Dhonden, an old monk, beckoning to me from the side of the road.

"Tashi Delek, Ani-la."

"Tashi Delek, Yeshe Dhonden."

For a moment our eyes lock. Looking into his dimming eyes, past the faded white at their rim, past the drooping lids, past the thin lines of sorrow beneath, I see the eyes of a young man. Clear. Proud.

I see him bend from his galloping horse to pick up a scarf on the ground and raise it with pride high over his head. I see him ride at the head of a long line of men, leading them into the hills. I see him enter the Great Hall at Chamdo, a Chinese soldier at his side, a gun pressed deep in his ribs. And in his eyes, furthest back past their faded lens, I see his body lying limp on a concrete floor, curled in on itself.

In those few seconds, each of our stories, the stories of our people, pass between us, as swiftly as wind through trees. There is no need to say more. He points to a space by his side. Silently I take it and crouch down on my heels.

"It won't be long now," a woman to my right whispers. I touch my chupa to be sure the scarf and incense are still there, then settle back against the hill to wait.

People pass by. Several men and women stop to talk. A young Tibetan man in Western clothes, a pressed white shirt, gray wool pants, shiny black shoes, walks quickly from the gate of the temple up the road, motioning people to either side. A murmur runs up and down each side. Far in the valley below, I hear the honking of horns. People fall silent, straining to hear.

The honking stops and for moments it is silent. A hawk flies above, circling the smoking urn. Far beyond, dark clouds move slowly over the high mountaintops, a gathering storm.

I shift uneasily from foot to foot. An old woman darts across the road. The young man in Western clothes walks briskly back toward the gate. Monks and nuns have gathered at either side. They stand, adjusting their robes, whispering to one another.

Thick blue smoke rises up from juniper boughs burning along the side of the road. A stick of incense is lit and passed through the crowd. Soon hundreds of fine thin plumes rise toward the sky.

Suddenly, as if out of nowhere, a car appears at the top of the hill, moving slowly down the road. It is large, tan, rounded on top, worn. On either side, above the outside mirrors, two small Tibetan flags are fluttering. Silently it advances, as people at each edge of the road bend down. As it draws closer, my heart begins to pound, my breath catches in my throat.

Slowly, inch by inch, as if crossing centuries of time, the car moves toward me. I lean forward, straining to see. The boughs of the overhanging trees cast shadows on the windshield. Through the shifting reflections I think I see the forms of two men, the one on the right closest to me bent slightly forward. Reflections of clouds, of birds, of sky slide toward me, as if carried on a golden throne moving silently closer.

Two people away. One. Now right in front. A shiver runs through me, as it does each time. There before me, looking directly at me, with an expression of indescribable compassion, His Holiness, Gyalwa Rinpoche, Jenzin Gyatso, Ocean of Wisdom—the Fourteenth Dalai Lama. My beloved master.

He raises his hand in a gesture of greeting, and in less than a breath passes by and is gone. The monks and nuns at the gate bow as his car enters the temple grounds. A caravan of cars, jeeps, trucks rush after. Men with radio phones, women in Western dress, monks, their robes flapping as the trucks sweep by.

In a few minutes it is over, like the storms that come out of nowhere and are gone. The brocade on the pillars comes down, the table with fruit taken away, and having welcomed him home, the crowd starts up the hill. Tomorrow they will return for his teachings.

I walk for a time with Tashi Norbu from Gonjo and Thinley Tashi from Kanze. They too are in Dharamsala near His Holiness, with thousands of Tibetans who fled the Chinese. We walk together in silence, but after a while I fall behind, lost in thought.

His Holiness's face is still before me. Whenever I see it, my sadness disappears, the loneliness and longing from so many years falls away. His face, like a radiant sun, has burned through the darkness. With his guidance, after so many years, I am finally free.

"You have seen Tibet's tragedy," he once said. *"You have lived its suffering. You must tell your story so others will know."*

2

Narrow Escape

In 1950, the Year of the Iron Tiger, my parents arranged to give me in marriage to the son of the chieftain of Markham. It was the sixth month of my seventeenth year. Our country was still at peace, though on the eastern bank of the Yangtze River Chinese troops were gathering. In a few short years, they would sweep over my country, changing it forever. In the name of liberating Tibet from "imperialist powers," they would destroy monasteries, plunder homes, burn sacred texts, and drive our people to poverty and despair. But at that particular time, late in the summer, Tibet was still free, and I was lost in concerns of my own.

All night I lay listening to the winds blow in from the west, howling against the shutters, hissing and whistling under the large wooden door. Each year they came at the turn of the season when the flowers had gone from the fields, and for days they blew. Down from the hills, bending tall grasses, churning the river, gusting up the road through our village until they reached our house at its eastern end. Starting high in the mountains at the edge of our country, they tumbled east across the great U-Tsang plain into our province of Kham. Some said they were winds of change.

Lying beside me, Mama slept soundly. Every so often she sighed, a shudder running through her slight body, as it does sometimes at the end of the day. Once she even fluttered like a small bird caught in a bush, and I moved toward her, raising the sheepskin over her shoulders, smoothing the hair from her face. In the dimming light her face was clear like a child's, though under her eyes fine lines ran down like tears.

Since marrying one of nine chieftains of Gonjo, her life had been weighted with duties. Laundry to be done in the river. Long hours cooking over a wood-burning stove. The supervision of servants. Attending to guests. It never stopped. All day people came to our house with disputes for their chieftain to settle. All day we heard their plodding steps on the stairs to his courtroom, heard their angry voices drifting down from the story above. Often they stayed for dinner, as many as a hundred extra people for my mother to feed.

Some said that my father's wealth and servants freed her, but in truth they only added to the burden. The more possessions there were, the more work was needed to care for them. It was an unending cycle.

Unable to sleep, I lay watching shadows from the dying fire slide along the wooden beams above my head. For moments I thought I heard the whisper of guests on the hiss of the wind. I looked, but the carpeted mattresses at the side of the room were empty and the small wooden tables had been cleared of the evening's meal by our servants.

Emptied of its human inhabitants, the great hall began to breathe its own lonely sounds. Doors creaked on their large metal hinges. Ghostly footsteps shuffled across the rough wooden floor. Whispers drifted down from the dark slippery stairway—voices from other times.

Generations of my family had been born here, generations had died. Sometimes I felt their presence in the darkened corridors between rooms: a cool breath on my shoulder; a flash of light in a windowless room; a door slipped open, a curtain pulled back, but no one was there.

Once on the fourth floor outside our chapel, I heard the voice of my great-aunt Kunsang chanting in low, windless tones. She was just my age when she died, and had already exhibited exceptional powers. It was said that on auspicious days, she locked herself in her room and had visions of letters. Large, curling, round shapes in the air above her head. The letters so filled her eyes that unless she wrote them down, she could see nothing else. I remember seeing several lines of them when I was young, but they made no sense. The Rinpoches, the reincarnate lamas, were the only ones who could decipher them, for they were the language of the deities.

As I lay trying to fall asleep in my mother's bed at the end of the kitchen, I imagined I saw them again in the shadows on the wall beside our bed. I shivered and drew closer to my mother.

*   *   *

Crack! The window blew shut. Or was it a gun? I turned to listen.

Far down the hallway I heard footsteps coming in our direction, growing louder. They stopped at the door. In the doorway I saw a dark form.

"Who is it?" I whispered.

For a moment the figure stood still. Then it stepped into the room. I curled against Mama as it moved toward the stove. The light from the dying embers cast light on the shape bending over. Tashi! Our old trusted servant. He poured tea from the pot on the stove into a cup, then left, limping out the door. I turned back toward the wall.

As the embers in the fireplace grew fainter, the shadows gradually faded and my attention returned to my own troubled thoughts. All evening I had been uneasy, like a boat on smooth waters being pulled toward a sudden drop in the land. A feeling of dread curled around me, at any moment my life might turn upside down.

In the quiet of the morning I prayed.

Blessed Guru Rinpoche, I am never far from your boundless compassion. Guide helpless beings, surround them with love.

The light from the butter lamps cast a ripple of gold across the statue of Padmasambhava. The chapel was still, the only sound the turning of the giant prayer wheel on the landing below.

Alone, my heart began its silent glide through space. In that stillness my spirit returned.

"We are as free as birds," Lhamo said, resting her head against mine, her arms outstretched. "Like when we were children."

We were high in the hills, looking out over the valley below. That morning after praying I'd met her at a bend in the river and we climbed to a place above Lemdha. From there, the town's fifty houses looked like stones scattered over a meadow.

After settling, we opened our picnic and spooned curd into small wooden bowls. Leaning back to back we savored its sticky, sweet taste in our mouths. Lhamo's back against mine felt reassuring, like when we were children free of concerns.

In those early years, we built houses of stone by the river, made dolls out of clay from its banks. We made yak-hair wigs, pebble jewelry, even drums like those used by the nuns. In the winters we skated on the river's frozen surface; in the summers we camped with our families near its edge. Now, having just finished school and not yet started families, our days were our own.

We rested peacefully against each other, gazing out over the surrounding expanse. Below us a thin silver ribbon glistened in the midday light. The day was tranquil, but at its edges an air of expectancy hung like a lengthening cloud.

"Free as birds," Lhamo repeated. "But how long will it last?"

Returning home, I pushed open the huge wooden gate at the entrance to the house and ran down several large stone steps to the barn on the first floor. When I reached the darkest corner in the back, near the stairway that led up to the kitchen, I walked softly by the small room for Lu, the demigod who guarded our house. Knowing he could become dangerous when angered, I kept a respectful distance. Once when I was younger, I thought I saw his human head and serpent body swimming close to shore in a nearby lake. Since that time, on auspicious days I took care to leave nuts and cheese outside the door to his room.

I ran up the steep steps to the second floor and stopped at the landing, out of breath. I felt a tug at bottom of my chupa and looked down. Dolma! My little white terrier, my hem in her teeth.

I bent over and picked her up. "Ferocious leopard!" I whispered, rubbing my nose in her soft white fur, "were you trying to eat me?"

I was about to open the door when I heard my father's voice. Something about it was different. Severe. I suddenly felt afraid, like at the beginning of a storm when without any warning there's a shift in the weather and the landscape becomes dark, unfamiliar. "Shh!" I put my hand over Dolma's mouth and leaned closer. Through the planks of the heavy wooden door I heard his muffled words.

"It's for her own good . . ." His voice was sharp. "When I'm no longer here she will need help governing our district of Gonjo. Rushok Pontsang has offered one of his three sons in marriage. I've accepted his offer and divided the wealth. Everything is finished. We have only to prepare the wine and consult the astrological chart for an auspicious day. The rest is done."

I pressed my ear to the door, scarcely believing what I'd heard.

"In time," he said with a particular insistence, "she will come to see it is for her own good."

I hugged Dolma closer and leaned against the doorway, confused by his tone.

I closed my eyes. In my mind I saw a great expanse of smile spreading over his ruddy face, I felt him lift me into his arms and stroke the top of my head. "You are our only child," he'd say, stopping whatever he was doing and patting my hand. "You are very precious."

"When will you tell her?" I heard my mother's anxious voice. I opened my eyes. Through a crack in the door I saw her straightening herself to her full height to meet his gaze, but he loomed far above, dwarfing her tiny body more like a father than a husband.

My father's mouth stretched across his face like a scar, purple and tight. His words were clipped. "They are coming next week. Not until then."

The grain of the wooden door began to weave, and I suddenly felt weak. Dolma squirmed out of my arms. I covered my ears and ran down the steps, up through the gate, and down the path toward the river Marchu.

Dolma came running behind. "Go home, go home." I waved her away, but she wouldn't turn back.

As I ran, I tried to think, but my mind felt frozen. Several times my foot caught on a rock in the path and I stumbled. Tears stung my eyes.

They've never done anything without asking me, now they're treating me like a possession to be traded at whim, sending me to a faraway town to live with a stranger. Images beat through my head. Children tugging at their mother's hems, women bent over their stoves, a stranger carrying me off to his bed. "No, no!" I felt desperate.

*   *   *

When I reached the river, I lay down on the large warm stones at its grassy edge and cried. My head was aching, my thoughts pulled in different directions. Papa wanted assurance his tribe was secure, Mama wanted grandchildren. I couldn't let them down. But the thought of losing my freedom gave me such a sinking feeling, I could barely breathe. I'll marry and make them happy. I'll refuse and devote my life to prayer. No matter which, the decision felt wrong.

Dolma crawled up beside me. I pulled her warm little body to me and we curled up together. I don't want children! I whispered, I don't want to feed endless mouths or be imprisoned by others' demands. Dolma licked the tears from my face; her soft tongue on my cheek only made me cry more.

I don't know how long I lay there, but after a time my breath came back, my mind grew clearer, I knew what to do. I will refuse to marry. The thought had a calming effect on me. The warmth of the stones on my cheek was soothing, and I lay with my arms around Dolma watching the river flow by.

The water was clear, and in places where the rocks stuck up the current turned back on itself and around. At times it looked like curling writing from the sacred texts, at other times like the faces of deities. Every so often by the banks where the water ran darker and still the silver fins of a fish appeared, glinting for moments, then sinking down again in the dark.

The sun was warm, the air soft on my face. In the fields across the water I could hear the hum of honey bees winding their way among the rows of barley.

My mind drifted to the monastery. Often on days like today I went there in search of peace. Climbing the narrow path and passing through its thick, cool walls, I entered a timeless world. There, in its temple with statues of the Buddha , I took refuge from the tensions of daily life.

In its darkened hall, light from butter lamps on the altar flickered across each golden face, showing expressions of such wisdom and compassion that I longed to remain in their presence. The soft rounded curve of each eyebrow, the clear eyes looking down, the full red lips slightly parted, filled me with peace.

In the silence of that darkened room and the ever-changing light from the lamps, I was reminded of my lama's teaching: *"The nature of mind is clear light, and our experience in the world only passing waves on its surface."*

I lay by the river until evening, alternating between feelings of peace and despair. The words of my father's sister, my beloved Ani Rigzin, ran through my head. *"Marriage is suffering. Once one is wed there is no turning back. The path is full of sorrow."*

My mother had taken that path. One day she had come home from playing in the fields to find people gathered in front of her house: her future husband's family, come to take her away. The next day, her family and a hundred of their men escorted her to the border, leaving her only a bridesmaid and a young boy to help. The day she arrived at my father's family, she was married. I have had other friends who tried to fight being taken, but to no avail. The marriages always took place.

I stayed by the river until dark. At night when I finally slipped into Mama's bed in a corner of the kitchen, I prayed to Lord Buddha to protect me. Unable to sleep, I listened to Mama cleaning up from the day and was awake when she slid in beside me. The smoke-filled scent of her skin, so familiar and often so comforting, offered no relief.

I lay still until her breath was even. Turning over, I looked at her face. Her mouth was curved like a baby's, partly open, her chin tiny and sharp. I felt an urge to protect her. At the same time I felt myself pulling away.

"Such big eyes," Mama said, teasing me, *"they can only stare."* I looked down at my plate.

"Ashe's a quiet one," Mama's friend said. *"Always apart."*

"Leave her alone." Ani Rigzin put down her cup and reached over to take my hand. *"She is shy."*

"Always apart." I lay awake, my thoughts in turmoil. I felt a loneliness I couldn't shake. Always apart. My mind drifted.

I thought of a bend in the river, where the water ran silent. I went there often before dawn. I would walk out onto the marshy shore, press my toes in the mud. I'd watch the sun streak the valley with gold; listen to dove calls; hawk cries.

There was always a pull at those times, a sliver of feeling, a sensation too fleeting to voice. Like a dream in the night. A calling.

The wind rose up into long high whistles, it dropped low like the chanting of monks far away. *Marriage is suffering,* it seemed to say. It moaned, it sighed. *"Once one is wed there is no turning back."* The voice of Ani Rigzin hissed in my ear.

Ani Rigzin. Her old bent shape moved slowly through the shadows, her bright eyes floated over my head. Come, she whispered, I will help you. Her crooked hand beckoned, come today.

Yes, I whispered, that's what to do. I'll ask Ani Rigzin.

As the room began to lighten, Mama turned over beside me. Thinking I was still asleep, she moved to the edge of the bed and slipped quietly out with no more noise than a spirit slipping through ether. I watched as her small stooped shape faded away from me into the darkness, and felt a tugging at my heart as if it were attached to hers.

I watched through partly closed eyes as she put on her heavy black chupa, tying the apron of a married woman around her waist. Quickly braiding her hair, she walked to the fire. She took dung from a metal container at one side and flung it onto the smoldering embers. In a few moments it burst into flame. Lifting a large metal pot from the shelf, she filled it with water and placed it over the flames. When she saw it was heating, she turned and disappeared up the stairs to our chapel.

I listened as her footsteps grew fainter. After I was certain she'd gone, I got out of bed. The floor was cold on my feet and I quickly put on my boots. I pulled my brown brocade chupa around me, took a sheepskin from the shelf by the bed and filled it with tea and tsampa, a fox-skin hat, my prayer beads, and one of my religious texts. I strapped a small gold charm box across my chest and fastened a knife to the silver flower belt around my waist. The room was becoming light. I had to move quickly.

As I walked across the floor the old boards groaned under my feet, and with each step I was afraid Mama would hear and come down. I tiptoed past Dolma asleep by the fire. Dolma! I wanted to scoop her up, take her with me, but not knowing what Ani Rigzin would advise I stiffened my back and kept walking.

Stopping for a moment in the doorway, I closed my eyes in prayer. *Om Mani Peme Hum, Oh Jewel in the Heart of the Lotus. Protect Mama and Papa.* Then with a quick bow in my parent's direction, I stepped across the threshold and out into the crisp morning air.

The old wooden gate faced east and beyond it a dusty road stretched through open fields, following the banks of the river north to Chamdo and Derge and on to the Yangtze River. To the west the road crossed the great open plain toward Lhasa. In ancient days it had been a caravan route running from the great cities of China south to India. Traders traveled it carrying deer horn and musk to trade in China for silks, tea, porcelain and tobacco, or for silver and gold in India. But now people moved back and forth on foot or horseback between the towns along the way, taking grain and woven goods to market. Pilgrims also followed it on their way from monastery to monastery.

I looked back at the house. Anya will be getting up, I thought. And Kunsang, my father's second wife. And the servants. Thupten will come down to care for the horses, Chimee will go to get water. Later the whole household will go to the all-day prayer service at the monastery.

As I started up the path to Khaley Monastery, I turned once more to look at our house. Behind, the hills looked dark and menacing. In the early morning mist they seemed higher than usual, their rocky ledges stuck out like the horns of an evil deity. Forbidding. Inauspicious.

"Ani Rigzin," I cried, rushing through the door of her room, bursting into tears when I saw her. "They want me to marry . . ." Half swallowing my words, I told her my parents' plan.

Her dim eyes shone with compassion, and she took my head in her lap. "There, there," she said, stroking my head. "I have heard of the plan but I was helpless to stop it. Everyone was unhappy but their pleading was useless, your father had given his word."

She looked at me with understanding. She too had refused to marry and had taken a nun's name, "Ani," at an early age. As my father's only sister she knew his strong will. "When he gives his word," she said, "it is final." I hung my head. Trusting her more than anyone, I knew what she said was true.

Often I visited her at the nunnery, borrowing her robes and joining the nuns in prayer, but after a few days away my father would miss me and order me home. Occasionally she came to stay with us, taking off her robes and joining in my mother's tasks. Like a mother, she sat with me while I ate, and took pains not to let anyone drink from my bowl. "You are precious," she said, "No one must contaminate your cup." Over the years a bond grew between us. We were alike in so many ways.

"Leave immediately for Gyalsay Rinpoche's monastery," Ani-la said, as if wanting to hide me away. "Leave while they're all at the prayer service. I am too old to go, I will stay and pray for you."

As we prepared to leave her room, she took my face in her hands and touched her forehead to mine. She pressed a small silver statue of the Buddha into my hands. "Take your father's servant, Tashi," she said, "he is old, but he knows the way. He can be trusted, you'll be safe with him." Tears welled in her eyes, one ran over her wrinkled cheek. She squeezed my hand, too sad to speak, and went out her door toward the monastery hall.

*   *   *

Tashi was sitting in the kitchen warming his hands by the fire when I arrived. When I poured out my plans he sat silently, turning his twisted fingers in the heat from the fire. His veiled eyes gazed into the flames as if he were seeing into another realm. His face was still, almost masklike, his skin like hide stretched over a drum.

I looked at his long thin arms. The vein on the top of his wrist was pulsing, one moment up, the next moment down.

For a second I thought I saw a shadow cross his face. I turned, but nothing was there, only the fire playing tricks. The room was silent except for the hissing of sap from the burning logs. I glanced down at my own arms. They were smooth, supple, but they were flesh over bones just the same, no more permanent than his. Today I am here, but tomorrow I could be anywhere.

Tashi stirred on his bench, rubbed his face in his hands. "Ah, Ashe Pachen," he whispered, "what you ask isn't possible . . . my duty is to your father Pomdha Gonor." He lowered his head onto his chest. "Don't ask me to do such a thing. He would never forgive me."

I wasn't usually denied. His refusal felt like a slap on my face. Spinning around, I stamped my foot. "Do as you please," I said, "but if you won't help, I have no other option. I will throw myself off the roof."

I paused for a moment to let the words have their full effect, then turned and ran up the steps.

I could hear his footsteps behind me as I ran two stairs at a time toward the roof. "Ashe . . . Ashe Pachen . . ." His voice was breathless as he struggled to catch up. I ran down the corridor and Tashi fell further behind.

On the roof, the sun was low, the air still chilled. I paused to catch my breath and looked out on the valley. It was autumn, and the reeds at the edge of the river had changed to orange like embers of a fire. In the distance I could see steam rising up from the hot mineral springs. Our trips to the baths would be fewer at this time of year, I thought, and surely Papa wouldn't let me bathe by myself. In the autumn wolves begin to come down from the hills.

"Ashe Pachen . . ." Tashi was coughing and panting behind me.

As he climbed the last step onto the roof, I moved toward its edge. "No! Ashe Pachen, no, no." He rushed at me and grabbed my hand in his birdlike claw. "Please, Ashe Pachen . . . I will go . . . your father is going to kill me for this, but I'll go . . . don't jump!"

He pulled at me and clutched me to his chest, his liquid breath rattling in his throat. His body, moist from exertion, gave off a metallic scent. I had never been so close to him, and his grasp made me feel faint. He must have sensed my discomfort. He took a step back, then raised his withered thumbs in a gesture of consent.

He looked so forlorn, his body quivering from the effort, his thumbs wavering up. Poor Tashi, I thought. For a moment I felt like relenting, if only to ease his discomfort.

We waited until dark so as not to be noticed. It was early evening when we left. Everyone was still at the monastery, but I knew the prayer session would be ending soon. We must hurry, I thought.

As I mounted my favorite horse, Shindruk, Tashi slowly opened the huge wooden gate. The full moon was rising in the eastern sky, and its glow lit our way as we rode out into the fields. Frost had gathered at the base of the fallen crops, and light from the moon cast a shimmer like jewels at our feet. As we rode toward the river the thin frozen crust crunched and sighed beneath the hooves of our horses. With each step I was afraid someone would hear, but my fears were unfounded and we reached the river without notice.

At the river's edge, we urged our horses into the water. They pushed silently against the current until we reached the other side. On the bank I turned once again to look at our house. From where we were it looked like a rock on the hill, small and inert. I felt a pang of sadness. So many memories. Was I right to be leaving? I thought of Mama and Papa still at the prayer service. Would they understand?

Mama. She was always protective, treating me as if I were the most precious person on earth. Even when I was too big to fit, she held me in her lap and stroked my head, singing songs in her high childlike voice, showering me with affection.

And Papa. He was gentler with me than with anyone else. Never too busy to see me, or to grant whatever I wished. Lifting me into his arms he'd touch his forehead to mine, saying, "You are my little chieftain, my favorite adviser."

My young brother died when he was only two months old, and it drew the three of us close. The times we spent together were dear to my heart.

The sweet fragrance of unleavened bread baking in the wood-burning oven floats over the bed as I slowly waken. I hear the spatter and pop of kapsey cookies frying in a pan on the top of the stove. Soon the air becomes thick with the pungent scent of yak butter as it churns in the tall wooden churner.

For days, Mama and the servants have been preparing for our annual trip to the nomads. Last night they worked into the early hours, cutting strips of dried meat and dried cheese, arranging them layer upon layer in rounded tin cases. And now, in the brightening light, dust swirls as they rush from shelf to shelf, gathering tsampa and tea, wooden bowls, silver spoons and chopsticks, which they pack into old wooden traveling boxes that had once belonged to my grandfather.

When everything is packed, Mama, Papa, Aunt Rigzin, our three big yellow dogs, my little white Dolma, and our servants gather in the courtyard behind our house. After loading the boxes on yaks, we mount our horses and ride into the hills. Our procession winds up through the meadows, a thin dark ribbon moving slowly across the hillside, the colors of supply boxes sparkling in the light.

After a day's ride into the hills, the nomads' dark yak-hair dwellings appear in the distance, rising from the ground like large black rocks. When we reach them we are greeted by whistles and calls. The men in their bulky raw sheepskins encircle our party, grabbing at the boxes to help us unload and set up our huge white tents. The women, peering out from their tents, bring us butter tea. The children, barefoot and ragged, run excitedly in and out, their large mastiffs barking close at their heels.

The days unfold each in the same slow way. In the morning we scoop thick sweet cream from containers of milk left over from the night before and sit by the fire eating tsampa and drinking butter tea. After breakfast I am free to go off with the nomads' children to wander the green highlands, while Mama and Ani Rigzin prepare food for the noonday picnic and Papa plays bakchen, dominos, mah-jongg with his assistant under the eaves of the tent.

At this time of year the grass is higher than a twelve-year-old child and the meadows are crowded thick with wild flowers. For hours we run through the bright-colored fields, catching soft petals in the creases of our toes. When we tire, we lay on our backs and watch puffy white clouds swirl across the sky, or gaze at the river winding across the flat valley floor like a slow-moving serpent. At night we sit by the campfire drinking butter tea and watching the stars spread across the sky. Day after day continues like this, strung one upon another like jewels.

As I stood by the river lost in thought, my spirit felt heavy. Those earthly pleasures so close to the heart create a special kind of attachment. It is not only unpleasant states that one must free oneself from. It is the tender, almost unbearably sweet ties that must also be cut.

I awoke with a start, in a strange room. I looked around me in panic. In the corner I saw a dark shape on the floor. I heard a low moaning sound.

As my eyes gradually became accustomed to the darkness, I saw it was Tashi. He was sleeping, the whiskers on his chin quivering as he snored. At the sight of him, I remembered where I was, in the home of his friend. "They are trustworthy," he had said. "They won't tell. We'll be safe for the night."

Still cold from the river, I tossed and turned on the rough mattress they'd given me. It was the best they had, but full of lumps and difficult to sleep on. The wind streamed in through the cracks, pricking my face, pushing my thoughts to the back of my head. In my stomach, a small frightened bird fluttered noiselessly.

The next morning we set off early. In some places people were already out getting water from the river. The chill from the night was hanging over the meadows. Still cold, I had difficulty shaking the feel of the night. An uneasiness hung just beyond reach. I leaned my head onto Shindruk's neck, letting the warmth of his coat soothe me. I rode like that, my head on his neck, until my back grew stiff. By then I felt better.

For a short while we followed the road, but not wanting to be seen, we soon veered off toward the hills. We traveled north in the direction of Gyalsay Rinpoche's monastery at Tromkhog, on the far side of the Yangtze River.

Occasionally, as we rode, I recognized a familiar pile of rocks, a familiar sweep of hills, reminders of my first trip to the monastery three years before. Off and on, I heard Gyalsay Rinpoche's voice.

"Regard everything as though it is a dream. Everything is ephemeral, ungovernable, and hollow. Work with the essential nature of your mind, pure and radiant. Keep your mind clear and aware in each moment.

"All activity should be done with one intention. To help, and not harm, others. Be gentle, be kind, be compassionate, be generous to everyone including yourself."

The memory of his voice reassured me.

For most of the day we followed a narrow trail into the hills, and for a time we rode through a wide open field at the top. We passed goats and sheep, but there was no sign of people.

As far as I could see, the soft curving hills spread away in every direction. A breeze rippled slowly through the grasses like waves. Overhead, the sky arched from horizon to horizon, and a few soft clouds floated above me like thoughts in the mind. Later, the broad smooth hill sloped gently down into a river valley and for a time we followed along the river's edge.

Late in the afternoon we came to a flat grassy stretch. Tashi settled near the river and I chose a place further back. Except for the sound of the river, the place was quiet; except for a small bird on a nearby rock, there were no signs of life. The silence made me uneasy. It was the first time I'd been so far from home without my father or mother.

The hours of quiet stretching ahead, which once brought peace, now felt uncomfortable and empty. I took a spiritual text out of my bag and tried to shift my attention.

> *In the boundless panorama of the visible universe, recognize whatever shapes appear, whatever sounds vibrate as nothing but projections of your mind, illusory and unreal. Without grasping at anything, rest in the peace of an awareness that transcends all concepts. This is the heart of the practice.*

"*Without grasping at anything . . .*" Words I had heard so often now seemed more difficult. Were Mama and Papa only projections of my mind, illusory and unreal? I felt confused, and wrapped my text up once again in its cloth covering.

Standing up, I looked westward toward home. The darkening hills rolled on and on as far as I could see. In a distant valley beyond the farthest hill, I imagined I saw my house, its earthen walls rising four stories tall at the edge of the village.

Soon Mama would be beginning the evening meal. I imagined her in front of the stove, bending over a large pot on the fire while one of the servants added pieces of turnip and potato; loose strands of hair falling down around her face, her eyes tired, her body listless.

Behind her, Anya would be making butter tea as she did so many times each day, breaking a piece off the tea block with her twisted fingers and brewing it in a thick iron pot over the fire; taking the old wooden churner from its place on the wall, pouring tea, salt, and yak butter into a long wooden tube, and plunging the long wooden stick up and down, until the liquid inside frothed and foamed.

Soon Thupten would take the oil stick lamps from the wall to light them in the flame of the fire. And soon servants would begin to place platters of food on tables in front of guests who were staying after attending my father's court; men on one side of the room, women on the other, bent over with their legs spread apart, scooping tsampa into balls with their fingers and drinking stew from the wooden bowls.

Up the darkened stairs on the third floor, Papa would be waking from his nap; his brow furrowed, his eyes dull. As he stirred, I imagined him rising from his bed, going to the window, calling his special pet name for me, "Nyu . . . little Nyu," looking out into the darkness with an expression of such sadness it was as if a part of his body, a leg, an arm, had been lost.

With a heavy heart, I leaned against the grassy draw. The sky above me began to get dark. Shadows from behind the boulders reached menacingly at me. Taking my prayer beads in hand, I crawled under the sheepskin. The wind had stopped, the night was still, the only sound the beat of my heart alone in its huge hollow cavern.

As the night closed in around me, I thought of Gyalsay Rinpoche's monastery. Once the thought of it brought solace; now it seemed hollow and dark. In my mind, empty corridors wound, damp and enclosed, in every direction. The mournful sound of a gong beat far inside. Its dimly held song was beating, beating. And on the floor below, there was the echo of feet shuffling across cold stone floors.

The air was cold on my face, my head was spinning. I reached for Mama's warm lap, Papa's broad smile. But as I spread my fingers in front of me, all I touched was the wind.

In the morning Tashi and I packed our belongings and continued north. Halfway into the day, I saw a town in the distance. We'd stayed away from towns in case someone from our village was there, so as not to be recognized.

"We're almost out of food," I said to Tashi when I saw it. "We have no choice but to go down." We headed reluctantly toward it.

Hoping I wouldn't see anyone I knew, I rode in with my head lowered. Merchants cried out, musicians clattered and clanged, dogs barked. People clustered around cloth merchants surrounded by lengths of glistening silk and tables piled high with jewelry, metal bowls, silver spoons. With wild gestures and half-crazed laughs they bargained. Slabs of meat covered with flies hung limply from poles. Large woven baskets of fruit, vegetables, and barley crowded in between.

I turned to Tashi for encouragement. He motioned me forward. "You're seventeen, old enough to go by yourself." I dismounted, hal-

ter in hand, and pushed my way through the crowds to a stall where
an old man was grinding roasted barley for tsampa. As he turned the
great stone wheel, fine dust rose into the air in small golden clouds.
Behind him, stacked against a crumbling wall, were cloth bags of all
sizes filled with the tsampa.

I pointed to one the size of three hands. "That one, for two
beads," I said in a tone I had heard my father use. For a moment he
hesitated. "Two beads and no more," I said firmly. His mouth
opened wide in a toothless smile, and shrugging his shoulders, he
took the beads and slipped them into a pouch by his side.

I paused to survey the other tables, looking for tea. Across the
square I recognized a man from our village. His large nose and
square-set chin were unmistakable. It is Samten's father, I thought,
the father of a friend from Lemdha, bargaining with a cloth merchant over a bright red piece of silk.

I wanted to run to him. "Take me home! Take me home!" I imagined leaping onto his horse behind him, riding in through the gate of
my house. But closing my eyes and taking a breath, I remembered my
resolve and stilled my response. Bending my head even more, I edged
to a tea stall nearby.

"That one," I whispered to the man on the other side of the booth,
gesturing to a small block on the shelf behind. He looked at me with
suspicion, but seeing the turquoise bead in my outstretched hand he
accepted it without question and turned to another customer. I hurried back to Tashi, at the edge of the town. Soon we were back in the
hills high above the village.

～

On the third day we passed several families of nomads, their large
black tents a familiar and welcome sight. Late in the day, at the top
of a hill, we came to a pile of Mani stones left by passing travelers,
offering them as they chanted the mantra of Chenrezig, God of Compassion, *Om Mani Peme Hum*. I added a small round gray one that
I'd carried from the river we left two days ago. *Om Mani Peme
Hum, let me reach Tromkhog safely.*

Behind, the hill rose steeply up. It was late in the afternoon and rather than continue, we decided to stop at a small level clearing near the pile of stones. From this point I could see in many directions. The grassy hills had gradually given way to more rugged terrain. Crumbling shelves of rock clung to the hillside. The valleys grew narrow and dark. In the distance, I saw another small village crowded in between two high hills, dim now, for the sun was beginning to sink in the sky, leaving only shadows on the valley floor. As I looked, a shiver ran through me. I recognized the town.

Two decades before my father had come along the same path, passing the spot where I was now sitting. There was a pile of Mani stones, he once told me, and beyond, in a steep ravine, a town. He was nineteen years old and tall, strongly built, on his way to the market. As he entered the village, the market square was crowded with people, except at the center. Once Papa told me the story.

At the center of the village, he'd said, *three Chinese soldiers bent over an old man. His face was swollen, his arms covered with blood, caked in places, moist and glistening in others. A mass of gashes crisscrossed the skin on his back, his legs lay limply at unnatural angles. Slumped on the ground, he was twisted and trembling.*

One of the soldiers pushed at the body with his boot. Another lit a cigarette. After a few moments, they bent down and, taking his arms, dragged him to a post at the side of the square. They propped him against it, lashing a rope across his chest to keep him upright. His head continued to droop forward.

His fingers and hands were wrapped in rawhide, keeping them stiff and unable to bend. Taking slivers of bamboo, they slowly pushed one after another into the soft flesh between finger and nail. Pushing, pushing them in as far as they would go.

The old man's head rose up with a jerk, his eyes opened wide and a sound came out of his mouth that was liquid, shrill, not human.

A murmur rose from the crowd.

The soldiers laughed and congratulated one another. But one was not finished. Taking a bundle of small paper flags from his pocket, he attached one to each of the long bamboo slivers and stepped back to watch them fluttering in the breeze. The others bent over with laughter.

Dazed and horrified, my father pushed through the crowd and be-gan to run. He ran, he told me, and didn't stop until he reached home. He ran for two days, up steep trails, across grassy plains, try-ing to erase the images from his mind. For weeks he couldn't sleep.

Though I heard him tell that story only once, the images stayed clear in my mind. And as the light began to fade, the memory wrapped around me.

I leaned up against the Mani stones, pulled the sheepskin over my shoulders, and closed my eyes. Tashi was settled at a respectful dis-tance. The wind cracked against the stones, whistled over the barren ground. I imagined I heard in the distance the sound of bandits ap-proaching. I put my hand on my knife and waited, but nothing came.

Later, I thought I heard the call of a leopard crying down from the mountain. I took my knife out of the leather holder. I called *Om Mani Peme Hum.* I heard horses' hooves thundering toward me, ten, twenty, an army of bandits. I sat up, my heart pounding. But no. It was only the wind. I looked in Tashi's direction for reassurance but he was fast asleep.

Past, present, I struggled to keep my mind clear. The threat of the unknown, the threat of marriage, blended together. Leaning back against the Mani stones, I took the turquoise beads from around my neck. *Om Mani Peme Hum. Om Mani Peme Hum.* One after an-other I moved the cold beads through my fingers as I prayed. *Om Mani Peme Hum.*

Colder now, the wind came in thin strands curling around the stones at my back. It lashed at me, sending slivers of pain up my fin-gers like flames. I pulled the sheepskin around my head and closed my eyes. The howl of the wind crept into my dreams.

The winds continue to blow, but now an eerie light spreads over the hills. The glow seems to emanate from the mountain ahead. A path, shining, leads to the top. At either side of the path, men in fine bro-cade cloaks and headdresses of gold stand beating large ritual drums.

My father is beside me, holding my hand, pulling me gently but forcefully toward the top. I move beside him as if in a trance.

The path narrows. We start to climb a steep incline of loose shale. The light is brightening now, and the sound of drums more intense. Rocks cut my feet; still we move forward.

Beyond the shale is a rock wall fifty feet high, almost vertical, with rough steps cut into its face. Step after step I stumble behind my father, his grip tightening around my wrist. The beat of the drums now deafening, the light blinds my eyes.

At the last step, my father stops. I look in the direction of his gaze. No more than twenty arm lengths in front of us, standing atop a stone altar, is an immense man, red satin robes hanging down from his shoulders in furls. His head is large and bestial, his eyes bulging red. Fire flows out of his mouth, his fat wet tongue hangs to one side, dripping with blood. Beneath him, a golden bowl filled with blood. In his right hand, a long silver sword.

An otherworldly light seems to emanate from beneath him. My father pushes me forward, then steps back as if offering me to him. The drums reach a fever pitch, then stop, and the wind dies down.

Reaching up to his head he takes it off to reveal the ghostly pale face of a Chinese soldier. He reaches for me, and taking my wrist he draws me toward him.

No, I scream. No.

He is shaking my wrist. "Pachen, Pachen."

"Pachen, Lemdha Pachen." The dream faded. I opened my eyes and saw eight of my father's men crowding around me.

Tupten, our servant, bent over me, his fox-skin hat pulled low on his forehead, his eyes pleading.

"Your father misses you," he said, "he has been sick with worry. There are bandits, wild animals, it is no place for a young woman to be wandering alone. He said there is no need for you to run away. He will break the marriage contract, you are free to live as you want. He made us vow to bring you back. He placed Mani stones on our forehead and made us lick spittle from our own hands."

I knew they had taken the most sacred oath, and there would be no way to dissuade them. In a way I was relieved, for in truth I was longing for home. But just the same, I felt uneasy. Perhaps I had an intimation of things to come.

3
Changes

My return home brought with it a mixture of feelings: embarrassment, anger, and relief. The feelings mixed together until they were almost indistinct from one another, the way feelings often do; all I knew was that I wanted to slip into the house without being noticed. But as I crept through the door to the kitchen, all eyes turned in my direction.

My mother dropped the spoon she was using and ran toward me, her arms outstretched. Seeing her arms reaching out, I stepped reflexively back, bracing against her eagerness to welcome me home.

She was smiling as if nothing had happened, seemingly unaware of all she and Papa had put me through. I felt suddenly angry from the strain of the last few days, and before she could reach me I turned away.

I felt her come up behind me, but refused to acknowledge her presence. I was dimly aware that I wanted to blame her, not my father. I felt like shouting, "You tried to trade me in marriage!" Instead I said nothing.

She moved to the side, and I looked at her out of the corner of my eye. Her head was slightly bent, like a small child who'd been punished and didn't know why. Sensing her need for me to embrace her, I felt myself stiffen, not wanting to be moved, as I often am, to protect her. I focused my eyes on the nearest wall and stared straight ahead.

The wall in front of me was black with soot from years of smoke. Halfway up, the eight symbols of good fortune were written in dots of tsampa stuck on the wall. Seeing the familiar designs, I began to calm. I traced their curling white shapes with my eyes, stopping when I reached the conch shell, my favorite.

Its rounded shape reminded me of the words I'd memorized in Gonlha's class. *"With pure speech like a right-turning shell of good fortune . . . may blessings radiate."*

"Right speech is one of the most important precepts," Gonlha often said. *"Speaking with anger and lies, speaking badly of others, all fill the mind with negativity. Speaking with compassion and truth bring blessings."*

"Pure speech . . . right turning . . . good fortune . . ." The words began to fade, and for a moment my mind was free of thoughts and

feelings. My anger slowly dissolved. I felt myself softening, and I turned toward my mother.

Anya came into the room. "Your father would like you to join him in his room." Immediately my chest tightened again, and despite my intention to watch my speech my response poured out before I could stop it.

"Why should I bother—he wanted to send me away." I felt like crying and bit my lip, hurt at his willingness to give me in marriage. "He doesn't care." Unable to help myself, I started to cry.

Anya walked from the doorway and took me into her arms. "Don't talk like that, Ashe. Your father missed you so much . . . he hasn't slept since you left. . . ."

Her arms were warm, and I felt myself sinking into her body. A familiar scent from her skin folded around me.

"In the meadow the flowers are blooming . . . flowers for sweet Ashe Pachen." Anya sprinkles flowers over my head until I am covered. She pulls pieces of tsampa out of a pouch and sticks them in my mouth. She pours warm milk from the terra-cotta jug into my cup. "The little lamb Ashe Pachen is safe in her Anya's lap. No one will hurt her. . . ."

Upstairs, the bright light coming through the window of my father's room blinded me, and I stood in the doorway, unable to see inside. A sound from the back startled me. It was my father clearing his throat.

"Nyu," he called, "my little Nyu Pachen, come in." Gradually the blue walls of his room appeared from the dark, then the red, green, and white of the trim at the top. Light filtered down from the old glass panes in the windows, and in the back, sitting on a carpeted mattress, I saw my father.

I felt shy, as I did sometimes when I first came before him. He was a striking man, tall, ruddy complexion, a long black braid wrapped around his head, dark flashing eyes. Though others in the village were awed by his presence, he was respected and loved, for everyone knew his heart was soft underneath his solemn appearance. Of the nine chieftains of Gonjo, he was considered the leader.

Seeing me hesitate, he beckoned me urgently toward him. I crossed and sat down on the mattress by his side. He clasped me in his arms and held me tight. When he finally loosened his grip, he lifted my hand and stroked it. My hand rested in his, like a bird asleep in its nest, happy to be home.

The next day he set off for Markham to call off the marriage agreement. My potential groom's family in Markham had heard nothing of my attempts to escape and had been making preparations for weeks. They had brewed one hundred basinsful of chang, the Tibetan barley beer, and had begun to cook for the wedding feast.

In order to appease them, my father went bearing gifts: one of our finest horses tied with a silk scarf around its neck, an offering to discourage their anger, a rifle, a brocade sheepskin chupa, a saddle, and more things, too many to describe. The negotiation must have gone on for some time. He was gone several weeks, and when he came home he looked tired. But after that, I heard no more about it. And I was safe from marrying, at least for a while.

"Chamdo has fallen!"

The words from the messenger ran through the house like a shock. Mama ran to get Papa, while people from all over Lemdha poured into the house. We crowded into the kitchen to hear the news.

"The battle for Kham is over," the old man sobbed. "The Chinese have arrived."

My father walked over to him and put his hand on the old man's shoulder. The room was still, and for moments the only sound was his muffled crying. After he'd composed himself, he wiped his face on the back of his sleeve and continued.

"Two days before the Chinese entered Chamdo, the cowardly Governor-General Ngabo abandoned his troops. Not wanting to leave provisions for the Chinese, he set fire to the government stores, destroyed weapons and ammunition, and fled. When he was halfway down the mountain, he met Tibetan soldiers coming from Lhasa. 'Throw your guns and bullets over the side of the mountain, and come with me!' he ordered. Two days later he was captured.

"Panic broke out in the streets of Chamdo. People were running in all directions, dragging their personal belongings behind them. The stalls of the main street were deserted. It was terrible to see." The old man began to cry again.

"It is happening as the Great Thirteenth predicted," my father said sadly. "The summer before he died, he spoke words that are now coming true."

Everyone listened intently as my father recited the prediction.

"*It may happen,*" my father quoted from memory, "*that here, in the center of Tibet, religion and government will be attacked both from without and within.*

"*Unless we can guard our own country, it will happen that all the revered holders of the Faith will disappear and become nameless, all beings will be sunk in great hardship and overpowering fear.*

"*The days and nights will drag on, slowly, in suffering.*"

"They have come," my father said solemnly, "and I have a feeling they won't be gone soon."

Chamdo fell in 1950, shortly after the Chinese crossed the Yangtze River into Tibet. For a time after the invasion, our daily lives meandered like a stream unsure of its course. Occasionally we felt their presence like an insect which bit, then disappeared, but it would be years before the full impact took hold. Whenever news of their activities came, I took a momentary notice, but soon returned to my practice without giving it much thought. Mostly I was relieved to have been spared the agony of marriage, and grateful to my father for having appeased my prospective groom's family.

His conciliatory gesture was typical of my father. Though more like a hermit than a chieftain, he never retreated from his duty to others. He often said that generosity begets love and respect, and he urged me to do my best to help others in need. He had no use for material things, preferring to give away what he had. "When you give generously," he often said, "you accumulate greater merit for your future life."

At times his generosity burdened my mother. Once, when a neighbor tried to steal food my mother had cooked for a festival, my father only laughed. *"Quick, you old rascal, you'd better hurry,"* he called out in a booming voice when he saw him, *"my wife will come back soon, then you'll be caught! There is food in the box by the table, get it and hurry out the door."* He laughed again, a deep hearty laugh.

Later, when my mother returned to find the food gone, she ran to my father's room in desperation.

"The food we prepared has disappeared!" she cried.

"Don't worry," my father said, patting her cheek, *"it was only Boogya. The poor man is less fortunate than we. Prepare some more food, we have plenty for everyone."*

My mother was incensed. *"If you continue to give everything away, we will have nothing,"* she wailed. But my father only smiled. *"We have enough . . . it is only food. Things of this world can't follow us when we die . . ."*

Perhaps if my mother had been free from the responsibility of providing food for the household, she would have been less concerned about my father's expansiveness, for she was a caring person by nature. Whenever somebody in our village needed help, whether orphans, old people, beggars, she never turned any away.

My father said it was rare to find a woman so patient and eventempered. She, in turn, was devoted to him. Even when he visited other women, she didn't complain. In all their years together, I don't ever remember them fighting. They often sat together in the evening discussing the events of the day. Most of the time she agreed with him, but occasionally she spoke her mind.

Each year they were together they seemed closer, and though they never showed affection in public I could tell that they felt it. In the morning when she braided his long hair, I often saw her fingers linger against his brow, stroking his hair gently away from his face. And in the evenings when there were no visitors, she would go up to his room to sleep, and sometimes I heard them talking and laughing far into the night.

I don't remember how old I was when my father married the second time. I am told that my younger brother died at two months old, and that afterward my mother and father explored every possibility for having a child. They even ate *Za yig*, precious scriptures, but nothing worked.

One night, years later when it was clear she would have no more children, my father asked her about bringing a second wife into the house. As he spoke to her a shadow momentarily crossed over her face. My father put his hand on hers and continued to speak. "For the good of the district" and "tomorrow" was all I could hear.

The next day strangers arrived at our door. A young woman, not much older than me, was with them. She was tall, her dark hair pulled back in the Gonjo style, a huge turquoise at the top of her head. Her name was Kunsang, the daughter of Norbu Pontsang, one of the chieftains of Gonjo. She arrived wearing the symbolic arrow of a bride around her neck, her eyes dark with fear.

Marrying her was not something my father did lightly. It was done at the urging of his ministers and subjects, who were concerned about losing the family lineage. Since I was not marrying and my mother had born no more children, a second wife should enter the family.

In the beginning, my mother took Kunsang wherever she went, explaining the household tasks, introducing others in the village. She treated her as a daughter, and as a result, Kunsang adored my mother and did whatever she asked.

For a while, I kept my distance. It bothered me to see my father with another. I felt replaced, and jealous of his time with her. But I slowly began to accept her. Over the years we became close, though the marriage never had the desired outcome, for she, too, remained childless.

∾

A month after the fall of Chamdo, a messenger arrived with news that Lhasa had been thrown into chaos. "The Chinese invasion has created confusion among those who are governing," he said. "There are struggles over who should lead."

"Taktra should be removed!" my father said with disgust, speaking of the seventy-five-year-old regent who was governing the country until the Dalai Lama could be enthroned. "He has become unpopular in the past four years and has lost his authority." But he knew that the young Dalai Lama, who was only fifteen, was too young to assume power, and he was afraid of what would happen with no one in charge. "It is a perilous time," he said. "We need someone to guide us."

Several days later a man burst into the kitchen. "His Holiness the Fourteenth Dalai Lama has just been enthroned!" he shouted.

He told us that the two state oracles had been consulted, and after some prodding, the Gadong oracle had spoken from a trance. "He said that the responsibility for both the spiritual and the temporal should be taken by the Dalai Lama," the messenger reported, "and on the 17th of November, His Holiness assumed power."

My father was delighted at the news. "Now we have our rightful ruler back on the throne. We have been too long without a spiritual leader."

Six months later His Holiness sent a delegation to Peking. "No sooner had they arrived," a neighboring chieftain told us, "than they were forced to sign a Seventeen-Point Agreement turning over all our country's policy-making to the Chinese in exchange for a promise that the Chinese would leave His Holiness's authority intact, and respect Tibet's religion and culture." The chieftain paced back and forth as he spoke. "The Chinese had the nerve to seal the agreement with a phony Tibetan stamp," he fumed, "and His Holiness was left powerless to change it!"

Daily, now, men came to our house, from all over Gonjo and Markham, and even from the north. They came with news for my father, news of the Chinese. One day while passing the door to my father's room, I couldn't help hearing a man's voice. It was quavering, almost tearful.

"Several nights ago in Chamdo five Chinese soldiers came to the door of my house. Late at night, after my family was asleep, they pounded on the door. 'What is it?' I called. My wife tried to hold me down in our bed, but I rose. Not waiting for me to open the door, they burst in. 'We have come for your children,' they said. 'They are going to a school in the Motherland.' My wife rushed in from the next room and threw herself at their feet. 'No, no, please, no, they are only children . . . they are young,' she cried.

"The taller of them stepped forward and pushed her aside with his feet. 'Your children are lucky,' he said with a sneer on his face. 'An education in the Motherland is an honor.'

"Two soldiers left to look for them. Soon we heard cries coming from the room above. 'Ama, Ama-la, Pala!' my little son cried. I stepped forward, but the tall soldier grabbed my shoulder. He struck me hard on the ear. 'Stand back,' he said, 'this has nothing to do with you. It's your children we've come for. They are lucky to be taken from your heathen home and shown the glories of the cultural revolution.'

"The other two reappeared with our two children, my daughter Pema, who is eight years old, and my son Paljor, who is five. My son was already crying, and Pema stood close to him, holding his hand in hers. When he saw us, Paljor pulled away and ran toward us, his arms outstretched. The soldier behind pulled him back. Paljor twisted and reached trying to grasp at my wife's robe, but each time he did, the soldier kept pulling him back.

" 'Please,' I begged, 'they are our only children, we are poor people and they are all we have.' The tall soldier stepped forward and hit me onto the floor. Over and over he kicked me. In the stomach, in the ribs, until I was doubled over and my breath had gone.

"With me on the floor and my wife sobbing beside, they carried our children out of the house. Pema turned to look at us, her eyes wild with fright. It was my last sight of her, but I could hear Paljor calling, 'Mama, Papa,' until they were far down the road."

The man burst into uncontrollable sobs, and I could hear the others trying to comfort him. That night, when I took dinner to my father, he was standing at the window. He didn't respond when I opened the door, and stood looking out until I left. It was the first of many times I would see him like that. And in truth, I think it was the beginning of his end.

For days after hearing the story, I couldn't get it out of my mind. The wild, frightened look in the eyes of the daughter, the cries of the son. Over and over I saw them taken away. I imagined a school, unlike any I knew. A large building, cold and made of cement, in a land far away from the warmth of family and friends. How different it was from my own "school" in the large sunny room on the fourth floor of our house.

Frost clings to the windows of the classroom this morning. I curl my fingers into the lambskin lining of my chupa, trying to stay warm. Lhamo, Sonam, and Tashi sit cross-legged on two long rugs nearby. In front of us, Gonlha walks back and forth. The long sleeves of his robe swing against his knees, making a sound like the flapping of wings as he walks. He is waiting for us to dust the black wooden boards in our laps with powder from the pouches hanging at our necks. Instead of reading from the sacred texts as usual, we are practicing our script, and as a special treat while we prepare our boards, Gonlha recites from the epic of King Gesar.

"I am Gesar, Lion King of Ling, the great conqueror and healer . . . I hold the sword of truth in one hand, and the medicine of peace in the other. . . . We are the promise of this world, we are the glory . . ."

Gesar, the manifestation of Guru Padmasambhava, the blessed saint from India who brought Buddhism to Tibet, and of Chenrezig, the god of compassion. This is my favorite part of our classes, whenever Gonlha recites the deeds of his wondrous courage. No matter how many times I hear them, it is never enough. But today my fingers are numb from the cold and I struggle to pick out the white chalk dust from my pouch.

As I pull at the pouch, I keep my eye on Gonlha's sleeves. Unlike other teachers, he never beats us, though he occasionally brushes our head with his sleeve if he sees us falling behind. It is more an embarrassment than a blow, but it works just the same to keep us mindful.

When I finally open my pouch, I pinch some dust, sprinkle it over my board, then take up my bamboo pen and begin to write. Gonlha continues to recite as we draw large rounded shapes of the Tibetan alphabet.

"I am Gesar, King of Ling, who brings prosperity, dignity, and joy, who destroys cowardice, delusion, and slavery . . . we are one in dignity, we are one in courage, we are one in gentleness . . . from today onward I have entered your hearts."

As I move my pen slowly over the dusted surface, I listen to Gonlha read and my heart swells with pride at the words. "We are one in dignity . . . one in courage . . ."

After our morning meal, Gonlha announces, "I'll be gone for a while, continue to practice your script." We pick up our slates and he disappears through the curtain, out the door. Tashi runs to the window. He watches until he sees Gonlha's stately form on the walk below, then raises his thumb to signal "He's gone." Immediately we jump up.

Lhamo reaches over and pulls the sash of my chupa undone. I dive toward her and catch her braids in my hands. Sonam throws her pouch of powder at us, I kick at it with my foot. The pouch breaks open, the dust sprays out and we fall to the floor into the dust. Tashi throws himself on top.

Squirming, squealing, giggling, shrieking, we roll through the chalk on the floor. We laugh so hard that we ache. Suddenly, without any warning, Gonlha reappears at the door.

"Well," he says, looking at the pieces of ribbon, cloth, bamboo, and chalk strewn in chaos across the room. "Well, what have we here?" His eyes narrow in disapproval.

"Tashi," I whisper breathlessly, "you were supposed to keep watch . . ."

But just as quickly, Gonlha begins to laugh. Rumbling up from his large belly until he is shaking all over. Deep, bellyful laughs. He swings his sleeves left and right at us, as we scurry around straightening the room.

When the room has been tidied, and we are each settled down on our mattress, Gonlha clears his voice and begins once again to recite as if nothing had happened.

"Gesar and his host of warriors gallop down the bridge of billowing smoke, like a thunderstorm sweeping across a desert plain . . . Gesar comes like a wheel of iron rolling across the sky to subdue the demonic hordes . . . And the earth becomes still."

Gonlha was an exceptional and compassionate man, good-natured, always smiling. He was a monk from the monastery on the hill above us, but had been in our house for as long as I can remember. He lived in a room next to the chapel as its caretaker, and seven days a week, year round, he held classes for me and neighboring friends. Originally from a humble family, he finished his Gelong degree in Buddhist philosophy, the highest degree one can attain, and because of that was celibate, with no wife or children of his own.

But beyond his character and intelligence, he had magical powers. He was a Ser-sung, a hailstorm watcher, and could control the weather through his strength of mind. Once, when a heavy hailstorm was destroying our crops in the field, he put on the black hat of the Ser-sung and a special dark colored chupa. He took a ritual sword in one hand and began to chant and dance. As he danced, his complexion slowly changed to a pale, otherworldly color. He waved the sword in the direction of the clouds, then with a huff and a puff, blew them away. There were flames on the tip of the sword and flames on his head. I know, because I saw them with my own eyes.

Another time, he protected our house from lightning and thunder. Great flashes of light lit the sky and the noise was deafening. Dancing in circles, he waved his sword, and soon it stopped, everything calmed down.

He also helped people in the village with cases of bites or sores that were badly infected and refused to heal. He heated a sickle until it was blazing hot, put his tongue to its blade, and licked it, then with blessed water in his mouth, he spit on the sore. That sort of cure was nothing unique, as there were many tantrics who could do the same thing; but unlike them, the power of a Ser-sung was truly amazing.

There were strict rules regarding the use of this power. It took years of study and retreat in the hills, and when the studies were finished, the Ser-sung had to take vows before he could start his practice. Even then, it could only be used to help others in need.

Gonlha must have accumulated a lot of good merit in his previous life to be able to be so talented in this one. But he never was arrogant or prideful. To me, he was the large, gentle man who looked after our chapel and taught me to read. I will always be grateful to him for that.

Despite continuing news of Chinese activities, life at home continued as always. In the springtime, the hills around our village came back to life. Everywhere the creatures and plants were waking. Tiny green shoots, so fragile it seemed they couldn't possibly last until summer, pushed up through the earth where only weeks before there were blankets of snow. Worms and beetles fresh from their long winter sleep staggered and squirmed from holes in the ground. The river, swelled from the melting snow, tumbled down and around, filling the valley with its song, and on its banks, baby foxes out for a romp with their mothers barked small raspy barks at the rippling water.

It was my favorite time of year, for the days became longer and soon we would go to the hot springs. At that time of year, many families gathered to camp at their edge and take long baths in their hot sulfur water. Often we walked to the springs, but on special occasions, when the whole family and the servants went there together, we loaded the horses with food, blankets, and tents, and camped in the open space of the pastures nearby.

That morning, six months after my return, there was one last snow. Luminous flakes, suspended mid-air, drifted through the sky like spirits in search of a home. They tickled the new little shoots. They filled up fresh holes in the ground. They froze the songs of the birds for most of the day. Webs on the gate were bordered in lace, fields were dusted with chalk. Despite the fact I wanted it gone, I couldn't help noticing its beauty.

All day I worried that winter had returned and that our first trip of the year to the hot springs wouldn't take place. But now, in the late afternoon, the sun had come out and spring had pushed itself back into the air. The change, so quick—snow in the morning, warm breezes now—could have only happened through magic. Perhaps Gonlha had been out, casting his spells.

We gathered in the courtyard at the side of the house after supper. Mama, Papa, Ani Rigzin, Kunsang, my friends Lhamo and Sonam, and their families. Tashi and Tenzin had saddled the horses. Anya and Pema were carrying baskets of food from the kitchen. The dogs were chasing each other in and out between the legs of the horses.

After everything was loaded, we started out along the banks of the river. The moon, rising in the sky in front of us, cast a silver light on the water beyond, and its beams spread over the fresh new grasses, giving them an unnatural glow. Our horses made a soft padding sound on the dampened earth; the dogs ran barking ahead. Surrounded by those I loved most, riding through meadows of silver, I felt as frisky as a newborn colt.

On the way, Papa called back to Lhamo and me. "See up there, in the bend of the road? It is the ghost of an old woman. She is wearing warm spirit clothes. . . . Watch out! She is gathering more for her children . . . hold onto your chupa or she'll pull it off. . . ."

Lhamo and I screamed and drew our horses together. I narrowed my gaze and peered far ahead, trying to see what lay beyond. The light from the moon played tricks with my eyes. For a moment I saw the old head bent over, the twisted arm reaching furtively out, but in the next, there was only a bush at the side of the road.

"There are ghosts out tonight," Lhamo's older brother whispers behind us. "They are hungry for mischievous young girls. . . . You had better be good or they'll eat you. . . . They are h-u-n-g-r-y ghosts, looking for food . . ."

Lhamo turned and threw her scarf at him, and we both flipped our reins on the neck of our horses and rode off.

After a short time, we reached the place in the river where the water rose up in steaming bubbles. Our servants, Thupten, Pema, and Chime, lifted the bundles of food and other belongings off the wooden carriers on either side of the yaks. Lhamo and I ran ahead to the place where the women bathe and began to undress.

As soon as we'd taken our chupas and undershirts off we huddled together, but before we could go further Sonam ran up from behind and pushed us in. The water was silky and warm. It curled around my arms and legs, licked against my bare skin, and filled my head with a pungent scent like eggs that have grown too old. Heat pushed into my pores and washed each small opening clean. The warmth on my body felt good after a long, bathless winter.

For a long time we floated as if in a trance, feeling the bubbles break on our backs, and looking up at the moon as it moved its small footsteps across the sky. Mama and Ani Rigzin were soaking several paces away. Further down the river, Papa and Lhamo's father sat in the shallows, drinking chang and talking in low voices.

Lhamo broke our silence. "I heard Mama and Papa talking last night," she whispered. "I heard them say they were marrying me to Tenzin Phunsok, Yure Wangmo's son." I looked into Lhamo's face, expecting to see it distressed. Her face was turned, and in the light of the moon I saw a smile creep over. "Lhamo," I said, "aren't you sad?"

"She's been hoping it would happen for years," Sonam whispered into my ear. "I've seen the way she looks at Tenzin . . ."

Lhamo turned her head further away, and in the fading moonlight I thought I saw a faint blush spread over her cheeks. I tugged at her arm again, shaking her back and forth in the water. "Is it true?"

Lhamo threw her arms around my neck, her mouth nuzzled into my ear. "Yes!" she whispered, "but you mustn't tell."

Her head quivered against mine, as if some strange current were flowing through. I could feel her excitement as if it were a living thing. For the first time in all our years together, I saw we were different. I looked at her broad forehead, at the strong square set of her jaw, and saw something I'd never noticed before. An earthbound cast to her body, rooted deep in this life. A body that wanted children, a body created to give birth.

Born in the same village, lives spent together since childhood. All the same influences, and yet something made us different. Perhaps it was the result of our previous lives, the karma we'd accumulated. Whatever it was, I saw we were headed in different directions. I wanted a life of stillness and prayer, she, a life of the world. From then on, though we remained friends out of loyalty to our shared history, our souls took separate paths, and I never again felt a sister-hood with her in quite the same way.

At times after that, I wondered what it was that made people different; what small voice entered that made us ourselves. Sometimes late at night I felt souls from the past hovering nearby, waiting to ride on a newly lit spark into this life. Who were they? Where had they come from? What wandering being was born? For days I pondered: this world, the world beyond; my father, my mother; the mystery that creates us.

The next year, a tea merchant arrived from the west with news of an ominous event. "A wolf was seen roaming on the ramparts of the Great Sakya Monastery!" he said. We gathered around him to hear more.

"The wolf was chased by the elders and young boys, and stoned to death in a dry river bed. Several of the elders carried him back to the monastery and stuffed him. They hung him on a post outside the gate. All who saw him said he was a sign that the Chinese were near."

"It was an omen," my father agreed. "So far Lemdha has been spared, but how much longer can it be?"

In the Spring of 1953, the storms were more ferocious than usual. Winds blew with a force not seen for many years. Dirt was churned into the air and sent raging across the valley. Several poles with prayer flags were torn down.

"It is an omen," many said. "The Chinese will soon come."

To the north of us in Amdo, we heard that the soldiers had begun to denounce local Tibetans. There were confrontations, arrests, executions, even isolated incidents of fighting, and as a result several thousand Amdoans were killed or sent to labor camps.

To the south, in the area of Gyalthang, the local population was divided into five different strata and a campaign of arrests was launched. People belonging to the first three strata, the lords, the landowners, and the lamas, were publicly humiliated or condemned.

Closer to our home, a motor road had been completed from Derge to Chamdo. Daily, Chinese entered Kham; their growing numbers were said to be part of a massive strategy to transfer people from crowded areas in China to the vast empty spaces of Tibet. The effort was so successful that years later, in many parts of Tibet there were more Chinese than Tibetans, and Tibetan life as we knew it was gradually eroded.

But in 1953, there was only a shadow of what was to come.

Two years after our time at the hot springs, Lhamo was married.

When the groom arrived with his family and friends to escort her to his house, I was with Lhamo in her room on the third floor. It was considered bad luck to look at the future husband on the day of the wedding, and even though Lhamo had seen Tenzin Phunsok many times before, her mother insisted she stay away from the window.

"Can you see him?" Lhamo asked, pushing me toward the window. "Does he look happy?" She pulled at the sleeves of her chupa, and fussed with the beads in her hair. It was the first time I had ever seen her nervous.

But later, as she walked down the stairs in her yellow brocade chupa with embroidered flowers at its hem, she was radiant. Her long hair was braided in two, intertwined with turquoise beads. Long golden earrings hung from her ears, necklaces of coral and turquoise at her neck. And her wrists were encircled with bands of jade, her fingers with onyx.

In the courtyard, she was surrounded by relatives. They wrapped a white cloth over her to hide her from view, hung an ornamental arrow around her neck, then helped her mount her horse.

Once we reached Tenzin's house, her relatives surrounded her again, putting traditional white silk scarves around her neck. The ceremony was conducted on the third floor of the house. Khaley Rinpoche led us in prayer. At the end, he blessed Lhamo and Tenzin, and food was served in the kitchen downstairs.

For three days and three nights, the celebration continued. Dance groups performed outside by the fire, gifts were spread around the courtyard for all to see. Guns, jewels, silver cups, horses, saddles, blankets, and more, too many to count.

On the evening of the last day as I was leaving, I looked back over the room. The decorative brocade on the pillars was beginning to droop. Empty cups of chang scattered over tables at the edge of the room. Dishes were piled high in the back, near large basins of water. And in every corner, presents, one stacked on top of another. A wave of discomfort swept over me when I saw them. The senselessness of so many things.

I heard, once again, the words of my father. *"If you don't put a limit to greed, whatever you do becomes worthless. . . . Material possessions can't follow you when you die."*

One day, not too long after, I woke up and the air had changed. It was nothing particular I could point to. But I could feel it in the pit of my stomach.

The feeling followed me wherever I went that morning. At times I would catch my breath in excitement, as if it were the day before Losar, the new year, or the start of a trip. But mixed in with excitement was a faint edge of dread, as if someone were leaving.

Late in the morning, I was down at the river with Anya when something caught my attention. On a hill above the river, a man was watching. Dressed in a short little coat, long thin pants, a strange round hat with a brim in front, he was unlike anyone I'd ever seen. For moments he watched us, then turned and continued up the road. I followed him with my eyes until he was out of sight.

"Ashe Pachen." Anya noticed my attention had shifted, and gave me a poke on my back. "What are you staring at?"

It was hard to answer. It was not what I saw with my eyes so much as a feeling tugging somewhere inside me. A loneliness under my skin, in my bones, and it made me afraid.

But unable to explain, I merely shrugged my shoulders and turned back to the piles of laundry at my feet.

Several days later, Anya and I returned to the river and were standing ankle-deep in the water rinsing the clothes we had washed. We let them twist and turn in the currents until the water ran clear, then threw them up on rocks by the shore to dry.

The water had lost its summer warmth and stung as it flowed over my feet. I shifted my weight from one foot to the other, trying to keep warm. At the same time I positioned myself on the slippery stones so I wouldn't fall in as I bent to hold the clothes under water. I had just managed to balance myself with one foot on a flat mossy rock, and the other on a larger round one, when I heard my name being called. "Ashe Pachen . . . Ashe . . ."

It was my mother calling. Her voice was shriller than usual, almost urgent. "Ashe . . . Pa . . . chen . . ." I could hear my name but the rest was lost in the flow of the water.

Just then, Sonam came running toward us. "Ashe, come . . . your mother wants you to come . . . the Chinese are here. . . ."

The Chinese. The words ran through me like a bolt of lightning. I threw the wash down by the edge of the water and ran. I left so quickly that I forgot to put on my shoes. Up the path, through the gate, down the stairs then up again, to the kitchen.

Five, six, seven men were standing at the back of the room near the stove. Each wore a short little coat, long thin pants, a strange round hat with a brim in front, like the man I'd seen several days before. One turned to look at me as I came in. At a closer distance, I saw that on the front of his hat was a small red star. At the time, it reminded me of blood.

The man gave a sharp bow of his head in my direction, then turned back to my father, who was standing in their midst. I leaned toward them to hear what they said, but they were speaking in a language I couldn't understand. A young Tibetan man standing beside them took what they said and changed it into Tibetan for my father, but he was speaking so softly that even with my hand behind my ear nothing was clear.

That evening, after they left, my father met with several ministers in his room. Through a crack in the door, I could see him pacing back and forth in the room. I put my ear to the wood and heard

Pema Tsering, one of his ministers, speaking, "They have offered silks, brocades, silver coins in exchange for grain. They say they have come to liberate us from foreign imperialists . . ."

"But they are soldiers," Shamo Chemi, another minister, replied, "in the north they attacked the monastery in Chamdo . . ."

My father continued to pace back and forth. "They are trying to win our trust with bribes and promises," he said. "They put words like honey on a knife. But wait . . . you'll see. If you lick the honey your tongue will be cut. They aren't to be trusted."

The square wooden butt of the gun pressed against my shoulder. It was hard. I squeezed its cold trigger as tightly as I could and was knocked back against my father standing behind me. There was a pain like the kick of a horse on my chest. I bit my lip and said nothing.

I was on the roof with my father. He was teaching me how to use firearms. Below on the ground, in the field by the side of the house, was a post with a small wooden box on top which I was trying to hit. My father leaned forward to see how close I had come.

"Over that way," he gestured, "to the left, and up."

He took the long metal barrel and, crouching beside me, guided my arm toward it.

"Hold steady . . . don't breathe. Now! Fire!"

Again the pain on the chest.

"You've got it!" He tousled my hair with delight. "But if that were a Chinese? Would you dare to kill him?"

Would I dare to kill? The words rumbled through my mind like thunder.

I hear footsteps behind me coming down the walk. They tap in sharp brisk steps on the stone. Like the shots from a gun.

I turn to look. In the shadows there is a man standing, out of sight. All I can see are his shoes. The shoes of a foreigner. I turn and run. I run into darkness.

The footsteps are always behind me.

*　*　*

I woke up in a sweat.

All day, I couldn't shake free of my dream. Late in the afternoon, unable to still my fear by myself, I went in search of Gonlha. I found him in the chapel, polishing one of the hundred brass bowls on the altar.

When I told him what I'd seen, he sat silent, his eyes cast down to his hands in his lap. We sat together in silence. At times I thought he was meditating, at times he seemed asleep.

Just when I thought he hadn't heard me, he stirred and whispered my given name, "Lemdha Pachen," turning it over in his mouth as if it were a prayer bead. "Lemdha Pachen . . ."

As he repeated my name, his eyes slowly raised to meet mine.

"The world you see with your eyes is fleeting, like lightning . . . like dew. Only the world beyond thought and appearance is true. You must make your mind empty—make it spacious as the sky. Without dwelling on fears or concerns, bring it to rest."

He reached out and took my hands in his, then bowed toward me until our foreheads met. We sat, our hands together, our foreheads touching. Then he rose and walked, in his slow limping gait, out of the chapel to his room.

The light in the room had grown dim. In the distance, horns from a nearby monastery wailed on the darkening air.

I sat by myself, and in the light of a hundred butter lamps, I prayed.

Om Mani Peme Hum.

4

To the Monastery

The Year of the Wood Horse began like any other. A new year brought a new beginning. But just as it is part of nature to begin again, it is part of memory to forget. And so, like the grass that forgets its winter freeze and returns to the world refreshed, the Chinese presence soon faded from my thoughts.

Had I understood at that time that things gone from the mind don't necessarily disappear from the world outside, I might have been more concerned. For the Chinese had no intention of disappearing. Having tricked a Tibetan delegation into signing away our independence, they took hold like a dog to a bone, and never let go.

For several years their flattery and gifts lulled us into a state of complacency. "Our authorities will not change Tibet's government," they said. But they lied. All over Tibet they created their own regimes. In the neighboring city of Chamdo they set up a People's Liberation Committee, headed by Chinese officials. My father was appointed to represent our district of Gonjo, but in truth, like other Tibetans, he was only a token member and was rarely included in their meetings. In other parts of Tibet the committees began to implement reforms, but for the time being our village was left untouched and life went on as it always had.

As the year 1954 drew near, the world of committees and officials held no interest for me, and though my village of Lemdha was only a day's ride away, the situation in Chamdo seemed as distant as a faraway star.

Twenty days before the new year began, we stocked up on oil. Roasting seeds of mustard, we beat them into paste, then boiled the paste to get oil. For days kapsey cookies spattered and fried in large pans of oil, and soon tables overflowed with the steaming crisp morsels, some red and green, some salty, some sweet.

As the first day of Losar, the new year's celebration, grew closer, other foods were stored in terra-cotta containers. Pickled radish, oatmeal and ground meat, potatoes with cabbage, the cooked heads of sheep.

On the day before Losar, houses were cleaned from top to bottom, the coverings on doors and windows were changed. Altars were decked in dried barley, with a sheep's head and rice set to one side. Fresh silk was put around the statues of each deity, pillars were covered with brocade. New mattresses and rugs were brought to the kitchen for guests arriving over the next ten days. Even the good luck signs on the walls were given a fresh coat of white paint. And in the late afternoon, offerings of kapsey, fruit, sausages, sheep's head were taken to the three local monasteries.

On that evening after all the decorating had been done, huge copper kettles of water and milk were lifted onto the stove, steaming the air with a milky fragrance. Later, the women bathed their bodies in the satin liquid, as the men had the night before, and while the water ran down their arms they turned east in the direction of purity and peace.

I remember the light on our glistening skin. The mist rising into the air. The smooth silky feel of my body, cleansed for the coming year. And as I slept through that night before Losar, whenever I raised my hands to my nose, the sweet perfume of milk mixed with smoke scented my dreams.

In the first morning of the Wood Horse Year I woke early, several hours before dawn. The air was so cold it stung as I breathed. I hastily put on my sheepskin chupa, tied the straps around my boots, and ran down the stairs.

In the kitchen, Mama had taken the large copper bucket from the pantry and was headed for the door. Before she had time to protest I snatched the bucket from her hand and was out the door, on the path to the river.

In the windows of several other houses, I could see the flickering light of torches and thin curls of smoke beginning to rise from a chimney or two. But nobody else was out on the path, as far as I could see. The moon, sliced in half, was hanging low in the western sky, and gave off enough light to walk without tripping. Resting the bucket on my hip, I hurried toward the river.

When I reached its edge, I stopped to catch my breath. Water flowed under a thin layer of ice at its shore, clinking and tinkling like small silver bells. Behind me, I heard a crunching on the path. Pema Gyaltsen's son, Dhonyu, not far away, ran toward me.

I grabbed my bucket and plunged it into the water before he could reach me, the ice splintering like glass. He arrived out of breath just as I lifted it back to my hip. His face was filled with disappointment, and for a moment I thought he might knock the bucket from my hands. But then his mouth curled into a smile and he gave my shoulder a friendly push.

"You've got it! The golden water! The first water of the new year. It is fortunate for your family." I bowed, and turned in the direction of my house.

As I walked away, I heard him say under his breath, "The family of a chieftain already has enough good fortune . . ."

"Wake up, wake up," we called. "Papa! Ani Rigzin! Kunsang! Anya! Happy Losar!" We carried a wooden box ringed with gold paper banners, filled with buttered tsampa and wheat. In a silver pitcher, we carried the water.

I took my clothes and jewelry from beside my bed where I'd placed them the night before. Seeing the crisp new brocade of my chupa, I remembered years in childhood when I woke to find that under my pillow, as if by magic, new jewelry and clothes had appeared.

One year, there was a little white chupa, lined with white fur, a white fur hat for my head, and two large *Dzi* on a silver chain, mysterious stones from long-ago oceans, with black circled "eyes." That day, my father called me his little snow princess.

"Stay away from the stove, my little snow princess, or you'll melt." He laughed his big bear laugh and picked me up in his arms, nuzzling his nose in the fur of my chupa.

But now that I'd grown, the pillow beneath my head was bare, and it was I who folded new clothes by my bed at night.

In the chapel of our house, a golden Thangka from the Tibetan government had been specially hung for Losar. On the altar in front a golden statue of Guru Padmasambhava sat big as life. Two graceful female deities peered from wooden cabinets at his side, statues of all sizes and colors crowded in close. Rose-colored pillars carved with gold dragons rose to the roof. Sacred texts lined the walls. And on benches nearby, bells, horns, drums waited to be used.

In the chapel's huge hall, smoke curled up from the hundred butter lamps. Light from their flames flickered across the face of Padmasambhava. At times it seemed he was actually breathing. We prostrated, bowing reverently onto the ground three times in front of his image, placed a ceremonial white scarf at his feet, and folded our hands, palm to palm, in front of our heart.

We prayed to be free of the graspings of our minds so we might attain the essence of our true nature, primordial wisdom. We prayed to be cleansed of the poisons ignorance, hatred, and desire. We prayed to develop a compassionate, gentle attitude toward others. We prayed to follow the path of liberation.

On that morning, on the first day of the Wood Horse Year, in the golden chapel at the top of my house, I vowed to devote my life to the transformation of my limited ego, to the attainment of the rainbow body and the world of pure light. Let me cut through the attachments of my thoughts, let me treat others with compassion, let me return to Gyalsay Rinpoche's monastery for teachings. As I prayed, his monastery shimmered in my mind, beckoning me toward it.

Off and on throughout the day, I bent toward my hand where the sweet smell of milk still lingered. Something just beyond reach rode on its scent. Like light passing through grass in the meadows, or wind in the branches of trees, like mist curling up from the river, it carried me. When the scent started fading, I blew on my skin and for moments the warmth brought it back. Bit by bit it faded, and gradually it left, though its traces stayed with me throughout the next day.

～

Papa had been drinking chang since morning and was laughing louder than usual. The chieftain's hat given him by the Tibetan government had slipped to the side of his head. His yellow brocade chupa sagged a bit to the left. He stood in the back of the kitchen near the basins of chang, his arms encircling his good friend Pema Gyaltsen.

"Pema-la," his voice boomed out through the room, addressing Pema with the honorific "la." "Pema-la, my good friend. Drink to our years of friendship, to our days of youth, to our deeds of bravery . . . we have ridden over the plains of gold together . . . we have shot the silver arrow."

My father was usually silent in groups, unless he had something worthwhile to say, or unless he'd been drinking chang, when the fermented barley loosened his tongue. On that second day of Losar, guests came throughout the day. They ate food in great quantity, drank basinsful of chang. They celebrated, dancing, singing, gaming, and by night all spirits were high. At one point, after drinking to his good friend, my father even burst into song.

> *The good steed is like a swift bird,*
> *The golden saddle is like its feathers,*
> *When the bird and its feathers are together*
> *Then the great Highlands are easily crossed . . .*

He threw his arms around Pema Gyaltsen again and embraced him, drinking once more to their friendship.

I stood removed from the rest at the side of the room and watched. At the center, a group of men and women, boys and girls had begun to dance. They moved their legs together in unison, their arms wrapped around each other's waists.

"Ashe, come!" Lhamo waved at me to join them. I shrunk back against the wall, my face flushing.

No, no, I shook my head, wishing they wouldn't look. I bent down, as if my leg hurt. But Lhamo continued to call.

Trying to make my body as small as I could, I imagined myself somewhere else.

Ashe's a quiet one . . . always apart. The words turned in my head and I closed my eyes.

*   *   *

The hum in the room grew louder. Sounds of laughter, shouts. The plinking of strings. I opened my eyes.

At the other side of the room, I saw Pema Gyaltsen's son, Dhonyu, looking at me, his eyes like a wolf's, watching its prey.

I slid along the wall to one of the pillars and stood half hidden behind it, but his eyes continued to follow me, staring intently in my direction. Just then, I felt a tug at my chupa and looked down to see a ball of white at my feet. "Dolma!"

Relieved, I sank down and took her into my lap. She was panting, her little pink tongue hanging out, shining and moist. She squirmed in my lap, unable to still. I put my hand on her head. "I know," I said, "too many people, too much noise." I turned her over and stroked her silky pink stomach, feeling her heart jumping from the commotion in the room. "It's all right," I said, putting my head next to hers, "its all right."

"Ashe Pachen . . ." From across the room I heard Lhamo's mother calling me. She was a large woman, and swayed back and forth as she walked. She crossed the room and stood over me, looking down until I got up. I held Dolma against my chest, half hiding my face.

"Tashi Delek, a happy Losar," she said. I nodded my head.

She waited for me to speak. When I didn't, she went on as if I had. "I saw Pema Gyaltsen's son looking at you." Her tight little eyes were like pins in my head. My tongue felt stuck to the top of my mouth.

When I didn't respond she continued. "He would be a good match, the son of your father's best friend." Her mouth was partly open. Like a baby bird, I thought, waiting to be fed.

I took a step back, then, seeing my mother across the room at the stove, I pointed as if she were calling, and hurried away.

"Lhamo's with child," she called after me. I heard, but I didn't stop.

Mama was piling spareribs and noodles on platters. The sleeves of her blouse were rolled up, and one of her gold earrings had caught in her hair. She seemed annoyed when she saw me and waved me away. "Don't stand staring by yourself on the edge of the room . . . talk to the guests . . ."

I felt trapped by her words, and answered sharply, "I'll do as I please." I walked past her to the side of the room, leaned against the wall, and looked out over the room.

I never tired of watching people from a distance. I liked to imagine what went on behind the appearance they wore every day. Whether they were smiling, angry, or sad, I always saw more than what showed on their faces. Sometimes when no one was looking their faces would melt, and for moments I'd see a small child, an old woman, someone totally different. Sometimes, without knowing, the slightest gesture would reveal a deep secret—what they were really thinking, who they were underneath. I made up stories for each. I was no good at chatter, had no use for questions. I preferred to stare.

Late in the evening, Choenyi Dolma, a Gesar singer from our village, arrived at our house. I sat at the side of the room, my dog in my lap, to listen as Choenyi sang of Gesar's deeds. In a high, wavering voice, she began.

> *If anyone does not know this place, it is the kingdom of Ling, the center of the world. If anyone does not know me, I am Ma nene Karmo. I live in the blue turquoise palace, in the divine paradise . . .*

As she sang, her eyes raised to the sky, her face had a light of its own.

> *You must go to the underworld and when you get there, beware of the boar-headed and the dog-headed spirits. You will also find the cold hell and the hot hell there. There, too, is a bottomless river only you and your horse can cross . . .*

A silence had come over the room. All eyes were on Choenyi Dolma. A few leaned forward on their mattresses, some with expressions of deep concentration, some with expressions of wonder.

*When you destroy your enemies, Padmasambhava takes them
to the kingdom of heaven. I, Ma nene Karmo, always feel compassion for living creatures and never hate for them. You, too,
must be active. Do not stay here in Ling. Go to the underworld
to save the living creatures. Follow the white light.*

Would I have the courage to face the boar-headed spirits, I wondered, to endure the cold and hot hell. I thought how much more noble it was to save the living creatures than to marry. I prayed *Om
Mani Peme Hum, give me the courage.*

*In this way Ma nene Karmo sang about King Gesar's descent
into hell. From the victorious golden throne, King Gesar, the
heavenly ruler, the earth's tree of life, looked upon the assembly
with watchful eyes. All the fathers and mothers, sons and
daughters of Ling offered their adoration and good wishes to
the king. They performed songs and dances. They drank tea
and barley beer in a festive mood. Om Mani Peme Hum.*

At the end of the evening, some of the guests had gone home, some
fallen asleep on mattresses around the room. Mama sat down on a
bench by the stove and rubbed her face with her hands. Pieces of hair
had come down around her face, her brow was damp and pale. Her
hands seemed weighted by the twisted gold bracelets encircling them,
her fingers swollen beneath the gold rings. At her wrist, where two
veins came together, her pulse was jumping.

The sight of her pulse beating so rapidly alarmed me. She is so
tired, I thought. She's had no time to pray or do a regular practice. Her health could begin to fail. I began to worry. If she were
to die, what would happen to her spirit? And what would I do
without her? I felt sorry I'd spoken roughly earlier; I knew she meant
well.

"Let me rub your back," I said, sitting down behind her. I lifted
her hair, her neck pale and smooth, like an infant, so silken. I bent
over and kissed the soft furrow at the base of her head, then gently
began to stroke her back. "Sweet Mama," I whispered.

*   *   *

The next day I begged my father to let her go to Gyalsay Rinpoche's monastery, and after much crying and wringing my hands, he agreed. Several days later, I asked to accompany her. Again he agreed.

We left without even a sip of water or tea. Mama, Tashi, and I had horses, but there were many others traveling to the monastery who didn't have that luxury, and went on foot.

Each day during the three weeks' journey, we would stop to gather wood for the evening's fire when the sun began to go down. But one day, in a valley where a large meadow spread out, we stopped early. While the others were unloading the packs and setting up the tents, I walked down to the river by myself.

It was a small river, winding in curves like a snake through the meadow. In places it was open, in places tall grasses hid the banks. Though the air was cold, the snow had almost melted; only the edge of the forest was laced in white. I sat down in a place where the bank was bare, and for a time contented myself with throwing pebbles over its dark water. I found flat ones that skipped two or three times over the surface. I threw handfuls that fell like rain and watched circles spread as they dropped.

Up the river, a white shape caught my attention. A bird of some sort, but not one I'd seen before. Standing very still, its tall legs like sticks in the water, it was lit by the sun in such a way that at times it looked half like a person. Perhaps it's a deity, I thought, part human, part bird. I watched longer than I knew, for when I looked up, the sun had sunk several notches in the sky, and from across the field I heard Mama calling my name.

The sound of her voice must have startled the creature. Its neck straightened up like a spear thrown into the air, its head jerked around, and with long-winged sweeps, it lifted itself up from the water. With a wingspan as long as two people and a sound like the flapping of prayer flags in the wind, it rose up into the sky and was gone. I watched until only a small bent line was left in the sky, then walked back to camp.

All night I heard the flapping of a winged expanse in the air over my head, saw the lifting of long, thin stick legs. Once I thought I heard the cry of a night bird on the wind. It's an omen, I thought. My spirit will soon start to soar.

In the morning I woke feeling blessed.

That day, as I was riding, my mind drifted back to the first time I went to Khaley Rinpoche for vows and initiation. I was eight years old, and it was shortly after I learned to read and write. At that time, Gonlha said, "The best way to begin with the dharma practice is to receive the Refuge Taking Vows and then the initiation of Dorjee Phurba." I was filled with awe at the thought, and for days could think of nothing else. I begged him to take me to Khaley Rinpoche for the teachings. But he paid me no heed and went about his duties tending the chapel each day, as if the thought had gone out of his head.

Then one day, several months later when I least expected it, he told me he thought I was ready. I still remember the day we set out. A sweet, warm breeze was rustling the prayer flags outside our house. The grass was thick under foot, and flowers were scattered like stars over the hills.

Half an hour up a steep winding path we reached a small clearing. It was an isolated place some distance above Khaley monastery and thought to have once been a sacred place of Chenrezig, the Buddha of Compassion.

Khaley Rinpoche was sitting alone in a tent he had pitched at the upper end of the clearing. The tent was nestled against a rocky outcropping, and as we walked toward it, the large pointed rocks seemed to arch over in protection, like fingers closing in on a hand.

Hearing our steps, Khaley Rinpoche came to the window. I had seen him before with my family at teachings, but never alone, and never so close.

A shadow glides toward the window. A dark form, coming forward from deep in the room. As the light from outside slides over his head and onto his face, I see that his eyes are looking at me. I drop my head. My arms come up from both sides, joining my hands together in devotion. I touch the top of my head, my throat, my heart. Then, bending, I touch my hands to the ground, then my knees, until I am stretched with my forehead touching the ground. Three times like this, I prostrate in front of the compassionate Khaley Rinpoche in a gesture of reverence.

As I finish my prostrations, Gonlha nods to offerings of kapsey and fruit at my feet. I pick up the basket and scarf and walk forward with my eyes on the ground ahead of me, my heart fluttering with excitement.

When I reach the side of the tent, beneath the window, I hold out the basket and scarf until they are lifted gently up. A soft stroke of a hand passes over my head, and I raise my eyes.

Khaley Rinpoche sits in the window before me, his red-brown robe around one arm and over his chest. His long smooth face and half-cupped cheeks light up as his eyes narrow into a smile. His lips part.

"Life is a series of rebirths, each life determined by actions in a previous life. This we call Karma. Karma is made all the time. When you act with good motivation, your life is rewarded. When you act with bad motivation, your life suffers. As long as you fail to recognize this cyclical quality, your Karma will continue to repeat itself, in this life and the next."

A shadow passes over Khaley Rinpoche's face; his voice drops to a whisper.

"Know that the world is impermanent, like the clouds of autumn. The speed of human lives, like lightning in the sky, passing swiftly as a stream down a mountain. Without this understanding, life is suffering. Only by clearing your mind of delusion can permanent happiness be found, only by following the path to freedom and liberation will you finally find peace."

He looks at me with an expression of kindness, and asks, "Do you wish to commit yourself to this path? Do you wish to take refuge in the Buddha, of pure mind and compassionate heart? Do you wish to take refuge in the Dharma, the teachings that liberate, the path to freedom? Do you wish to take refuge in the Sangha, the spiritual community which will support you as you follow the path? The Buddha, the Dharma, and the Sangha. Do you wish to take refuge?"

"Tro la!" I say with all the conviction of my being. "I do!"

I bow my head forward. Khaley Rinpoche snips off a piece of my hair. "You are now Doctrine Holder Dharma Lamp," he says, addressing me by the spiritual name he has chosen. "Some day you may become an 'Ani,' a nun."

He touches the top of my head with the feathers of a peacock, and puts pieces of rice in my closely cropped hair.

"You have been given a precious human life with freedom and blessing," he says. "Be grateful, make the most of your opportunity. Practice well. Be compassionate to all living things."

A wave of happiness passes through me. I bow to the ground.

Later that day I was initiated into the deity practice of Dorjee Phurba. When I had done preliminary prayers, Khaley Rinpoche asked me to visualize him floating in the air in front of me. His three blue-black heads, his six hands, his four legs, his magnificent wings, before me in all his wrathful splendor. Light rays beyond imagination spun from his heart with the luster of molten sapphire, bodies of ego which tried to destroy him lay defeated at his feet.

"As you are watching," Khaley Rinpoche instructed, *"this wrathful and ferocious-looking being enters your body, filling you with the power of his compassion and enabling you to annihilate all inner obstacles standing in the way of freedom. His forceful compassion is now within you, cutting through the delusions of your mind. Merge yourself with his strength and power. He is now your protector."*

I left that day feeling a new sense of purpose. I was eight years old. Since then, that purpose has stayed with me wherever I've gone. It was that sense of purpose that accompanied me at the age of twenty-one as I traveled with my mother to Gyalsay Rinpoche's monastery.

On the last day of our journey we came to the Yangtze River. We reached the river's edge by late afternoon and dismounted. The river flowed swiftly from the melting of snows in the mountains and broke against boulders by the shore. Crossing was difficult. While men pulled boxes and bags from the yaks and drove the animals into the water to swim to the other side, Mama and I sat down on a packing box to await the coracle ferry.

Soon we heard the voice of a boatman echoing from around a bend in the river. It was shrill, like the call of a bird, announcing his approach. Shortly he appeared, rowing against the current, his boat sunk low in the water. The boat was made of yak skin lashed onto willow boughs, and curled up on all sides like a dumpling. When it got to the shore, eight men and two donkeys stepped out.

After clearing the boat of their packs, the boatman gestured to Mama and me, and with the help of a man from our party we climbed over the coracle's edge. A brackish scent from foam on the shore was heavy in the air. I leaned unsteadily against the side of the boat while our packs were loaded and others got in.

The boatman, a wizened old man with a ragged chupa and a worn fur cap, paced back and forth on the sandy shore as he waited for the boat to be filled. When we were finally ready, he scrambled up onto his perch at the front of the boat and, grasping two wooden oars in his weathered hands, began to row us across.

The current quickly caught us, and for a moment we were carried on the waves of a small rapid. We were thrown against one another as the boat rolled from side to side, and the spray from the boatman's oars dampened our faces. I clung to the smooth wood of the willow boughs, my fingers white from the cold of the water, and imagined Dorjee Phurba at my side, protecting me. Seeing his ferocious three heads gave me courage, and I soon got used to the roll of the boat.

We reached the other side in safety and began to climb into the hills. The path was well traveled but narrow, and we hadn't gone far when we were confronted by a long line of pilgrims descending from the monastery above. We moved to one side to let them pass by. A few steps farther, the tinkling of bells alerted us to a pack caravan coming round a bend in the road, and we stopped to make way for traders, their yaks weighted down with goods for the markets in Chamdo. As the path swung steeply up, we nearly collided with several young children carrying bundles of branches on their backs. Scrambling agilely over the large boulders, they hurtled toward us like rocks tumbling down the hillside, laughing and calling out "Tashi Delek" as they passed.

The path wound its way for miles ever more steeply up the side of the mountain, high above rushing streams. Occasionally, the echo of bells rose up the canyon wall from the pack trains below. Several times, Shindruk stumbled and stopped, refusing to move until I urged him on.

After an hour we reached the first stand of pine trees and, tired from the difficult climb, we stopped for a rest. Through the moss-clad firs, I could see a thin strand of silver winding far below; with my hand to my ear I could still hear the rush of the water. As the others sat down to eat dried cheese and pieces of meat, I leaned my head down on Shindruk's mane and stroked his matted coat with my hand. Good Shindruk, I whispered, rubbing my face in his pungent hair.

The scent from his damp flesh, mixed in with the sweet smell of pine, stirred in my head like incense. Years later, whenever I thought back to that day, the memories always came wrapped in the scent of damp horse and sweet pine, the image of Gyalsay Rinpoche's monastery always fused with those smells.

After climbing a short while further, we rounded a bend in the road. There, like an apparition, was the monastery. It was immense and glowing, stretching like a sacred mountain of stone, layer upon layer up the hillside. Already butter lamps had been lit and thousands of sparkling lights glimmered against the darkening hill. A gong echoed in a rhythmic pulse, and the low guttural chanting of monks floated down through the chilled evening air, deep, primal, as if arising from far inside the mountain. The sight filled me with awe.

We entered the large stone courtyard. A monk in long red robes appeared from a door at the side. He greeted us, clasping his hands in front of his chest and bowing his head.

We followed him up a flight of stone stairs, past a towering line of prayer wheels on the terrace and into a vast vaulted hall that echoed with the scurry of feet and the high, thin ringing of gongs. Hundreds of butter lamps shone from the walls and ceiling. Corridors stretched long and cool in every direction. The sweet, spicy scent of incense was thick in the air. Stillness enveloped me. At last, no one to disturb my mind. No one to see how I look, what I do. I am free!

The small room was dark but adequate. There was a mattress on one side by the wall, a table for an altar on the other. And in between, a small window opening out onto the courtyard two stories below. A chill hung in the air, as if the room had been vacant for some time. Dust and the ashes of incense mingled together on the table. The mattress was damp.

For a moment, the bareness of the room made me anxious. Alone with myself, I didn't know what to do. I stood uneasily in the middle of the room, sat down on the mattress, got up again. The room smelled musty. Taking a cloth from my bag I wiped the table clean, folded the cloth, paced across the room.

Ah, my altar. I searched through my bag until I found nine brass water bowls. I put them in a row at the front of the table, making sure the spaces between were the same. Behind them, I placed a small gold statue of Chenrezig, Buddha of Compassion, and on the wall I hung a Thangka of Dorjee Phurba. I stood back to look.

I moved Chenrezig and Dorjee Phurba several times until they were in just the right place. Prostrating in reverence three times in front of them, I then sat down to pray.

In the quiet of the room, silence filtered through the window like light. My breathing slowed down. I felt calm.

"Ashe," Mama called down the hall, "see what they've brought." A table in her room had been specially arranged in anticipation of our arrival, filled with dishes of meat, butter, tsampa, and pots of tea. Red and gold brocade covered the altar. Richly woven rugs lay on the mattresses. For a moment I regretted I was staying in the modest room of a nun.

"Simplicity is part of the spiritual life." Khaley Rinpoche's voice reminded that what I had was enough.

That night, as I got into bed, I looked around the room. My eyes followed along the crease where the ceiling joined the walls. Unobstructed by hangings or paint, it ran straight and clear around the top of the room. Below it, light from butter lamps on the altar spread a golden glow over the wall's empty surface. There was something about the emptiness of the walls, the straight crisp lines, that moved me, and gazing at them I fell into a peaceful sleep.

The face of a man drifts up through azure blue water. Young. At first indistinct, partly hidden. Then clearer, until he bursts through the surface, shimmering in gold. His eyes meet mine, and I gasp.

"His Holiness!" I said when I woke.

"I saw His Holiness in a dream," I told Mama over breakfast. "He was surrounded in gold."

"A sign," Mama said. "He is watching over you."

My heart leaped. I felt blessed.

A novice monk brought butter tea to our rooms, and later hot water in a bucket for washing. A short time after, one of Rinpoche's attendants appeared and gestured to Mama and me to follow him. My heart was pounding as I took my offerings and set out after him down the dark, narrow passageways that wound through the monastery.

Our descent took us through immense kitchens, where great iron kettles of tea steamed on high stone ovens. The walls, covered with centuries of soot, were black as night. The faces of monks attending the fires were even blacker, but as we passed, their eyes brightened in greeting.

We hurried through the winding corridors past stuffed yaks, bears, and tigers suspended from the ceilings; past swords, spears, brightly painted shields mounted on walls; stopping briefly before the main temple where hundreds of monks sat cross-legged, bowed in prayer. Light from the windows mixed with the smoke of the butter lamps. From where we stood, the endless rows of rounded robed shapes looked like boulders in a giant cave. The room filled with the muted hum of their voices in prayer. Far away I heard the distant call of a trumpet.

We continued, sliding one foot in front of the other to be sure of our footing. I could see only a short distance ahead, and with each step my vision grew dimmer until all I could see was the glimmer of butter lamps far in front. In the dimness I reached for Mama's chupa.

Farther on we passed an altar of Dorjee Phurba. He stood in a circle of flames, the bodies of our mind's enemies at his feet. Rivers of blood flowed from the mound he was standing on, weapons of destruction to slay the ego were clasped in his many hands.

A shiver ran through me when I saw him, and I stopped to prostrate. *"Blessed Dorjee Phurba, help me to cut through the grasping of my mind."*

After what seemed like an eternity of walking, we arrived at the inner chamber. On either side, fierce demonic deities carved of wood guarded the entrance. The attendant opened the door, and we stepped in.

After a moment I summoned the nerve to look up.

Gyalsay Rinpoche was sitting on a simple mattress in the back of the room, a red cloak wrapped around his large body. His face was illuminated by a tiny beam of sun, filtering down through the darkness from a window on the upper wall. Like the golden face of the Buddha, his face was radiant; I quickly lowered my eyes. Filled with an almost unbearable happiness, I fell mute with my hands in my lap, my head bowed.

His attendant served us sweet rice, curd, meat to welcome us. Mama spoke to him of our trip. Before leaving, we presented the offerings and traditional white scarves we'd brought him. I glanced quickly around his room as we left. It was simple, only a small altar and two plain Thangkas, one Lord Buddha, one Padmasambhava.

For days the simplicity of the room and the radiance of Rinpoche's face guided my mind as I prayed.

That night at dinner I noticed that Mama looked better. The color had come back in her cheeks, the lines around her eyes had eased. "Aren't you glad we came?" I asked. She smiled and looked down, like a small child who'd been given a treat. Before leaving, I bent down and laid my head on her shoulder. She nestled against my cheek. "I'm happy we're here," I said, and could feel her smile.

The next morning, I was awakened by the rhythmic beating of monastic drums from the top of the roof, announcing the start of a teaching. I hurried to dress, joined Mama and others from nearby rooms, and went down to the courtyard. We made our way between a hundred participants sitting on the ground in prayer. The air was filled with the sound of the long brass trumpets from the roof and the chanting of monks in the temple beyond. Rinpoche was already seated on a great wooden throne facing the courtyard. Shortly after we sat down, he began.

"Whomever is alive today will be dead in a hundred years. Like a hair pulled from butter you will leave all you've accumulated. What riches you've earned will be left behind.

"But even with wealth the size of an ant hill, if you become selfish, it will bring suffering the size of a mountain. Keep your wishes small and be happy with what you are, then you cannot be controlled by ill fate."

Lhamo floats effortlessly down the stairs in her yellow brocade chupa with embroidered flowers at its hem. Her long hair is intertwined with turquoise beads. Golden earrings hang from her ears. Necklaces of coral and turquoise at her neck. Her wrists are encircled with bands of jade, her fingers with onyx.

At the end of the day, the decorative brocade on the pillars begins to droop, empty cups of chang scatter on tables at the edge of the room, dishes pile in the back, near basins of water. In every corner, presents, stacked one on top of another.

The senselessness of so many things.

I remembered Rinpoche's room. The small simple altar. The empty walls. The light on his radiant face.

Through the long afternoon of prayer, these images guided me. When I returned to my room in the evening, I glanced at my small altar. One statue, one Thangka, nine water bowls, that is all I need.

*   *   *

The next day, Rinpoche continued.

"Nothing is permanent. You are like lightning in the sky, like the bubbles on water, like dew on the leaves of the trees. But if you see death in everyday life, it will give a foundation to your practice. Thus it is important to understand the nature of death and the transitoriness of all living things.

"All beings are submerged in an ocean of suffering, caused by false beliefs, anger, and greed. If you wish to free yourself of this suffering, like seeing a doctor to become free of an illness, you must seek out a lama and practice his teachings.

"First you should learn to observe your mind and simplify how you see things. Bring your mind into a state of calm. Whatever thoughts or feelings arise, allow them to rise and settle, without following their path. Like the wind that comes and goes without changing the sky, let them flow through your mind without affecting it. Rest your mind lightly on an object of beauty."

I watched the light sparkle down through the leaves on the trees. It moved in tiny gold butterflies over the ground. My back began to ache as I watched. I changed my position but the ache wouldn't leave. My attention shifted to the pain. I remembered feeling it while Shindruk was climbing the mountain. My thoughts began to wander . . . Shindruk . . . has anyone remembered to feed him? My thoughts slipped away so quickly, I barely noticed. Soon I was lost in memory.

A little white colt nuzzles its mother's leg. It is several days old, and still wobbling on tiny legs. "Oh, Papa, look." I point to the colt. "Can I have him for my own?"

"Remain focused." Gyalsay Rinpoche's voice brought me back with a start.

"Whatever thoughts or feelings arise," he repeated, "allow them to exist without following their path."

Mindful of Gyalsay Rinpoche's words, I let the memory drift away, and returned my attention to the present.

"Each day, avoid wrongful acts," Gyalsay Rinpoche continued.

"Even a very small misdeed will have an effect, and its consequence will come back one day to haunt you."

Once again my mind drifted.

Gasey-Gyama's son leans against his father's arm, his eyes looking down at the ground as if hoping not to be noticed. I sneak up behind, reach around, and pull the sash to his chupa. The chupa comes loose. The boy's face flushes; he pulls the chupa around him and ties the sash. I reach over and pull it again. "Stop," he pleads, almost in tears. I can't stop giggling.

"It is like a fruit that will come out when ready. If your actions are good, the fruit of your life will be good; if your actions are bad, the fruit will be spoiled."

"You are a mischief-maker, some day you'll be sorry." Mama's voice echoed in my mind.

I turned my attention back to Gyalsay Rinpoche and listened intently.

"You cannot change your life until you change your mind, therefore everyone should strive to have good mental attitude"

Rinpoche paused. "I will tell you a story to illustrate.

"Once upon a time, there was an old mother crossing a river with her daughter. As they were crossing, they were carried out by the water. As they were being washed away, the mother thought that whatever happened to her didn't matter if it was possible to save her daughter. And the daughter was thinking the same thing, it didn't matter what happened to her, if her mother was safe.

"In the meantime, while each was thinking about the other's safety, both were washed away and drowned. And though both drowned, because they each had a compassionate state of mind at the moment of death, they were lifted back to life by the god Sang Pa.

"Therefore, you should be willing to give up your life without hesitation to help others. Every day concentrate on others as a mother on a child, thinking of others before yourself. Each day that should be your motivation. Try not to let a prideful mind run your life, but instead place yourself at a modest level, coming from the heart.

"Remember the words of Buddha: 'In separateness lies the world's greatest misery; in compassion lies the world's true strength.' To make the world a better place, practice compassion, tolerance, and respect; this is the basis of religious activity. These actions help in your present life and are an asset for the next. Their qualities, like precious jewels, can never be destroyed, even by death."

"I want to be kinder," I said to Mama at dinner. She looked up with a curious expression, as if waiting for me to say more. But when I was silent, she smiled, and returned to her soup.

Later I prayed: *Let me control my unruly behavior, let me accumulate merit to wash away my negative actions.*

Several weeks later, a young woman arrived with her family. I noticed her one afternoon in the dining hall while we were having our midday meal. She was taller than I, her long dark hair pulled back and hanging loose down to her waist. Her complexion was clear with a rosy tint, her eyes dark and intense.

The next morning, she sat down beside me in the chapel. I saw the way she clasped her beads when she prayed, the look of adoration on her face, and I couldn't help thinking that she reminded me of myself. When she got up to leave, I followed her. She walked out to the open courtyard and sat on a stone ledge looking out over the spreading green pastures below.

"You have just come?" I ventured.

"Yes, from the other side of the Yangtze River in Derge," she replied. "I have been here twice before. Gyalsay Rinpoche is my main guru."

"I've been here before too!" I said, delighted by our common experience. "Rinpoche is my guiding light."

After that initial exchange, we were curious to learn more about each other and sat for hours talking. We talked of our early teachings, of our desire to follow a spiritual path, of the temptations of pleasure, the impermanence of life.

I was surprised how easily we understood each other. I had only to
say a few words and she grasped what I meant. When she spoke, I
understood before she even opened her mouth. I had never had such
an ease in conversing. With others I found myself repeating my
words over and over until they understood what I was feeling, and
some never did. With Dekyong, the comprehension was instant. Our
outlook was so similar, our feelings so alike, that we barely needed to
speak.

"Do you feel sad, sometimes for no reason?" she asked as we were
getting up to leave.

"When I'm separated from the spiritual teachings," I said, "or
with people who are only concerned with material things, I begin to
feel a sadness I can't explain."

"Yes," she said. "I understand."

Dekyong and I quickly became inseparable. Though we were often
in silence contemplating the teachings, a bond began to form between us, linking the most delicate part of our spirit.

We were close, but I knew even then that "togetherness" is an illusion, that between the closest beings a boundless space continues
to exist. No matter whom we cling to, what we grasp, it is like
fingers grasping the wind. Open them up and nothing is there. No
thing. No I.

And yet just as a flock of geese wave their long winding V across
the sky, I knew we were also connected. The tiniest insect, the tallest
mountain. Held together by invisible threads. An intricate web.

After I had been at the monastery more than a month, Gyalsay Rinpoche sent word that it was time to complete my preliminary practice. I leaped off of my mattress, grabbed a piece of fruit to give as an
offering, and ran down the dark corridors behind his attendant.

When I reached his room, I found him sitting alone in silence. I
slipped in through the door, prostrated three times, and sat down on
a mattress in front of him. After a few moments I summoned my

courage to look at his face. His eyes were partly closed in meditation. Not wanting to disturb him, I sat for some time fingering the Mani beads, counting. One bead, one mantra. *Om Mani Peme Hum,* I repeated silently to myself. *Let my mind open to receive the compassionate blessings of Chenrezig.*

Gyalsay Rinpoche continued to sit silently, never losing concentration. His hands were resting lightly on his folded knees, the nails of his fingers long and carefully rounded. His garnet robe wrapped over one shoulder, his saffron blouse covering his arms, he sat in stillness like an enormous statue of Lord Buddha.

Just when I thought I'd made a mistake in coming, he began to speak. His eyes stayed in the same half-open position, his face was serene and immobile, his lips barely moved as his words came out. He slid from meditation to speech so effortlessly, the states were no different; remaining in the place of expanse and calm, his mind clear as a sacred lake.

As he began to speak, his voice filled the room with its resonant tone.

"All joy in the world has come through wishing happiness for others. All misery, through wanting pleasure only for oneself.

"The grasping mind hides one's true nature. When anger, ignorance, and pride are removed, basic wisdom can be revealed. Wipe away negative qualities through meditation; treat others with a compassionate heart."

Rinpoche paused, as if wanting to be sure I understood. I did.

I feel my face flush with anger. The meat on my plate is lean, unappealing. The sight of it annoys me, and I push the plate away.

"I want meat that has fat on it," I say, pouting my lips and crossing my hands over my chest. "Come! Take this away."

Anya rushes to my side, with Thupten close behind.

"Ashe, don't cry," Anya pleads, seeing the tears forming in my eyes. "This is the meat that was cooked. Your mother told us to feed you. Girls who are eight years old shouldn't cry."

"You must eat what's prepared," Thupten adds. "We can give you nothing else."

"I won't!" I say, knocking the plate to the floor. It bounces on the

hard wood surface and pieces of food scatter like broken glass over the rug.

I rise and stand in front of them, my hands at my waist. "I will tell Papa, and you will be punished."

I stamp my feet defiantly and turn toward the door. Glancing over my shoulder, I see them huddle together, their faces white, their hands trembling. "I will show them," I think. "They will be sorry."

"A clear mind, and compassion toward others," Gyalsay Rinpoche continued when he thought I'd absorbed his words, "that is the essence of the teachings."

I felt ashamed at my willful nature, and looked down.

Rinpoche shifted slightly on his mattress. But except for the meager movement, he remained in the same state of quiet while continuing to speak.

"The preliminary practice contains all paths," he said with special emphasis. "It starts with trainings to help the mind turn toward the Dharma, and ends by uniting it with the enlightened wisdom of Buddha. Every effort should be made to complete the practice."

His eyes still halfway closed, he leaned forward.

"You have begun the practice. Are you ready to continue?"

Feeling badly about my self-centered acts, I merely nodded my head.

"We will start with the cleansing of channels."

Rinpoche told me to visualize the wisdom air, directing it in through one nostril. Force air down one side, up the other, and out the opposite nostril. Then the reverse.

"With each breath you are cleansing the channels of anger, desire, and ignorance, expelling the diseases of wind, bile, and phlegm," he said at the end of the practice. "Now, go back to your room and practice."

"You are a fussy eater," Mama said at dinner, noticing my plate still half full. "You should finish your food." I felt my face flush. "I'll eat what I please!" I got up and went back to my room.

In front of my altar, I struggled with my feelings.

"A clear mind, and compassion toward others . . ."
"Who is as fussy as you . . ."
My feelings flipped, like a fish on dry land. Shame, irritation, remorse, anger.
"With each breath you are cleansing the channels of anger . . ."
I breathed in, imagined wisdom flowing into my lungs. I breathed out, felt anger leaving my body. In. Out. In. Out. I struggled.

"Today we will awaken loving kindness, compassion, joy, and equanimity," Gyalsay Rinpoche said.

"Visualize a clear light with nectar coming down on you from Guru Rinpoche. The light touches you. It blesses you and all sentient beings, it purifies your body, speech, and mind. It enters you. You and all beings rise up like a great flock of birds, all dissolve into Guru Rinpoche. Rinpoche, in turn, dissolves into the great expanse, the ultimate truth. All dissolve into the bodhicitta of great emptiness."

Day after day, I contemplated Gyalsay Rinpoche's teachings, struggling with the habits of my mind. His words were inspiring, but putting them into practice was as difficult as pushing a ferryboat up a steep hill.

One morning, I woke earlier than usual. For no clear reason, I felt out of sorts. The stone floor was colder when I prostrated. The water in my bowls spilled when I emptied them out. The strap on my boots broke when I wound it around. My head ached. My temper, which had been silenced since coming to the monastery, poured back in full force. Nothing I could do made it stop. I threw my boot on the floor. I stamped my foot. Meaningless things! I thought.

Am I lazy? I wondered after I'd calmed down. I want to live quietly, undisturbed by worldly things. Am I concerned for myself and nobody else? Have I the strength to follow the path? For a long time I sat quietly struggling to bring my mind to rest.

At times my mind soared. My thoughts swept away.

Other times, I was so sleepy I could barely open my eyes.

*   *   *

Seeking relief from my thoughts one morning, I walked to the courtyard and looked out at the rolling expanse. The sky was just beginning to lighten. In the east, a thin row of clouds had turned
purple-pink in the rising sun. They waved across the horizon like serpents in flight.

Moments later, like a spark igniting a fire, the rest of the sky came
alive with color. A soft, veiled pink arched above and around on all
sides. In the distance, the pines on the surrounding hills were black
and feathered. Below, I heard the call of a mourning dove.

My being, weary from struggle, softened. For a long time I watched
the sky change color, listened to the echo of gongs from the temple.

"Do you feel troubled by the life your parents have chosen for you?"
Dekyong asked as we walked down the corridor hand and hand. "I
feel pulled between what they expect and following my heart."

Dekyong put into words the struggles I felt in myself.

"They want me to marry and have children," she continued. "I
want a life of silence and prayer."

It was hard for me to answer. I felt a calling to leave worldly dis-
tractions behind, but I also felt a duty to family. I struggled between
the two.

"My aunt Rigzin always tells me to follow my heart," I finally
said. "She says that serving the Buddha brings more riches than having a husband and child."

"My parents would be unhappy if I refused what they wished.
They might even be angry," Dekyong said. "If I marry who they
choose, it will strengthen our family. If I follow a spiritual path . . ."
She didn't finish.

"I know," I whispered. "I have felt the same way."

We walked on in silence, past the sacred shrines and temples of the
monastery, past the giant prayer wheels lining the courtyard, to
the path around the outer wall. For the next hour, we circled the holy
building in reverence, prayer beads in hand. *Om Mani Peme Hum.*
A thousand times we said *Om Mani Peme Hum,* until the sky grew
dark.

The days settled into a routine. I received teachings. I met with Mama for meals. Dekyong and I walked the long path encircling the monastery.

Daily there were struggles with my mind. Daily I practiced to bring it to rest.

At the end of the preliminary teachings, Gyalsay Rinpoche summoned me before him once again.

"Imagine the face of Padmasambhava, Guru Rinpoche, before you," he told me when I had settled in front of him, his eyes filled with compassionate love. "Imagine yourself melting into a ball the size of a pea. Shoot up like a spark and merge with his heart, then dissolve into his enlightened mind. Like pouring water into water, there is no difference between you and Guru Rinpoche. Remain in this state, experiencing his wisdom."

He leaned forward, and I felt the warm pressure of his fingers, his precious hands in a cap over my head. No words were spoken, but in my heart, a torrent of feeling released.

That night when I prayed, I felt the boundaries of my skin fall away. My spirit flowed out through the room.

Later, I dreamed.

I am soaring through a vast expanse. Below me the hills are a thin scar on the earth. At my side, winged arms rise slowly, and fall. In this spaciousness, the sky stretching in every direction, I feel part of all beings.

The next day, Gyalsay Rinpoche asked if I had completed the preparation for mind training.

"One hundred thousand prostrations. One hundred thousand mandala offerings. One hundred thousand deity practices. One hundred thousand mantras of Refuge. If those aren't done, you can't receive further instruction."

Remembering my hands scraping against the cold stone floor, sometimes a thousand times a day, my fingers keeping count on the Mani beads, my lips cracked dry in prayer, I said, with assurance, "I have."

Every day after that I gathered with others in the courtyard to receive instruction. The first day, Gyalsay Rinpoche read from the "Flight of the Garuda."

> *I will now sing this song about the view . . .*
> *It enables one to swiftly traverse all the levels and paths.*

I sat listening beneath the giant prayer wheels at the courtyard's edge. Overhead, clouds were rushing across the sky. Like supplicants they blew, their heads stretched out on long twisting necks, their tiny hands hanging beneath them in prayer. All morning, the pale winged creatures passed overhead.

"What is the view?" Rinpoche asked. "It is being able to see things as they actually are. It is understanding that the nature of the mind is the nature of everything, and that that nature is the absolute truth.

"And what is the nature of mind? It is like a sky: empty, spacious, and pure. Like the sun: luminous, clear, not obstructed. It is always present, it is everywhere."

When he had finished speaking, we formed a single line to receive a mantra. As I passed by his wooden throne, he whispered in my ear, "Luminosity is the nature of one's mind, no amount of confusion can darken it."

After receiving his words, we walked slowly down the rough stone steps toward the forest. In one valley the men gathered, in another, the women. There, we formed a circle around our instructor, a nun for the women, a monk for the men, and hour after hour they patiently went over with each the words we'd been given.

All day, all night, in prayer, at meals, before sleeping, after waking, I contemplated Rinpoche's words to me. "Luminosity is the nature of one's mind . . ."

Luminosity, the nature of my mind. A bright glowing light, traveling through each part of my body. Each golden strand, creeping into my blood and my bones. Dazzling the darkness of my thinking, dispelling my selfish desires. No matter how confused I became, how grasping I grew, my mind's true nature would remain, indestructible, everlastingly luminous.

Each day I felt the sensation of light grow through me, like a rainbow spreading over the sky. A luminous heat lodged near my heart.

"Light," Dekyong said to me one morning, "we are all made of light."

As the months passed by in the monastery, I began to feel that was true. Thoughts came and went, at times I felt heavy and stiff. But often they dissolved. At those times I felt myself rippling, like ribbons of light.

Tat-tat. Tat- tat. "Lemdha Pachen Dolma." Tat-tat.

I turned in my bed.

"Your father has sent a servant to bring you home." The voice of Gyalsay Rinpoche's attendant was loud on the other side of the door. Tat-tat.

I turned in my bed. The room was still dark. Under the crack of the door I could see the light of a flickering lamp, tiny flame-streaks over the floor. Blown by the wind, it wavered, almost went out, wavered, came back.

"Lemdha Dolma." The voice grew louder. "Your father is asking for you home."

"Ah-lay," I called back, "ah-lay, I hear."

"The servant is waiting in the courtyard below."

"I will come," I replied.

The light flickered once more, then gradually dimmed. His footsteps faded away down the hall.

I turned over and looked toward the ceiling. In the darkness, the lines at the top were hidden from sight. I felt an urgency rising and filling my head. My feet felt like lead.

*   *   *

In the courtyard, a dark form walked toward me out of the morning mist. As he came closer, I could see it was Thupten, a paper rolled under his arm.

"A letter from your father, Pomdha Gonor," he said as we met. I could tell he preferred to have me read my father's words than tell me himself.

> "*My dear Lemdha Pachen,*" my father wrote, addressing me in a formal manner. "*It has been six months that you have been gone. It is time to come home, and begin to learn your duties as heir of a chieftain.*
>
> "*Gyalsay Rinpoche asks that your mother stay to finish her practice. But you are young. You will be able to return another day. In the meantime, he will ask Khaley Rinpoche to continue your training.*
>
> "*Thupten will accompany you.*
> *Your Father, Pomdha Gonor, Chieftain of Lemdha*"

My heart sank, but I knew it was my duty to go.

I left the next day. The morning was overcast, and clouds hung in clusters overhead. The wind was blowing in from the east, and there was the feeling of a coming storm in the air. Mama cried as I hugged her good-bye. I could feel her thin shoulders tremble beneath my hand, and heard a small animal sound in her chest. I stroked her cheek and kissed her forehead, but was unable to look into her eyes.

Thupten was anxious to leave before the rains began, and gestured at me to come right away. I gathered what little belongings I had, and as we were mounting our horses, Dekyong came running down the large stone stairs.

She threw her arms around me, and we clung together as the rain started falling. Her body was warm, tinged with the scent of sweet grass. I felt her heart beat against mine. Beating and breathing the same rhythm, we stood holding each other until it felt we were wrapped in one body.

I don't know how many moments passed as we stood like that.

But when we finally came apart, it seemed my blood and breath stayed behind.

As I got on my horse, her hand rose to wave. I could see it fluttering above her head as I rode through the gate. Like the wings of a moth it waved overhead as I began down the path.

I turned one last time to look back. In a monastery window two stories up, I saw the face of Gyalsay Rinpoche looking down at us. His face was clear and calm. His eyes were filled with kindness. He bowed his head slightly and raised his hand. It was then that I began to cry.

That was my third meeting with Rinpoche. It was also the last.

5

A Growing Threat

I fell into a state of despondency in the days following my return from the monastery. Although nothing was different at home, something had changed. As if a thin silken veil were separating me from the others around, I felt invisible.

Papa was gone attending meetings when I returned. He left no instruction, no indication why he'd summoned me, and I was frustrated to find myself home for no apparent reason. The others were absorbed in their everyday chores. At night when they finished their work, they sat by the fire gossiping about neighbors and talking over the events of the day. I sat at the edge of the room feeling strangely apart.

Bit by bit I withdrew into myself, neither sad to have left nor happy to be back. Preferring to be left alone, I retreated upstairs to a room by the chapel.

"Ashe! Ashe!" Anya and Kunsang would come to the door, trying to draw me out. I joined them to help with the chores, but their idle chatter brought me close to tears, and I soon fled back to my sanctuary. It was only when I saw the peaceful faces of Ani Rigzin or Gonlha that I felt a glimmer of what I'd experienced at the monastery. It was as if their faces were mirrors, reflecting my own true nature back to me. And trying to hold on to that rapidly fading sense, I wandered the halls and stairways at night, hoping somehow to rekindle it.

One day, I ventured out of the house and down toward the river. In the distance I saw Sonam and Gosay Pema Tsering washing their clothes. When they spotted me, they rushed toward me waving their hands in the air.

"Ashe, did you fall in love?" Sonam called.

"Were you pregnant and hiding away?" Gosay Pema Tsering giggled.

When they reached me, they pulled playfully at the sleeves of my chupa and poked my ribs. I felt at a loss for words, but they didn't seem to notice. They chattered away, telling what had happened since I'd been gone.

They rolled each bit of news in their mouths, savoring it, chewing it over, then spitting it out. "Old Ama Rinchen died and her son ran away ... Lhamo had a baby ... Dechen and Tashi are lovers ..."

I nodded, they talked. In my head there was a tingling as if thousands of bubbles were bursting. The more they talked, the more I felt myself drifting away, beginning to disappear.

With an effort, I pulled myself free. Not far away, at the edge of the river, a woman was sitting with a bundle in her lap. A tiny hand was clasped onto one of her fingers. She rocked back and forth, one hand on the baby, the other rinsing a long piece of cloth in the water.

At first I didn't know who it was. Her hair was pulled tightly back. Fine lines curved over the side of her brow.

Then I recognized the familiar profile. "Lhamo, is that you?"

Her mouth moved upward into a faint smile, and she nodded. As I got closer I saw loneliness in her eyes. Her body was fuller, her face worn. The carefree girl I had known for so many years was no longer there.

We tried to talk to each other, but the words were heavy and lifeless, and after a few pleasantries we parted. How quickly we had grown in different directions.

The feelings that had been so alive in the monastery began to grow dim. I said prayers, did prostrations and offerings, but it wasn't the same. The light and expanse that had filled me felt far away. The unspoken kinship with others seemed lost. Whenever I thought of Dekyong or beloved Gyalsay Rinpoche, I felt an ache I couldn't explain, something so close to me gone, like veins being pulled, one by one, from my flesh.

Papa continued his travels away from home. Caught up in the events to the north, he rode from village to village attending meetings. Whenever he came home, even for a day, he was locked in his room with his ministers.

I tried to do things to make him notice me. I picked a bouquet of flowers and brought them in with his tea. I taught Dolma to carry his belt in her teeth. I practiced shooting his gun from the roof. But nothing worked.

"It was four years ago that His Holiness sent a delegation to Peking," I heard my father telling his ministers as I passed by his room one day. "At the time, as all of you know, the Chinese promised to respect Tibet's religion and culture.

"That was in 1950, the Year of the Iron Tiger. Now, after four years of broken promises, we have had enough! It is rumored that His Holiness has been invited to China. It is also rumored that the Tibetans in Lhasa are opposed to the trip. I pray he won't go."

"His Holiness the Dalai Lama is coming to Chamdo," a messenger cried as he ran through the kitchen in the direction of my father's room. Like dust kicked up by his passing feet, words began to swirl through the room. "His Holiness is coming ... arriving in Chamdo ... when is he coming?"

Without waiting to hear more, I jumped from the bench by the fire and ran, two steps at a time, up the stairs. I arrived, out of breath, in my father's room in time to hear the messenger repeat his announcement.

"His Holiness the Dalai Lama will pass through Chamdo on his way to China in three weeks. I have been sent to request that Chief Pomdha Gonor join the eight other chieftains of Gonjo district in traveling to the capital city of Chamdo to receive His Holiness's blessings."

Hearing the name of His Holiness, I was filled with an indescribable happiness. Almost instantly, the despair I'd been in since returning from the monastery disappeared.

His Holiness! The emanation of Chenrezig, god of Compassion! My heart leaped at the thought. Shortly after he had been enthroned we received a photograph of him and I knelt before it for hours. He was seated on his throne, the great wheel of life beneath him, his shoulders covered with a rich gold and maroon robe. He was leaning slightly forward, his lips parted as if about to speak. His eyes looked straight into mine. They were filled with such genuine interest that I felt he was seeing my innermost thoughts.

From that time on I felt understood by him, and believed he was looking out for me, guiding my path.

"Tell my ministers to prepare." My father's voice broke into my thoughts. "I will leave tomorrow with eight attendants and servants."

The messenger bowed and turned so abruptly that his short brown chupa flapped at his knees, stirring the air by my feet.

"What is it you want, young Nyu?" my father asked, when the others had left.

I pulled at the belt of my chupa, uncertain how to ask him in a way that would get his consent.

Behind the stern lines in his face, I could see a slight smile and a twinkling in his eyes. "Could it be that you want to travel with me to Chamdo?"

I put my arms around his neck and kissed both his cheeks.

"All right, you can come," he said, laughing and tousling my hair, "but you'd better be ready by morning."

I will see His Holiness, I thought. I will also be with Papa.

The next morning we left. Papa, eight chieftains, their attendants, and me. It was late in the summer during the heavy rains, and all day rain blew, layer after layer, across the high meadow. At times it blew from the side, coming at me so hard I had to bend my head down to keep it from lashing my face. It trickled over my head and under my chupa, rolling in tiny wet beads down my back. As the day wore on, the dampness spread through my clothes. By the time we stopped for the night, even the saddle blanket I sat on was wet.

We stopped at a place where the hill began to slope down to a valley. There was a cluster of rocks at its side which provided shelter of sorts. Several of the men wrapped a tent over the tips of the rocks, others built a fire with yak dung, and we huddled underneath, close to the fire, to dry. Later, the smell of damp wool still around me, I drifted into an uneasy sleep.

Pale and transparent like rain, a line of men, five hundred long, ride on horses across the high plain. Noblemen in rich brocade chupas, a turquoise earring dangling from one ear. Religious leaders in robes of maroon, triangular hats pointed up toward the sky. Servants and attendants in chupas the color of rich darkened earth. And in their midst, surrounded by rainbow light, the Dalai Lama on a snow white horse.

They move as if blown by the wind, in layers of mist, slanting forward. Their heads are bowed toward the east, their feet flung back to the west. As if pulled in a tug of war between where they are going and where they have come from, they drift ahead out of sight.

"I have just come from the forests of Poyul to the south," a young man cried, as he galloped up to us the next day. "I saw His Holiness and his party. They were traveling on a road the Chinese are building along the side of a gorge high above a river. In many places it was washed out. The party had to get off their horses and walk for miles through ankle-deep mud, while boulders fell around them like hailstones."

The young man looked weary. His horse and his chupa were spattered with mud. He wiped the sweat off his brow and shifted in his seat.

"One day five mules slipped over the edge of the trail," he continued. "They pulled two of their handlers to their death on the rocks below. Later that day, another in the party was killed by a falling rock. Several officials quickly gathered to discuss the situation.

"They decided it was pointless to go on, and asked their Chinese escorts to permit them to return to the old Tibetan trade route. The Chinese would not hear of it, and insisted they continue on the unfinished road.

"As I parted ways with them, His Holiness and his party were being transferred into trucks and jeeps at the command of the Chinese. If lucky, they will arrive in Chamdo in less than a week. But their spirits are low."

A silence fell over our group. My father's eyes flashed in anger. "We must hurry, to reach Chamdo in time," he said. "We must pay our respects to His Holiness. He needs our support."

As he urged his horse on in the direction of Chamdo, he said under his breath, "It is a bad omen. It does not bode well for His Holiness's trip."

*   *   *

For the next five days, we pushed our horses hard, traveling from early morning until late at night. My knees were sore from holding tight to my horse's sides, an ache ran up my back to the top of my spine, but I thought of His Holiness's compassionate face and rode on.

My father rode at the front of the line, his body bent forward as if trying to shorten the distance ahead. The others, not wanting to fall behind, pressed on with the same sense of urgency.

I soon fell to the back of the line, where my only view was the swaying tails of horses, the raising and lowering of hooves. As the distance between us grew, I felt a sinking inside. Papa includes me like a son, I thought, often taking me riding and shooting with his friends. As his daughter, he is protective and keeps me close at his side. But now he is riding without me, not turning once to see how I am.

As he rounded a bend in the road and I saw myself falling farther behind, I burst into tears of frustration. I tried calling, but the wind drowned my words. Realizing that tears were no help, I wiped them on my muddy sleeve and flapped my reins against Shindruk's neck. After stumbling and slipping on the wet rocks for some time, we were able to catch up.

When I thought I could go no further, we arrived in Chamdo. We camped on the edge of the town that night. The next day we prepared to greet His Holiness. It was a warm summer day. The rains had stopped and the sun was rising over the hills to the east. The air, washed clean by the rains, was fresh and filled with damp grass smells.

I took my brown brocade chupa out of my pack and put it over a new white silk blouse, with a silver charm box around my neck. Papa and the others put on their chieftain hats and unwound the braids from around their heads in honor of meeting His Holiness. Wanting to bring him objects that reflected spiritual richness, we put a golden cup and silver pitcher in a pack overflowing with offerings and mounted our horses.

When we got to the streets of Chamdo, they were filled with people like us. On horseback, on foot, carrying boughs of incense, baskets of food, garlands of flowers.

As we drew closer, the crowd became so thick that my father motioned to us to get off our horses and leave them with two of the servants. I rushed forward and took hold of his chupa and held on tightly as he pushed through the crowd.

In places the crowd parted as people recognized his chieftain hat, in other places it became so thick that we were pressed tightly against one another, unable to move.

The heat became more intense as the sun began to rise. The air disappeared around us, and tempers grew short. Beside me, two children pushed at each other and began to cry. Their mother gave them a swat on the ear, and taking each by an arm pulled them ahead. A man behind me complained that I'd stepped on his foot. Another in front had a fit of coughing. For a time we moved together like a wave of water. Forward, to the side, back, forward, as if part of a larger body.

A sound rose above the murmurs of the crowd. It was a man's voice coming from somewhere above us. We stopped to look. For the first time I noticed large gray buildings surrounding us. They were bare, without prayer flags or color, like trees shorn of their branches. Their shape was perfectly square. Their windows, without awnings, were plain. Like intruders in a place where they shouldn't be, like unfriendly spirits.

My father pointed at them and said to a fellow chieftain, "The Chinese."

"The last time I was here," he told us, "Tibetan houses were standing where those monsters now stand." He pointed to one that had been built so close to a statue of Buddha that the face was hidden from view. As he pointed, his other hand went to his gun strapped to his side. For several moments he and Anak Pon talked heatedly about what they'd like to do.

"Tear them down with my hands," my father said. "Shoot them to pieces."

Above their voices I heard the man's voice continue to shout. Loud and echoing. Sometimes the voice spoke our language, sometimes a language I couldn't understand. I looked in the direction of the sound to see who was speaking, but the voice appeared to be coming from boxes mounted on high wooden poles. From what I could understand, it was praising the joys of working for the great Motherland, and directing people where to report for that work.

Who is the Great Mother, I wondered, where is her land, what kind of work did people do there? I wondered if she was coming to Chamdo like the rest of us, to celebrate His Holiness's arrival. But as I listened to my father's conversation with his chieftain friends, I realized the Great Mother had something to do with the Chinese. Much later, I would hear of little else, but in 1954 I was only twenty-one, and the words were still unfamiliar.

All day we stood in the crowd. At times my father pushed forward, but by afternoon thousands had gathered and there wasn't any place left to go. Slowly we moved toward the center of town. We passed several temples. Huge pictures of a large smiling face hung over their entrances. Again my father put his head together in heated conversation with Anak Pon and Norbuk Pon. "Chairman Mao," was all that I heard.

It seemed strange to have a picture other than His Holiness or one of the lamas, and I wondered if Chairman Mao was a lama from China. But weary from the heat and the crush of the crowd, I let it pass through my mind without much more thought.

Late in the day, a murmur ran through the crowd. "He is coming! He is coming!" The words spread like flames. In the distance I heard the faint sound of music, like the buzzing of insects, rising and falling in measured beat.

Just as I thought I could stand still no longer, the crowd fell silent. My father raised up on his toes to look, then lifted me over his head. Looking in the direction his hand was pointing, over thousands of heads, I saw faint puffs of dust. Once I caught a glimpse of a drab-colored motorized car.

I strained to see more, but soldiers in brown uniforms had come forward and were waving sticks at the crowd, trying to move us back. At the same time the masses of people shoved forward, and I was jostled from side to side as we were pressed even tighter together.

My father, swearing beneath his breath, took my hand and, turning against the sea of faces, struggled back toward the edge of the city. I was puzzled and wondered where His Holiness was, but followed Papa, still not sure what he had pointed to or what I had seen.

Later we were told that His Holiness had entered Chamdo in a procession of Jeeps. At the center of the city he was greeted by an orchestra of accordion players and a group of smiling Chinese women with flowers in their hands. He'd given his blessings to the crowd, with a line of Chinese soldiers behind him, then was hurried into a Jeep and driven off again, to the east.

All night the image flowed through my head of thin puffs of dust, the blur of a chalk-green motorized car. It fused in my mind with the compassionate gaze of His Holiness.

"The Chinese have insulted the Tibetan people," my father fumed the next day to anyone who would listen as we began the journey home. "They have shown disrespect for His Holiness, they have desecrated our temples. There is nothing in their hearts but a lust for power."

That night, as we settled around the fire to eat a soup of barley, turnips, and meat, he contrasted the travesty of this day to the day he witnessed the procession of the young five-year-old Dalai Lama as he was escorted from his home in Amdo, a district north of Kham, to the Potala Palace in Lhasa.

I had heard the story of His Holiness's discovery many times before. In 1935, the story went, a search party headed by Regent Reting journeyed from Lhasa south to the sacred lake Lhamo Lhatso. There in its crystal waters, the story said, he received a vision leading him to a modest home in a farming community in Amdo. In the village of Taktser, he was led to a three-year-old boy.

The young boy was presented with a series of articles, some belonging to the Thirteenth Dalai Lama, who had died four years before, and some carefully crafted duplicates. The boy invariably chose the authentic objects. Having passed that test, the story went, the boy was examined for the physical marks which were signs of a Dalai Lama. Large ears, tiger-skin streaks on his legs, a spiraling conch shell on the palm of his hand. When those too were discovered, there was no doubt of the young boy's identity. He was clearly reincarnated as the Fourteenth Dalai Lama, and was taken two years later to his rightful home, home of other Dalai Lamas before him, the grand Potala Palace.

Though I had heard the story of his discovery as often as the tales of King Gesar, I had never heard the story of his journey to Lhasa.

My father was twenty-five when he heard that the newly discovered Dalai Lama would be traveling to Lhasa. Leaving his young wife and six-year-old daughter, he rode with three other chieftains to the Doguthan Plain, two miles east of Lhasa. There, on a radiantly clear day in early fall of the Year of the Tiger, he stood with thousands of others lining the road the procession would take.

The air was filled with the plaintive blowing of oboes, the clarion call of trumpets several yards long, the rumbling and thundering of large kettle drums announcing the beginning of the procession.

Yellow and white chalk lines were drawn at the edge of the road. On either side bowls of incense were burning. Towering overhead, poles hung with prayer flags stood like giant trees of color, thick as a forest along the way.

As the procession began, a band from the Tibetan army marched by, playing "God Save the King." Tibetans at either side of the road rang bells. Hundreds of attendants in green satin tunics, lamas in robes fringed with gold, officials in multicolored mantles, walked slowly forward.

Dust rose up and turned gold in the sunlit air. Long trumpets borne on the shoulders of monks cried out. Out of the mist a gilded wood palanquin appeared. Behind its curtains of gold and bright paper flowers the young Dalai Lama rode, hidden from sight. A tall peacock umbrella and a gold umbrella were borne above him by no-

blemen running at his side. Accompanied by bleating horns, swirling incense, the gilded palanquin passed by. All bowed and felt his holy presence.

The day before we reached home, we met an old man walking up the road in our direction, with a pack slung over his back. His brow was deeply lined, and thin white whiskers hung in wisps from his chin. His red robe and saffron blouse identified him as a monk, and from the look of his well-worn boots, it was clear he had walked a long distance.

When we reached his side, he put up his hand for my father to stop.

"Have you word of His Holiness?" he asked. "I was told he was passing this way."

My father told him of our experience in Chamdo. "The Chinese showed His Holiness no respect," he repeated with vehemence, the strain of the trip etched on his face.

"Ah," the old monk said sadly, "in the north, I've been told, the Chinese have begun to turn against our religion. They have said that it is 'useless to society.' They have entered the monasteries, taken our precious statues and sacred texts, and sent them to China."

My father got off his horse and crouched down on his haunches as he listened to the old man talk.

"In the south," the old man continued, "they have forced men to work on their roads, they have even ordered them to kill helpless creatures. With shovels Tibetans have beaten field mice, with their bare hands they have had to twist the necks of small birds, with their feet they have stamped on beetles and spiders." He raised his eyes in anger. "Our vow to protect all living things has been violated."

∾

I returned home with a heavy heart. Instead of seeing His Holiness's face, I caught a glimpse into the souls of the Chinese. For the first time since their arrival, I felt their dark spirit seeping into our home.

Bare gray buildings, drab-colored cars, thin puffs of dust mixed together in my mind with the broken necks of birds. And often, on the darkened stairway, or turning a corner in the dimly lit hall, the face of Chairman Mao floated up through the darkness.

At the same time, being so near His Holiness helped reconnect me to my days at the monastery. Once again the teachings of Gyalsay Rinpoche came alive in my mind. At times when I least expected it, I heard him saying, *"If you see death in everyday life, it will give a foundation to your practice."*

As the reality of what was happening in our country began to enter my awareness, the teachings helped ground me in the truths that endure. But I also became aware, in a way I hadn't before, that daily practice involved more than the saying of prayers. Sitting in meditation was no good if I couldn't bring it into action. I was mindful of Gyalsay Rinpoche's words, that *"to make the world a better place you must practice tolerance and love."*

From then on, I tried to have compassion for those around me and tolerance for their differing ways. But I found that was easier to think about than to do.

Every day I spent time in the chapel in my house or visited Ani Rigzin in her room at Khaley Rinpoche's monastery. Increasingly, much of my time was taken up with my religious practices, and I felt a sense of peace and clarity in ways I never had before.

One day, when I was leaving the house on my way to the monastery, a young woman appeared at the gate. "Lhamo has asked you to visit her," she said, "her baby is sick. Her husband and his family are busy with the fall harvest and she needs someone to help." I felt unable to refuse the request, but was frustrated at the thought of interrupting my practice. After struggling with an urge to ignore her and continue on the way to the monastery, my vow to act with compassion prevailed, and I reluctantly followed her down the road to Lhamo's home.

I found Lhamo sitting by the fire in the center of the room, alone, with her baby in her lap. The baby was crying and Lhamo looked as if she hadn't slept for several days. Her chupa was covered with stains of food; there were empty pots on the floor by the fire, plates of half-eaten food on the table at her side. The room was dark and filled with smoke; the fire needed tending.

My first impulse was to turn and run. But the expression on Lhamo's face was so forlorn that I took a deep breath and rolled up my sleeves. "Let's get this cleaned up," I said to her. "A clean room will make you feel better." I sound like my mother, I thought.

For most of the day I washed dishes and clothes, holding the baby for moments while Lhamo tried to rest. But his loud wailing kept her from falling asleep, and she spent much of the time moving back and forth from her bed, getting up when his cries rose too loud, trying to nurse him to sleep, lying down when he'd quieted, getting up again when he screamed.

In between her efforts to calm him, I carried him around the room, swaying him back and forth, trying to rock him to sleep. Whenever I stopped, for even a moment, his little face turned red and he let out a high-pitched shriek. It amazed me that something so small could make so much noise. At times I felt like screaming myself in dismay. But each time, when I thought I could stand it no more, Lhamo appeared at my side.

By the late afternoon my head had begun to pulse with a dull pain, and my back ached from carrying the baby. My temper became increasingly short. I almost shouted at Lhamo when she asked for a cup of tea, and I couldn't bear to look at the baby. With his little red face and wide-open mouth, he looked increasingly unpleasant. When I could take it no more, I made an excuse about helping my mother, and left.

On the way home, I felt despondent. My feelings of peace and clarity had gone, and the words "compassion for others" had lost their uplifting meaning.

∽

Messengers continued to come to our house almost every day with news of the Chinese. One told of a town to the east where forty-eight babies, each less than one year old, were taken by soldiers and sent to China to be indoctrinated into the communist way of life. Their parents were told that with their children gone they were free to work longer hours. When several spoke out they were taken to a nearby river and drowned.

One morning a man appeared at our front doorway. His face was streaked with dust, his hair tied back in a knot. His eyes were wild. I recognized him as a trader my father had befriended several years ago.

"Pomdha Gonor," he said vehemently. "I must speak to the honorable chieftain. It is urgent."

I was caught by his insistence, and took him straightway to my father's room. My father was sitting on his bed in meditation, but quickly rose to greet the distraught visitor.

"Oh Pomdha Gonor." The man, unable to contain himself anymore, burst into tears. "My precious Lama Dhondun . . . my blessed Lama . . ."

He was unable to continue, his body shaking with sobs. My father came over to him and gently guided him to a seat. Sitting beside him, he waited for him to regain composure.

"In Kyiedo, just two days ago, I saw a terrible thing," the old man said when he was able to speak. "I had come to the monastery to pray with Lama Dhondun when four Chinese soldiers broke in. They dragged him out of the temple. In front of a large group of monks and townspeople he was forced to kneel. His face kept its radiant calm, and he looked up into the eyes of the soldiers with a look of compassion, his eyes soft and caring.

"That seemed to unsettle one of the soldiers. Coming closer to Lama Dhondun, he raised his foot and brought it down several times on my poor Lama's head. When Lama Dhondun continued to look patiently at him, blood beginning to flow from his mouth, the soldier kicked him again and again, this time in the ribs. Lama Dhondun let out a soft moan and fell to his hands.

"At that, the soldier mounted him, put a cord around his neck and pretended to ride him as if he were a horse. He held the cord tightly, jerking it back several times. As he was doing this another soldier came over, unbelted his trousers, and urinated over my Lama's poor battered head. The other soldiers doubled over with laughter and gestured to the nearby monks as if this would be their fate too, if they continued their religious practices. Oh Pomdha Gonor ... words cannot tell ... it was awful!" His voice broke off again into sobs.

That night my father gathered his ministers in his room. He asked me to join them. I was reluctant to be included. I was afraid that the more I sat in with the others, the more they would expect me to lead. All I want, I thought when he asked me, is to do my practice. But I felt that I couldn't refuse.

"The Chinese have not yet entered Gonjo," my father said, his face looking haggard and pale. "But it is only a matter of time." He asked the others to voice their concerns, and by the light of the torches, they talked late into the night.

Gosay Tsering, my father's eldest minister, spoke first. "For centuries, like the body following the head, we in Gonjo have paid taxes and obeyed the laws laid down by the government of Tibet. But in a few short years"—he raised his hand in emphasis—"the Chinese have changed all that. Now our decisions are forced to be made by the fraudulent 'Chamdo Liberation Committee.'"

The mention of the committee in Chamdo brought heated response, for it was well known that though the committee was composed of Tibetans and Chinese, the Tibetans were represented in name only, and the governing force was Chinese.

My father stood up. "I have been appointed chairman for all of Gonjo, but have I ever been consulted about decisions that affect us? You all know the answer—it is NO! Like a big insect eating a small one, they have no concern for our thoughts."

After a respectful silence, Shamo Chemi, another trusted minister, spoke. "I have heard that they have invaded the lower lands, and in the towns of Kanze, Lingkha Shipa, they have 'borrowed' grain reserves of the government, requested 'loans' of silver and gold to feed their troops."

"Loans! Borrowed!" Gosay Tsering spat the words out. "They borrow with guns, not words ..."

"They are recruiting beggars off the street," Shamo Chemi interrupted him, "sending them through the countryside to relieve people of their possessions."

"Ah, the thieves and the lowest," my father said with disdain, "they are acting like kings, strutting around in Chinese brocades . . ." He spat on the floor to show his distaste. "The Chinese soldiers are clever, they are killing us slowly, as our fingers fall, one by one, off the hand."

"Not slowly," Gosay Tsering growled. "In Amdo, in the village of Doi, five hundred landowners were taken into the center of the town and before the rest of the crowd three hundred were shot in the head. Those that remained were told they would meet the same fate if they opposed the order to turn over their land to the 'Liberation Army.'"

"This is what I think of their army." My father spat again on the floor. "They tell us that they have come to liberate us from outside oppressors, while like a spider, they enclose us in their web. We can no longer sit on the side watching. We must begin to make plans."

That night my sleep was troubled. Once again I dreamed of shoes tapping on the floor outside my room. I heard them coming down a long cement walk. Tapping against the cold stone surface, in short brisk steps. Click-click. Click-click. Louder, louder as they neared my room. But this time they stopped at the door. Then I woke.

Throughout the following year, news of Chinese activities continued to pour in from all around us. For a time the Chinese cordoned off an area east of the Yangtze River, making it impossible for my mother to leave Gyalsay Rinpoche's monastery. I comforted myself with the thought that she would be pleased to have more time to pursue her practice. But knowing that her return was out of the question, I missed her terribly.

It is strange, the tricks the mind plays. She was no more absent than she had been the month before. It was not so much her presence I missed, it was more the thought of her absence.

No one else seemed to feel the same sadness that I did. Kunsang took her place. The house ran smoothly without her and my father seemed not to notice. Consumed with his own duties, he rode tirelessly from town to town meeting with leaders from our area. He met with lamas, chieftains, local townspeople making plans to counter the Chinese. Together they swore to one another that no matter what the outcome, they were prepared to resist. Each chieftain committed a number of men and arms. In addition, it was decided that each well-to-do family should prepare three armed men with horses to be used in the effort.

While he and the others were preparing, the Chinese continued to confiscate property from people in areas east of the Yangtze. They began to set up communes in Tibetan villages, and at the same time they trucked hundreds of peasants from all over China to settle in Tibet. Outraged by these events, leaders in Derge, Kanze, Nyagrong, Ba, and Lithang assembled thousands of their people. Armed with swords and rifles, they rode into Chinese army camps, killing and looting. The Chinese suffered massive losses and were forced to retreat, but not without consequence.

"The monastery in Lithang has been bombed," the messenger cried, not waiting for formal recognition.

He was half-talking, half-crying, and my father rose from his mattress to calm him. Taking the poor man's hand in his, he led him to an empty seat, and, bending over, put his hands on the young man's shoulders. After a few moments, the man's breath grew calmer and my father stood back.

"Tell us," my father said in a steady voice, and the man poured out his story.

"Three months ago, the Chinese ordered the lamas of the monastery in our village of Lithang to draw up a list of its possessions. The lamas refused and called a meeting urging the men from our village to bear arms against the Chinese. The men organized an attack against a Chinese camp that was in the valley beyond our town. They were able to steal a supply of weapons before being routed away. But with the Chinese riding after them, hard on their heels, they took refuge in the monastery.

"The Chinese surrounded the monastery and, in an attempt to lure the men out, made a proposal. In exchange for the surrender of men and monks, they would agree to postpone the creation of any more collectives for two years. If the men refused to surrender they would be bombed."

At this point in his story, the young man burst into tears. My father leaned over and, laying his hand once again on a shoulder, gave it a gentle pat. After a cup of chang, the man continued.

"You know, Pomdha Gonor," he said, still sniffling a bit, "our men hadn't any idea what the Chinese were threatening. They didn't understand the consequences of their actions, and they refused. Then out of the sky came something we'd never seen before. Flying machines with wings like birds swooped down. The air was filled with thunder, buildings exploding, people screaming inside. Six thousand people were inside the monastery at the time . . . four thousand of them died. . . . Men, women, children . . . four thousand were killed."

When he was finished, a quiet fell over the room. The news was more than our minds could absorb. For quite a long time nobody spoke, and except for the man's quiet crying, it was silent.

In the beginning of the Year of the Fire Monkey, 1956, we heard that a program called "Democratic Reforms" was being introduced all over Amdo and Kham. "Properties and herds of the landholders and monasteries have been seized," my father said, hitting his fist into his hand. "They are being redistributed without any understanding of how it will affect the people. They say it is 'for the good of all,' but what good can come of it?"

We heard that reforms were introduced in public meetings, and that those accused of putting up any resistance were brought to a public place in chains. "After forcing everyone in the village to attend," a visiting monk, who had attended one such meeting, reported, "members of the crowd were encouraged to criticize, to humiliate, to attack the resisters. We monks were encouraged to turn against our abbots, village people to turn against their leaders, children against their parents. It was awful."

"The Chinese are trying to create dissension among the people," my father said, "but it is having the opposite effect. It is creating further fuel for the resistance!"

Almost weekly, my father's ministers gathered in our house to discuss the situation. The meetings were coming so frequently that as soon as I saw Gosay Tsering's tall, thin form appear in the doorway, I knew what to expect. Soon I would hear the heavy steps of Shamo Chemi, and Atsang coming up the stairway behind him. Sometimes Anak Pon, Norbuk Pon, and other local chieftains would arrive close on their heels. All would disappear to my father's room, for chang and discussion.

At times I joined them at my father's request, but I never felt entirely accepted by the others. From time to time I noticed them watching me when they thought I wasn't looking, with a mixture of curiosity, disbelief, and dismay on their faces, as if they thought their meetings were no place for a woman.

Their reactions didn't bother me, for I had no desire to be there, and would have much preferred to stay in the chapel praying, or reading spiritual texts in my room. But my father wanted to prepare me in the event I would be called to take over for him, and he mentioned the possibility to me from time to time. I felt overwhelmed at the thought. How would I know what to do, when would I have time for my practice? *Oh Lord Buddha, I pray it will never happen.*

In the spring of that year, the joint Tibetan-Chinese committee ordered leaders from all over Western Kham to attend a meeting in

Chamdo. Lamas, chieftains, heads of important families, people's representatives came together, and for several days the meeting went on.

During the meetings, Wang Chimi, the Chinese representative, asked the assembled leaders to assist in implementing the Democratic Reforms. "If you refuse to help," he threatened, "the reforms will be carried out by force." My father was one of those who spoke out vehemently against the reforms. He stood up, declaring, "I will only carry out the orders of the Tibetan government in Lhasa, and the wishes of the Tibetan people," he said. "I will never accept the reforms on recommendation from the Chinese. Tibet is a free country ruled by His Holiness the Fourteenth Dalai Lama. It is only his orders that I'll obey."

Cheers filled the room, and many of the other chieftains, inspired by his example, rose up to speak against the reforms proposed by the Chinese. A vote was taken. One hundred voted their support, more than two hundred opposed it.

Soon after, the meeting was dismissed The leaders were sent home with gifts of picture books, pens, and soap.

"Bribes!" my father fumed, pacing up and down his room. His face was red and beads of perspiration dampened his forehead. "They think their pictures of China, their fancy ink pens, will seduce us and weaken our resolve. . . ." He had worked himself into such a state that his breath was short, and his hands, as he waved them in the air, were shaking. The force of his anger seemed to be tearing him apart.

For days he stayed up in his room, refusing to eat. Every day I went to his door, but he waved me away. Then late one evening as I was getting ready for bed, I heard Gosay Tsering's voice as he passed through the kitchen on his way to my father's room. There was something about the tone of his voice that roused my curiosity, and, throwing my chupa around me, I followed behind, up the stairs.

My father was sitting on a mattress in the corner of the room when we came in. He was slumped over, and in the dim light I saw that his eyes were dull. They were focused ahead, looking far into the distance.

At first he took no notice of our presence, and we stood uneasily in the doorway, uncertain what to do. After a few moments, Gosay Tsering cleared his throat. "Pomdha Gonor, I have come with more news of the Chinese."

Like pulling in a line that had been cast far away, my father slowly came back to himself. A shiver ran through his body, he shifted his position, then raised his eyes to meet ours.

Gosay Tsering began to speak. He spoke late into the night. What more can they do, I wondered as I listened to story after story of tragedy. At the time, I was unaware that in response to the continuing tragedies, people had started rising up in resistance.

In the town of Nyagrong, to the south of us, Chinese soldiers arrived at the home of Gyurme, of the Chipa family. He was away on business and his family had just sat down to the evening meal when the soldiers knocked on the door.

"We have come for your weapons," the soldiers demanded as they entered. Gyurme's old mother rose and turned to face them. Looking them straight in the eye, her voice firm, she replied, "We have none."

Without speaking another word, without giving any warning, the soldiers raised their rifles and shot them dead. Gyurme's mother, his wife, his young son, and a family servant, all dead.

The people of Nyagrong were enraged. Two weeks later, Dorjee Yudon, the beautiful young wife of Chieftain Gyari Nima, decided to launch a revolt. She gathered her husband's men and, after they'd collected their weapons and mounted horses, she led an attack on the castle of the Female Dragon where the Chinese soldiers had secluded themselves. The Chinese were well fortified with supplies and refused to come out. The fighting went on for days.

When Gosay Tsering finished telling his stories, my father let out a sound like the air whining through a crack in the wall. Then a tiny cry, barely audible. His gaze fell down to the floor, and for a moment I thought he might faint. But after a few moments he raised his eyes, and straightened.

"We must send help," he said, as if coming back to life. "Call a meeting of chieftains and ministers," he said to Gosay Tsering. "Bring us food," he motioned to me.

The wind was blowing down from the hills as Papa and I mounted our horses and rode to a place on the border between Gonjo and Dagyab. There, we met chieftains from all over our district. Among them, I recognized Chime Gonpo and Raru Tennan of Derge, Chungbhum Purpa of Markham, and many others from local villages.

As the rain began to fall they huddled together on their horses, fox-skin hats on their heads, swords at their side. Each had a wild look in his eye, wild like the eyes of their horses. True Khampa warriors.

I sat on the side and watched them making their plans. They resolved to unite in driving out the Chinese. They agreed not to send workers for the road being constructed through Gonjo. They pledged to withhold meat, grain, horses, and ammunition when asked to supply them. They vowed to disrupt Chinese activities in any way possible.

When the discussion was finished, each got off his horse and walked over a piece of raw hide, still red with blood, taking the most solemn oath in Kham. "That seals the agreement," my father said.

He ended the meeting saying, "The words 'liberation of Tibet' are a deadly mockery. Tibet has been an independent country since the time of King Nyatri Tsenpo. We have history as a witness to that fact. Let us all resolve never to allow the bandit Chinese to take over our independence through force." He raised his rifle above his head and shouted, "Freedom to Tibet!"

"Freedom to Tibet!" the others roared back.

Events followed swiftly, one upon another. All over Kham people rose up in resistance; knowing the terrain, they were often successful. The Chinese began to bring massive numbers into Tibet in attempts to stop the attacks. Their soldiers were well trained and well equipped; one on one the Tibetans were no match for them. Soon many people left their villages and fled to the hills. By the end of 1956 the number of Khampas who had taken to the hills had grown from hundreds to tens of thousands.

In 1957, one thousand men under Chief Chime Dorjee of Lingkha Shipa arrived at a nomad encampment in the hills above our town. He and his people had lost their land to the Chinese, and they arrived in search of shelter.

My father rode up to meet them. Dressed in a black chupa, with a fox-fur hat on his head, a rifle tied to his back, a sword at this side, he galloped through the tall waving grass into the hills.

Papa stood at the back near the pantry, calling out items of food from a long list of paper.

"Ten sacks of barley flour. Three of dried meat. Four bags of rice . . ."

Thupten and Tashi carried the bags from the pantry and stacked them in piles at his feet.

"The horses will require fodder," my father continued, and gesturing to Kunsang and me, "and extra clothes for all men, women, and children."

In the commotion, no one noticed my mother had entered the room, and for moments she stood at the side, surveying the scene. Arriving unannounced from the monastery, she had plunged into chaos.

Everywhere people were scattered, sitting on mattresses, crouched on their heels by the fire, leaning against the wall. Strange dogs were chasing our small dogs in and out of the room, children were crying for food.

My mother's mouth dropped in alarm, her eyes blinking and watering like a mole risen from its den in the earth into the bright glare of the sun.

"Mama!" I cried out when I saw her. I dropped the load I was holding and bounded across the room. As I reached her I leaped, almost knocking her over. Throwing my arms around her neck, I pressed her frail body to mine; her heartbeat, a faint tentative jumping against my chest. I reached down and lifted her face in my hands, touching her forehead to mine.

That night, curled in her arms, her warm skin with its familiar milky scent touching mine, I felt at peace for the first time since leaving the monastery.

"Mama," I whispered over and over.

I kissed the tips of her ears and stroked the hair from her brow. We talked about Gyalsay Rinpoche and his teachings. She told me about the Great Liberation and the Path of Clear Light. As she spoke I felt myself back at the monastery.

Gyalsay Rinpoche sits on a simple mattress in the back of his room. His face is illuminated by a tiny beam of sun, filtering down through the darkness. Like the golden face of Buddha, it is surrounded by light, so radiant.

"Let there be no mistake," my father read from the letter of Lama Nyenjik that was circulating among the chieftains, "the 'Liberation' of Tibet is nothing but a form of brutal colonialism . . . in a few years Mao Tse-tung plans to bring eight million Chinese into Tibet. This can only mean the complete obliteration of an ancient culture and people.

"It was a blot on the conscience of the world when not a single finger was lifted by any country to prevent the occupation of a free people; a matter of the deepest shame that not one country has raised its voice against the butchery of the Tibetan people. . . ."

My father set the letter down on the table in front of him. He rubbed his large hand across his face. "It is good," he said to us after giving the contents of the letter some thought. "It is good that someone has taken time to write the Indian government. We need help from outside, for we cannot survive alone."

"Surely now," I said hopefully, "aid will be sent. When others hear what is happening, they will send their support."

At that time, I was young and did not understand the way the world worked. I was so removed from the land beyond our high mountains that I had no experience, no images, no education to help me imagine what a larger world might be.

The only thing I knew for certain was that people who came from away were not to be trusted.

As the year wore on and the devastation by the Chinese increased, my father's health began to deteriorate. He was worried that it was only a matter of time before the Chinese reached Gonjo.

"The Tibetan government has no strategy for confronting the Chinese," he said. "We have nothing. Few weapons, no army to speak of. In contrast, the Chinese are immensely powerful. Therefore it is going to be very difficult." This was his main concern.

The worries began to aggravate his blood and wind disorders and soon fluid started accumulating in his body. Several times doctors came from neighboring towns. They took his pulse, said prayers, gave him pills wrapped in silken cloth. They did the best they could, but nevertheless my father continued to weaken.

When the Year of the Earth Dog began in 1958, Papa's hands and feet had become so swollen that he had difficulty walking across the room. Almost daily, he had headaches and shortness of breath. Often, when not pacing, he sat on his mattress, his shoulders bent, a faraway look in his eyes.

Mama, Kunsang, and I stayed close by his side in case he needed assistance. We read passages from the spiritual texts. We even asked Gosay Tsering to come to play dice with him, but no matter what we did, he continued to fail.

"If I recover from this illness," he said, on the days he was speaking, "I will destroy the largest Chinese arsenal in the north. I will not leave this earth without performing a deed that for generations people will say, 'This is what Pomdha Gonor did.' I will fulfill my duty to Tibet!"

*   *   *

One day, late in the spring, Papa was unable to get out of bed. It was the first day since the beginning of his illness that he'd remained in bed, and it seemed to Mama and me as if his spirit had finally collapsed.

All day the lamps in his room had been burning. From time to time, as their light flickered across his face, it seemed that he was changing from solid to liquid and back. At times he drifted off to sleep, at other times he lay looking ahead, his eyes unfocused and dull. Every so often, Kunsang bent over him, putting a fresh damp cloth on his forehead, but he seemed not to notice.

Just before dinner, Mama arrived with a doctor who had come from a nearby village. He was an elderly man, and he walked with his shoulders stooped, as if carrying a heavy load. Behind him, an apprentice carried his medical pouch. The young man's head was lowered, his eyes cast down toward the floor, as if it were his first time on such an assignment. He fumbled with the bulging pouch, and the doctor gestured impatiently for him to set it on the table in front of my father's bed.

The old man sat down at my father's side and lifted his hand, placing three fingers above the wrist. He sat silently for a few moments, reading Papa's pulse, then turned and opened his bag. As he lifted the flap on the large leather pouch, the pungent smell of herbal remedies poured out, filling the room.

Reaching deep into the bag, he took out several vials of different size pills and gave them to his helper to crush in a cup of water. When they had dissolved, he put the cup to my father's lips and, tipping it upward, coaxed the mixture into his mouth. My father choked a few times, then swallowed. With that, the doctor patted his hand and, holding my mother's shoulder, guided her out of the room, whispering into her ear as they left, "Be sure that he rests."

Later, in the early evening, Ani Rigzin returned from the monastery with Khaley Rinpoche. Rinpoche was dressed in a sleeveless brown robe, with prayer beads around his wrist and a heavy outer robe draped over his shoulders. As he approached the side of my father's bed, his large dark form looked like a mountain of calm in the dim light. He leaned over and touched my father's head with his hand.

After a few moments, he lifted a text wrapped in brocade out of his bag. He unwound several layers of the brocade from around the text, then, opening its rectangular wooden cover, he began to read.

The basic nature of your mind is inseparable luminosity and emptiness. It dwells as a great expanse of light, beyond birth or death. It is the Buddha of unchanging light.

He leaned closer and took my father's hand gently in his and held it with such tenderness that his touch itself seemed to give my father strength. Indicating that my father should repeat the words to himself, he continued.

Now when the bardo of dying dawns upon me,
I will abandon all grasping, yearning, and attachment.
Entering undistracted into clear awareness of the teaching,
I will send my consciousness into the space of unborn awareness.
And as I leave this compound body of flesh and blood
I will know that I am at peace.

He closed the text and leaned toward my father. "Pomdha Gonor, you have been a strong leader, a loyal husband, and father. As you begin your journey, may you be a protector to those without protection, a leader for those who journey, and a boat, a bridge, a passage for those desiring the farther shore. May you be the doctor and the medicine for all sick beings in the world. Like space and the great elements of earth, may you ever support the life of all boundless creatures. May you go forth from this place of your birth in peace."

After he left, my father seemed better. For a time his mind regained some of its old zest and he began to recount events of the last few years. He was particularly drawn to his last meeting with the Dalai Lama several years before. The recollection gave him energy and he was insistent on telling us.

"All the chieftains of Kham had gathered to ask his blessing. In our audience, His Holiness smiled and looked at us with affection." The memory of this meeting brought light to my father's eyes.

"Before our departure he gave us each a ceremonial scarf and blessed us by placing his warm hand on our heads. At the time I prayed from the bottom of my heart that he would come to no harm. But when I turned to leave, a deep sadness came over me and tears flowed from my eyes." As he said this, his eyes filled with tears. His lips, still pale, trembled as he spoke. "Now it seems both Tibet and His Holiness will fall under Chinese power."

Later, struggling for strength to speak, he whispered, "You must never trust the Chinese, they have come to destroy."

The next day, he was too weak to talk. All night my mother and Kunsang had taken turns being with him. In the morning when I came into his room, my mother was near the head of the bed, stroking his forehead. Kunsang had a hand on his shoulder. Anya and Gosay Tsering were standing at his side, and Ani Rigzin by his feet.

The color of his skin had changed overnight, and he was now a pale gray. Propped upright, barely visible in the dim light, his mouth was open, like a small dark hole against his graying skin. I looked at his thin neck. The muscles around it were loose and his throat looked as if it was caving in above his breast plate. I sat down by his side and reached for his hand lying limp over his chest.

His eyes were almost closed, his cheeks sunken in, as if with the passing of each minute the fullness of life was slipping away. I studied his forehead, the faded rough spots on the top, the curve of his cheekbones, the clear fine line of his nose. My eyes filled with tears.

He reached over, slowly, with great effort, and put his hand over mine. He is trying to tell me he loves me, I thought.

The rest of the day we sat by his side. For a time he seemed to get better, and I felt hopeful again. Late in the afternoon Ani Rigzin took my hand. "We must go to pray," she whispered. I reluctantly followed.

Early the next morning, as Ani Rigzin and I were making our way down from Khaley Monastery, Tashi came running toward us, waving his hands. "Ashe Pachen! Ashe Pachen!" he called. "Come quickly! Your father's condition is deteriorating."

I started to run. "What has happened?" I cried frantically.

When I reached him, Tashi was standing, winded, by the side of the path. "Tell me!" I said urgently, shaking his shoulders. "Is he going to live?"

Tashi seemed disoriented and stumbled over his words. I threw up my hands in frustration and ran toward our house. When I reached the house, I could hear people crying inside. The cries were so loud that it created a strange vibration in the air.

"What has happened?" I asked, grabbing the arm of a neighbor standing by the door. "Is my father all right?"

"Our luck has run out," she sobbed.

I pushed my way through the crowd of people who had gathered inside the house. "Let me see him!" I called out. "I must see him!" I felt numb as I ran up the stairs.

When I reached his room, I saw one of his ministers, Shamo Chemi, sitting in my father's chair outside the door. I started to run past him into the room, but he got up and blocked the door.

"I must see him!" I said frantically. "I promise not to create a scene." Seeing my distress, Shamo Chemi stepped aside.

Inside, Papa was lying on his bed. As I walked toward him, I saw that his face was hollow like a mask, and his skin drained of color.

At his bed I bent over to touch his forehead. As my fingers touched his head I startled. It felt empty and hard. Beginning to cool, the skin set like butter in a lamp whose flame had gone out. The current that had always been between us, like the draw in a stream, was gone.

I looked down at him and imagined . . .

His body was losing strength, as though he was falling, sinking down, crushed by an enormous weight. He couldn't move his head. His eyes felt dry.

All the warmth of his body was seeping away. There was a rushing sound in his ears, a great wind, sweeping the world, consuming the entire universe. Sweeping him away.

"Papa," I whispered, "don't leave me."

*   *   *

Late in the day, Tashi was sent to ask Khaley Rinpoche to carry out the pho-wa service, to extract my father's consciousness and guide his spirit on the white path to the paradise of peace.

In the evening, Mama and Kunsang washed his body, wrapped it in a pure white cloth, and knelt down to pray. I sat with my hand on his arm. He hasn't gone, I kept thinking. Someday he'll be back.

For three days, my father's body was kept in the house while monks and important lamas arrived to pray. They sat in the kitchen, in the chapel, they sat in a circle around his body, saying prayers. I was busy helping Mama in the kitchen and didn't have time to join them. But when I went to his room to fill his bowl with fresh food, I bent over when no one was looking and whispered a prayer in his ear. Go always toward the light, I whispered.

During the three days, preparations were made for his cremation. Mama prepared his favorite dishes to set by his side; Kunsang and the servants cooked food for guests. A thousand butter lamps were kept burning in our house, and in each of the surrounding monasteries we offered thousands more. The local astrologer was consulted about the appropriate prayers and a pyre was prepared on the roof of the granary.

At the end of three days, when it was certain his spirit had fully left his body, my father was given the funeral of a high lama. A platform had been built with a cylindrical space in the center for the body to be placed, and underneath there was space for the fire. At the side of the platform, Khaley Tulku, Dorzong Tulku, and Ngulra Tulku stood in brocade robes waiting for the ceremony to begin.

I stood with other guests on the roof of our house and watched as they lit the fire. Flames exploded, shooting into the air, and as the body was engulfed and started to disappear, cries and wailing burst out around me. My mother and Kunsang were moaning so loudly they were almost unconscious. I stood still as if stunned, my eyes closed, my spirit joining his.

His family was crying, but he could not hear. His body had ceased to feel pain or sensation. His thoughts and emotions had come to an end. The familiar environment faded. Floating in a space without form or dimension, he passed into radiant light.

He was dazzled by sound, by color. Blue, white, red, yellow, green emerged like rays then coalesced into fine points of light. The light they emitted was dazzling, the sound tremendous, like the roaring of a million waterfalls. Slowly dissolving, he moved like the spray of ocean on an endlessly rolling wave.

He was returning to his original state. He was no longer afraid.

That day I passed from my childhood. In a moment, I knew that my dream of a life devoted to meditation and prayer was no longer possible. Unable to follow my heart, I was bound by duty to carry on my father's work. With my country threatened and my family in danger, I set about making preparation for war. From that time forward, my life was never the same.

6
In the Hills

The day after my father's cremation, he came to me in a dream. In the dream it was dawn, the year freshly born. Everywhere new shoots of green were pushing up through black earth. Tiny white blossoms spread in clusters for miles. The air was thick with meadow larks, sparrows, blue birds, all singing together.

I saw him in the distance, riding toward me. He was dressed in his black chupa, fox-fur hat on his head, rifle on his back, sword at his side. As he came toward me, his eyes had a look of such tenderness I began to cry.

He opened his mouth and words came out in rushes of air. "Dear daughter . . ." he whispered, almost pleading, "what are the instructions?"

When I realized he must be asking for spiritual advice, I told him as best I could. "Leave all attachments behind. Stay free from fear. Take refuge in your teacher and the Three Jewels. Purify all negativity. If you are able to do these, someday you may reach the supreme liberation."

"Is there anything else I can do for my father?" I asked Lama Ratri. "Has he attained the ultimate release?"

Rinpoche was hunched over his texts and didn't look up. His robe was wrapped around his huge frame, and the long rectangular pages were spread out in his lap.

After what seemed like a long time, he put the texts to one side and took up his beads. He held them between his thumb and second finger and counted them off, two by two. "Your father Pomdha Gonor has already joined the Vajradhara," he said solemnly after eyeing the remaining beads, "but if you wish to do more to help him, I will give you some additional prayers."

He gave me a hundred blessed strings, a hundred small packets with pieces of his clothing and hair, a hundred small clay figures as amulets for the neck as offerings. At the same time, he pointed out that under my father's leadership, our tribe was the best organized in all of Gonjo.

"Your leaders are able, the people are well-off, your men are strong, and your horses are swift," he said. "But now Buddha Dharma is facing extinction. It is a matter of the survival of the teachings."

Survival of the teachings! A new sense of purpose came over me when I heard the words. Centuries of wisdom, innumerable sacred texts, all threatened. If I can contribute something to protecting the great teachings of Buddha, I thought, I will do whatever is asked. Even kill.

By the time I reached home, I was overwhelmed. I didn't know where to begin. Lama Ratri's words were uplifting, but carrying them out was something different. It is easy, I thought, to be inspired, but not so easy to act.

Everywhere I went, people welcomed me as their leader. "Pomdha Pachen," they called when they saw me. "Pachen our leader." Their faces showed such love and support I felt I couldn't deny them, but I was afraid I could never fill my father's shoes. At times I longed to return to the quiet of prayer.

In the days that followed, I felt totally alone. When I walked by his room, I expected to find him sitting on his mattress. Several times I turned to look in as if he were still there, but always the mattress was empty. In the kitchen, I waited for the sound of his step on the stairs. I listened for his voice calling "Nyu, Nyu," and at times I imagined I heard it.

Every night I walked to a desolate and wind-blown stretch by the river. I talked, I sang songs, I cried, but mostly I stared. At the black moving water. At the clouds overhead. At the otherworldly light.

It was a strange thing, my father's death, his absolute absence. And stranger the way the world came alive with his spirit. The day he died, a ribbon of geese waved across the sky. Days later, a faint band of color in the darkening clouds, traces of him everywhere.

*   *   *

The routine of our household continued without him. Mama kept her sadness to herself and went on about her daily tasks as usual. At times I saw her crying silently as she bent over a pot on the stove or took food from the cupboard. Kunsang cried openly, sitting down with her head in her hands when she could no longer stand. I was silent, and grieved by myself.

For forty-nine days after his death, we prayed continually. His soul was in limbo between liberation and the cycle of life. To help him on his journey to the field of clear light we performed rituals and made offerings to the lamas. Let him be reborn in a higher state, or freed altogether, we prayed.

Rain beat down the next fifty days without stopping. A fury of wind spit dust, rocks, and grass into the air. A darkness settled over the house. It's Papa, I thought, still angry at the Chinese.

In those days, I began to grow worried. My father had handled his duties so gracefully that I barely knew what they were. Now, every day someone came with a new demand.

"More horses are needed." "A thief stole the grain." "You must collect taxes for Lhasa."

How will we manage without him? I thought.

I walked through the house, struck by all that we had. So many things.

"Let us give what we have to the monasteries to collect merit for him," I said one day to Mama. "With all these belongings, we're burdened. They possess us, not the other way around."

For a short time, I dreamed of leaving on a pilgrimage to all the holy sites with only a pack on my back.

"The times are becoming hostile," Ani Rigzin said when she heard my musings. "It would be difficult to move freely. The Chinese have occupied lands to the north and south of us. Their soldiers are everywhere, it is not safe to travel alone."

"Gyalsay Rinpoche might help Pomdha Gonor attain Nirvana," my mother said. "If we visit we could continue our practice."

"The Chinese have taken control of the Yangtze River," Ani Rigzin reminded, "it's impossible to cross to the monastery."

"Even if we could leave," I said, remembering Lama Ratri's words, "I have to stay here. It's up to me to continue Papa's work."

I called Papa's ministers Gosay Tsering and Shamo Chemi to assist me. When I heard the familiar sound of their footsteps on the outside stairs, it seemed as if nothing were different. For a moment I felt reassured.

But when Gosay Tsering entered the kitchen I was shocked to see how he had changed in the intervening months. A line ran between his eyebrows, pulling them up in an expression of puzzled distress. His eyes were strained, as if holding back tears. His mouth ran in a thin line below his mustache, curving down at the edges. He looked like a small child who was lost.

Behind him, Shamo Chemi shifted his weight from one foot to the other, glancing at Gosay Tsering then at me, like a dog concerned for its master. Of all my father's ministers they were the most capable, but at that moment my heart sank, for they seemed no more confident than I.

"I have just come from Lama Ratri," I said, hoping to roust them from their gloom. "He told me that it was up to us to offer aid. He said our religion and culture are imperiled. He asked us to lead the struggle."

I reminded them that before he died, my father had started sending men from Lemdha to fight the invading soldiers in Lower Gonjo. He had distributed a pamphlet to every home listing the number of men, horses, swords, and guns each family should contribute.

"A minimum of three weapons and men from the larger families, two each from the medium-sized, one each from the smallest," I reminded. "His foresight made our task easier, but it is up to us to continue his work."

For a moment they were silent, then Gosay Tsering raised his head and straightened his shoulders as if understanding I needed his help.

"The Chinese are blasting roads through the hills in the lower regions of Gonjo," he said, thinking as he spoke. "Once the road is built, trucks with supplies for their troops will pour into Gonjo. We have to do whatever we can to stop them."

"We must send fifty well-armed men at a time," Shamo Chemi joined in. "Our tribe has more than six hundred, we can well afford it."

"We will go to each house as my father planned," I said, relieved by their response. "I will gather the men together and make sure each has a sturdy horse and a usable weapon."

As he was leaving, Gosay Tsering took me aside and spoke confidentially. "The people of Lemdha are happy you're taking on the responsibility of your father, Ashe Pachen. But some are worried. They know your devotion to the spiritual path, and they say you won't fulfill your commitment. . . ." He looked as if he had the same thought.

I knew there was truth in what he said, yet at the same time it angered me that anyone would doubt my loyalty. "You can tell them there is no need to worry. I always live up to my word."

When he left, I sat for a time in the dark. "Papa," I whispered. "Why have you gone?"

Guru Rinpoche, I prayed later that night, *guide me on the path.*

In the distance I see a dark shape. It walks toward me, through layers of mist, across a vast field. Bigger and bigger. There is no place to run.

It is almost upon me when its face becomes clear. I look in amazement.

It is His Holiness. He reaches out and takes my hand, his grasp gentle but firm.

It will be all right, I thought when I woke. His Holiness is with me.

For the rest of the year, we worked on developing strategies. With my father gone, Anak Pon, a chieftain in a nearby village, was the most powerful. It was up to him to work out an overall plan. I sent Gosay Tsering and Shamo Chemi to attend his meetings instead of going myself.

"You worked on the plans with my father," I said, "you will know what he had in mind. I trust your ability to represent me." But in truth, my reasons for not going myself were different. I wanted to stay home near Mama and Ani Rigzin, I wanted to be sure they were safe. And I hoped I'd have more time for stillness and prayer.

At the same time, I knew I had to do everything I could to defend the country. For the sake of my father, for His Holiness, I plunged into organizing the forces of Lemdha.

I began to call on others who had helped my father. One, named Dhondrub Norbu, had been a favorite of my father's, and I sent a messenger to his home in the nomadic region asking him to come to a meeting. Getting no response, I sent another message. I sent three more messages summoning him to my side, but each time there was no reply.

In the past, he always came at my father's first summons. His lack of response was a sign of disrespect. I sensed that because I was a woman, he did not respect me and was trying to undermine my authority. As the days passed, I grew increasingly angry and vowed he would not go unpunished. He must have heard of my displeasure, for one day he arrived at our door.

I was up in the chapel when Anya appeared and announced his arrival. "Tell him to wait," I said curtly. "I will be down when I'm finished." I took my time and said several more prayers than usual, to be sure he was kept waiting.

When I finally appeared in the kitchen and saw him standing by the stove, I was momentarily swayed from my anger. His jaw was chiseled square and curved in below his high cheekbones, his forehead was broad and smooth, his cheeks ruddy from his time in the hills. Red strings were woven through his long dark hair, and wound up and around like a turban. He stood straight, with his head held high, clearly someone to be admired. But there was something about his proud stance, almost defiant, that angered me, and my irritation came back.

I walked up to him, crossed my arms, and stood silently in front of him. He brought his hands together in front of his chest and bowed his head. "I wasn't trying to undermine your authority," he said. "You have my utmost respect."

I cut him off before he could go any further. "I don't want to hear your excuses."

It was true he'd appeared voluntarily and offered an apology of sorts, but I had no desire to grant him the usual amnesty. The thought kept entering my mind that he'd disobeyed me because I was a woman, and I felt enraged. If I let him go unpunished, I thought, rationalizing my desire to punish him, others might disobey. With the fighting nearby, that wouldn't be wise.

I narrowed my eyes coldly, then turned to Thupten, who was just coming out of the pantry with a bag of grain on his shoulder. "Thupten," I said in my sternest voice, "bring the whip!"

Thupten dropped the bag and looked at me in disbelief. Anya, hearing my words, stopped stirring the pot by the fire. Mama started toward me, then thinking better of it, took several steps back.

Whipping was a punishment reserved for severe misbehavior. I had never felt it myself or used it on anyone else, but it seemed important to let others know that I could mete out punishment as well as a man.

Pretending not to notice their reaction, I continued to stare into Dhondrub's eyes. He looked right back into mine with no indication my words had had any effect. This only angered me more. I ordered Thupten, "Call Samten and Phunsok from the fields. I'll need two strong men to hold him down."

Thupten ran down the stairs toward the fields while I stayed focused on Dhondrub.

We stood across from each other, a few hands apart, face to face. He had his arms to his side, his legs slightly bent in an effortless stance. With my arms crossed in front, I continued to stare into his eyes like a wild animal staring down its prey.

His eyes remained clear and unmoving. They were dark brown, but around the pupils there were speckles of yellow, which softened his gaze. As I looked into them I saw a gentleness which unsettled me.

For a moment I shifted my eyes to his brows. They were an upsweep of tiny dark hairs, and between them, hair that was lighter, like down. It is the kind of thing that a mother would notice, I thought, the fine hairs on her little child's face. With that thought I began to lose my resolve, but continued staring at him nonetheless.

For quite some time, we stood with our eyes locked. But as we looked into each other's eyes, subtle flickers, sudden bursts of expression, passed between us. In a wordless way we began to speak to each other.

"I am here with the whip and the men, as you asked." Thupten suddenly appeared in the doorway. In his hand was a whip, shoulder high, with a wooden handle and woven leather strips. Beside him were Samten and Phunsok, their chupas covered with bits of the grain they were threshing, their heads hung down in remorse for the deed they were about to commit.

A panic rushed through me. Seeing Kunsang appear in the back of the room, I gestured to the others to wait, and quickly crossed the room.

"Kunsang." I drew her into the pantry. "I've ordered a beating and can't back down. I need your help. As Thupten is raising the whip, run to me and beg for his forgiveness. I will grant your request and order Thupten to stop."

Kunsang looked at me with uncertainty. "Please," I said, taking her shoulders and pleading, "I don't want to cause pain." Kunsang gave a sigh, and reluctantly nodded her head. Taking that as an assent, I clasped her hands, then returned to the room.

"I am ready," I said to Thupten. "You can begin."

Thupten stepped into the middle of the room and gestured Dhondrub to lie on the floor. Dhondrub, his expression unchanging, fell to his knees and stretched his body face down. Samten knelt at his feet, bound his ankles together, pulled the legs straight. Phunsok placed his head in his lap, held his shoulders to the floor.

Shifting his weight from one foot to another, Thupten raised the whip. He lifted it above his head. Its tip rose another three arm's-lengths into the air, the long woven strands swayed to either side.

I looked for Kunsang.

Crack! It came down. A ripple went through Dhondrub's body

from his shoulders down his legs. Crack! The leather strands lashed at his back. Crack! Crack!

Kunsang! I looked frantically toward the pantry.

Crack! Crack! Crack! The surface of the twisted leather caught the lamp light and glistened as it curled through the air. Crack! Crack!

After ten strokes, the whip came to rest at Thupten's side and the room was silent, except for the sound of Dhondrub's breath, which had grown louder.

I stood, my shoulders curled in tight over my chest. My anger was gone. Instead I felt pain, as if I were the one who'd been whipped. I looked at his body stretched out before me, faint stains of red rising up through his shirt. *Om Mani Peme Hum,* I whispered again and again, under my breath. *Forgive me.*

All night I couldn't sleep. Over and over, I saw the long dark shaft rise up. I saw the slick leather strands, like a quivering serpent, coil and twist through the air. I heard its slap on the flesh of Dhondrub's back.

What came over me? I wondered. What have I done?

"When pride is removed, basic wisdom can be revealed. Treat others with a compassionate heart." Gyalsay Rinpoche's words echoed in my mind.

Later I asked Kunsang why she hadn't come out. "I was afraid," she said.

In the months that followed, the situation in Kham and Amdo got increasingly worse. We were told that the People's Liberation Army had moved in great numbers down into Kham from the north, while their troops based in Sichuan and Yunnan were moved up. The Chinese called this tactic *"Korjong Chenmo,"* meaning "Big Circle." Following this strategy, they planned to "crush the rebellious Khampas" in an ambush from all directions.

Within Kham, the fight dragged on in Lower Gonjo. Every day we heard news from passing tradesmen. Troops from all the tribes entered the struggle, but as the Chinese began overwhelming them, the troops took to the mountains. Derge lost territories, Lingkha Shipa lost territories, the Prince of Derge and fighters from Lingkha Shipa fled into our area. We did what we could to supply them with food and other supplies, but our provisions were limited.

In other regions of Tibet, we heard that agricultural and nomadic areas were turned into communes. Tibetan leaders continued to be purged, monks and lamas denounced.

The situation became so extreme that a group of resistance fighters came together into one large army in Lhokha, a town south of Lhasa. It was called *"Chushi Gangdruk,"* "Four Rivers, Six Ranges." Weapons were purchased from India, and eventually the American CIA provided support.

"Prison for anyone who helps Chushi Gangdruk," Gosay Tsering called as he came up the stairs. "The Chinese have forced our government to issue that proclamation."

"It will not be long," he said, entering the kitchen, "before they begin to bring their full force to bear. They will try anything to stop us."

In the first part of 1959, the Chinese sent their airplanes over the plains of Jangthang, which lay to the south, several days' ride from our village. Their bombs overwhelmed the area and more than one thousand lost their lives. After hearing the news, we met with the leaders of Derge and Lingkha Shipa, who were camping in the hills above our house. We decided to form a base camp up in the nomadic lands.

We gathered in an area south of our village called Nachen Thang. On a cold, clear day, the ground still dusted with snow, we stood in front of a pile of Mani stones and watched while the smoke from incense rose into the air. Lamas from a nearby monastery chanted for our success and survival. They made offerings and gave us a blessing.

We mounted our horses and rode into the hills, a gun strapped to each back, a sword at each side, a red fox-fur hat on each head.

We rode in a line, several men wide, winding for almost a mile across the meadow. I rode near its head, behind three who were carrying our flag. The sun was bright and cast a glare on the snow. The hooves of our horses crunched the frozen surface with each step, the sound echoed hollow and cold inside. With each step I felt myself carried further from the peace of my practice. As we rode along the banks of the river, one thought wouldn't leave my mind. Could I really kill?

After crossing the river, we came to a stretch of pasture that was familiar. It was a place my father had brought me to when I was first learning to ride.

"KI KI KIHEE! Lha Gyal Lo!" Papa's voice behind me makes me urge my horse on. I slap my reins back and forth on my horse's neck as Papa has shown me, to make him run faster. I lean over and whisper, "Go! Go!"

Looking back, I see Papa racing toward me, his long hair blowing behind him, one arm raised over his head. His teeth flash white in a broad smile. "I am coming, Nyu," he cries, "you'd better watch out!"

"KI KI KIHEE!" He reaches my side and leans over to take my hat off my head. "KIHEEEE! Lha Gyal Lo!" he cries, and charges past up the meadow.

He reins his horse in ahead of me and sits laughing as I ride up. His black eyes flashing, his cheeks flushed red. "Well, little Nyu," he laughs, reaching over to give me an affectionate push, "you almost had me."

I look at him sitting beside me. The beauty of his face, the straightness of his seat, are striking, but I narrow my eyes, giving him a look of determination. Tossing my head, I challenge, "Next time I will!"

*   *   *

In the early evening we reached the nomad camp. Exhausted from the day, we could barely exchange a kind word and kept to ourselves. I found a place apart from the rest, where the ground curved into a natural bowl. Clearing away the snow, I set up my tent, unrolled my sheepskin, and set my gold charm box in a place at the head.

The others had started a fire a short distance away. The warmth of its flames drew me to it. Hours passed as we sat drinking tea. Occasionally someone stood up and threw a small bit of dung on the fire, being careful to keep the flames low so as not to attract attention.

It was the dark of the moon, and the night was blacker than usual. The only light was the flickering fire. I focused on its flames in an attempt to keep my mind free of worry. But as the flames turned to embers I became more and more uneasy.

The responsibility of so many lives began to weigh heavily. I was the only woman among many men and was not sure I knew how to proceed. I looked at the others sitting around the fire; each face had the same expression. In truth, it was the first time any of us had been part of an "army." None of us had a clear idea what we should do.

Later, as I crawled under the bedding to sleep, I longed for Mama's warm skin next to mine.

Each day, men left for the south. Many of them were young, their faces full of pride. The thought of fighting was exciting to them, not yet real. It pained me to see them go. I knew some wouldn't come back.

Each day I met with the other leaders. Each day we received reports from Lower Gonjo and dispatched men to the south. But after the morning meeting had finished, there was nothing left to do. Some told stories to pass the time. Some talked. Some prayed. I did my daily recitations. Beyond that, nothing happened until the next day, when a messenger arrived bearing news. Some days no messenger appeared and our meetings were brief.

One day, several weeks after we had left for the hills, Shamo Chemi rode into camp. I could tell by his expression that he was bringing bad news.

He leaped off his horse and handed me a letter. It was written in

Tibetan, but the signature was Chinese. "Return to your family," the letter read, "and I will guarantee that nothing will happen to your possessions. Furthermore, if you surrender all the weapons that are listed in Pomdha Gonor's pamphlet, you will be awarded an appropriate rank for your deed. Send word through Shamo Chemi."

I was incensed. Far from any thought of surrender, my resolve to stay hidden and continue to prepare only increased. As I read the words over, I thought of all those killed in Gonjo and all those suffering throughout Tibet at the hands of the Chinese. I was reminded of my father's constant words of advice: *"We should not be deceived by the clever lies of the Chinese."*

"It is better to die than to surrender to the Chinese," I told Shamo Chemi in anger. "Because I'm a woman, they think I'll hand over the weapons of my people. It's an insult. Go back to them and tell them I will never surrender."

Shamo Chemi begged me to come back to my house, and promised to see that nothing happened to me or my family. "Please surrender. Please surrender," he kept saying. "If you stay, it will come to no good."

The Chinese continued to attack our troops in Lower Gonjo. Many battles were lost and many Tibetan people killed. "The Chinese are able to replace their ammunition regularly," a messenger told us, "while our men must rely on what they are carrying. Occasionally," he said, "we are able to take weapons from the Chinese soldiers we have killed, but even with ten extra bullets in our guns, after firing the ten there is nothing."

With little ammunition left, and no back-up supplies, our troops began to weaken.

One day, as we were discussing the situation, I couldn't stand it any longer. I was doing little in the camp and felt useless. I begged the other leaders to let me go to the south and join the battle. "There is no point to stay removed in this camp while the fighting is going on elsewhere," I said with frustration. "I feel I am doing nothing here. I want to join the troops in the south and fight for Tibet!"

Without my knowledge, one of the leaders sent word to my

mother of my wish to fight. As soon as she heard, she and Gosay Tsering rode to the camp to dissuade me. They pleaded with me to change my mind. My mother cried so loudly, I finally relented.

"The Chinese are only a day away!" the messenger cried as he rode into camp. "They have crossed into Upper Gonjo. It won't be long before they are here."

Men ran out of their tents. There were calls for others to come. We huddled together to discuss what to do.

"Lemdha Pachen," Anak Pon said, addressing me by my formal name. "Go down into Lemdha and gather as many families as you can. The rest of us will go to the upper lands and wait for you to join us. We will then all continue toward Lhasa."

Many who had left their homes in Kham to fight the Chinese had begun to move toward Lhasa or flee to camps of Chushi Gangdruk, the principal resistance force. Not knowing what else to do, we put all our hopes into reaching Lhasa and possibly joining with Chushi Gangdruk.

That morning after the meeting, I rode down to alert my household of our plans.

Our house exploded in panic at my announcement. Like a rock thrown into a flock of birds, people scattered into every corner. Gonlha and Ani Rigzin ran to the chapel to collect the statues, Thangkas, and texts. Mama and Kunsang went to the treasury to gather jewelry and gold. Anya, Thupten, and Tashi searched the pantry for food. And I supervised the other servants, collecting animals and preparing to load them with packs.

We planned to bury as much as we could, but the ground in the basement was still frozen solid. Kunsang nearly bloodied her hands clawing at the half-frozen earth. Thupten joined with a metal hoe, and they dug for hours. All day, as I supervised the packing, I heard the sound of feet on the stairs, of metal against dirt, of sacks dragged across floors.

By the end of the day, a huge copper water container, the size of ten people, had been filled with precious texts and covered with shovels of dirt. Six trunks with precious statues, golden idols, trumpets, drums, and silver ornaments were buried in shallow graves. Jewelry too heavy to carry was slipped into chinks in the wall.

That night we went one last time to the chapel. Stripped of its statues and hangings, it was a big empty room, like any other. The light of one butter lamp cast shadows of those bowed in prayer on the bare earthen wall. Gonlha's voice was the only sound.

"The more helpless beings are, the more important it is to love them, therefore liberate all beings in this dark age.
May the source of benefit and goodness spread and expand,
May the doctrine of the Buddha be everlasting."

Late in the night before going to bed, Mama and Ani Rigzin pleaded with me to leave by myself. "You can get farther if you go ahead. We are elderly and will only slow you down."

I refused. "If we die, we all die together. If we live we should not be alone. Whatever happens, we are going to stick together."

In the morning we loaded as many of our valuables as we could carry onto the backs of dri, yak, and mules. We strapped what jewelry we could to our bodies and stuffed the rest into saddle bags. Gold was wrapped and hidden beneath the jewelry. The special family Thangka given by the Tibetan government, stating the position of our family, the size of our land, our rights as chieftains, was rolled and packed on the back of a mule. Scriptural leaflets with pictures of Buddha painted in pure gold were put in a special box on the back of a dri. We even brought along an extra cow for milk.

We left just as the sun was spreading its light behind the hills. When we were halfway to the river, I turned once more to look at our house. A bundle of white sat near the gate. "Dolma!" I cried. Mama gave me a look; we had already discussed it, a servant was staying to care for the dogs. "They will be safer at home," Mama had said. My eyes filled with tears, but I wiped them away and rode on.

I turned several times to look. The white figure grew smaller with each step. When we reached the river, all I saw through my tears was a dot.

At the edge of the river we gathered with other families from Lemdha. Thupten, who had been sent to get my grandmother in a neighboring village, arrived leading her horse. The ice had broken early that year; the river ran black and smooth. We crossed in a place where the water was shallow, and reached the other side without getting wet.

Farther up in the hills, we joined groups from the towns of Lingkha Shipa, Markham, and Derge. There were thousands in the group as we set off in the direction of Lhasa: mothers, fathers, children, dogs, horses, yak, dri, mules, and many belongings. Like an ancient caravan crossing the plains, we moved slowly westward.

After traveling several hours, we realized our large numbers could be easily spotted by Chinese planes in the air and decided it was better to break into smaller units. Our group from Gonjo planned to meet those from Derge and Lingkha Shipa in the nomadic region of Dagyab the next day. Those from Markham planned a different route.

I sent a small advance team ahead to see if there were any Chinese along the route our Gonjo group was planning to take. The team was instructed to find the best trail for us to follow through the mountain. When they returned with news that the paths were clear, I sent fifteen men ahead to defend us from possible attacks. Once I saw that several had reached the peak of the hill, and several had gone on to the pass, I instructed another six men to bring up the rear, to protect us from possible attack from behind. Without a cloud in the sky and with the bare, treeless plains stretching in front of us, I could see no place that we could take cover in the event of an attack.

Several times we saw a plane in the distance. Having only heard about them, at first I thought it was a giant bird. Then a man next to me whispered, "An airplane," and I realized what it was. It flew without flapping its wings; the sound it made was like no other I'd heard.

Each time one came into sight, our anxiety increased. Once when we had stopped for tea, a young girl dropped the lid of the pot on a stone and all of us panicked, imagining a plane had crept up unnoticed and was bombing us.

Late that afternoon, we left the plains and climbed back into the hills. The path grew steep and boulders jutted out on either side. For a while the trail was so rough that we had to get off our horses and lead them on foot until the path smoothed out again.

Sending my family and the others ahead with the best of the troops, I stayed behind with the remaining men to guard the rear. When we were sure they had safely crossed over the top, we prepared to follow.

As we were mounting our horses, Thupten pointed frantically toward a nearby hill. Three Chinese soldiers in yellow-green uniforms were scrambling over the top, their guns raised in the air.

"Chinese!" I shouted in panic. Before we had time to seek cover, they opened fire. The sound of their machine guns startled the pack animals, and many broke loose and ran down the hill.

"Spread out!" I cried. The others dashed for cover behind nearby rocks. I ran to a huge boulder at the side of the road. I crouched low, and with the reins of my horse in my hand, pulled my gun from my belt and waited, my heart racing.

Tat-tat-tat! The sound of machine guns came again, this time closer. I raised my gun, my hand trembling. I aimed at a point by the soldiers, but my gun wavered and wouldn't stay fixed. I put my other hand on my wrist to steady it, and pulled the trigger. Dirt flew into the air, and one of the soldiers retreated. I fired several more shots. The other soldiers disappeared.

I leaned back against the rock and wiped sweat from my forehead. I gulped at the air. *Om Mani Peme Hum.* No one was killed.

Time passed with no more shooting. I stuck my head out and waved to the others. We crept up the hill, following the tracks of those who had gone ahead.

That night, we rejoined them in Dagyab. Later the Prince of Derge and the chief of Lingkha Shipa arrived, tired but unharmed. We sat in the dark, each talking about what had happened that day. Afraid we'd be noticed by lighting a fire, we ate dried mutton and bread and drank warm milk from our cow.

On that first day, we lost many pack animals and much of our wealth. I was most saddened when I found that the Thangka from the Tibetan government and the special gold scriptures had been on one of the animals that ran away.

I thought of going in search of it, but the others said I was crazy. "We can barely keep ourselves alive," Mama said, "let alone holding on to our possessions." Later I learned that the dri had found her way to our nomads' area, and one of the nomad families was keeping the treasures for me. But it wasn't until many years later that I retrieved it.

That night I pulled the sheepskin over my head and lay awake in the dark. Out of sight of the others, I cried for the first time since we left. Mama turned in her sleep, but didn't wake.

The next morning I rose early. The first rays of the sun had just touched the peaks of the surrounding mountains. Farther up the valley, I could see the tents of the Derge division, and to the side of them the tents of those from Lingkha Shipa.

In our part of the encampment, most of the people were still asleep, but smoke rising from a nearby tent was a sign that a few were up and beginning to make tea. Partly asleep, I slipped out of our tent, careful not to wake Mama, Granny, Kunsang, or Ani Rigzin. I crept toward the neighboring fire with a cup in my hand.

The sound of a cannon shattered the silence. A group of Chinese soldiers ran toward us, shouting and shooting their machine guns. Columns of dirt rose into the air, bullets falling like hail. Everywhere people started shouting. "Get up!" "Control the horses!" Everywhere there was confusion, frantic screams, whinnying horses, bleating yaks.

A young boy ran by me crying for his mother, his eyes wild. A moment later he fell to the ground, his shoulder ripped open. A horse broke loose just in front of me. It reared up and was shot in the neck. Cries came from every direction, everywhere people struggled to flee. Some leaped on horses without saddles, some ran by without boots.

Mama! Granny! I ran toward the tent. "Kunsang!" I screamed. "Help Granny . . . Mama . . . Ani Rigzin." I ran toward the horses. The belt from my chupa came untied and dragged on the ground. I tripped as I ran.

The horses were reeling, rearing up, tearing the ropes trying to break loose. I grabbed for my horse's halter. Crack! My hat flew off my head and landed on the ground. *Om Mani Peme Hum, blessed Dorjee Phurba protect us.* I snatched the hat, and with horses in hand, raced back to our tent.

Kunsang pulled Granny up from her bedding and stood at her side, holding her arm. The old woman was having trouble standing, her eyes wide with fright.

With no time to saddle Shindruk, I picked up Granny and lifted her onto his bare back. I jumped on behind, laid my body over hers, and motioned the others to follow.

I pushed Shindruk in the direction of the hills. Others fled in the same direction; in the confusion one collided with us. I focused my eyes on the hill ahead and urged Shindruk forward. He shied several times, almost knocking us off. We rode past a dead horse and a man whose face was half off. Another, whose foot was gone. And others . . . too many . . .

We didn't stop riding until we reached a stand of trees near the pass, which could provide shelter. Mama, Ani Rigzin, and Kunsang came right behind, and soon others joined us. We got off our horses and huddled together as I tried to think what to do next.

As we were waiting, the shooting died down, then stopped. A little while later a young man from Lemdha passed by and told us that the Chinese had left. With the danger past, my head began to clear and I realized we'd left all our belongings behind. We had escaped with only the jewelry that was strapped to our bodies, but not even a spoonful of tsampa to eat.

I worried that without food Mama, Granny, and Ani Rigzin might die of starvation. "There is no other choice but to go back and retrieve whatever is left," I said to Kunsang. As we rode down, there were a few people still climbing the hill from the camp, but already several thousand had left.

The deserted camp was strewn with bodies, some with their chests blown open, some with their heads bloodied, some with an arm or a leg missing. None were moving. Here and there a horse, a yak, a mule lay limp. Everywhere clothes, sacks of food, sacred texts were scattered over the ground, bits of dirt on some, splashes of blood on others.

I took a deep breath and looked at Kunsang. For a moment we both hesitated. But I urged Shindruk forward, keeping my eyes focused straight ahead to the place where we'd pitched the tent. Almost everything was still there.

As we were loading our horses with meat, butter, and tsampa, Shawaramo, one of my favorite mules, came running toward me, mewing and braying as if happy to see us. He nuzzled his nose into my chupa. "Shawaramo," I said in surprise, "where did you come from?" I leaned over to scratch his ear.

"Hurry." Kunsang looked nervous.

We loaded the rest of the food on the mule's back and rode up to the pass. There, we found that the others had gone on ahead and followed their trail into a valley.

After several hours, we reached a place where the ground leveled out into a meadow. A woman was standing in the middle of the road not far ahead, her horse tied to a bush. She was tall, lean, and she paced back and forth as if passing the time while she waited for someone to arrive. As we got closer, I recognized her. It was Dekyong.

I dropped Shawaramo's rope and rode toward her. She stood watching me approach. When she recognized me, her lips parted into a smile. Tears formed in her eyes, but she blinked once and they were gone.

Seeing her again, I was overcome with longing and sadness. For the first time since my father died, I felt the full weight of all that had happened the past few months.

I wiped a tear from my eye and slid off my horse. Dekyong and I stood silently with our arms wrapped tightly around each other. For an instant, the faces of my father and Gyalsay Rinpoche flashed in front of me, mixed together with faces that were bloodied and torn.

We loosened our grasp and took a step back. "You look tired," she said, brushing my cheek with her hand. "I was worried."

I gestured for Kunsang to go ahead with the food. Dekyong and I lay back against rocks on the side of the path. The day was clear, the air crisp but windless. We looked off toward the hills.

Dekyong rubbed her face in her hands. "It's like a dream," she said. "I keep hoping I'll wake."

I noticed fine lines had spread under her eyes, lines of worry at the corners of her mouth. Her face was fuller than before, but strained.

"My family lost their land," she said. "We fled to Dagyab and joined with people from Lingkha Shipa. When I heard that your family was ahead, I came into the camp looking for you. But so many people . . . then the attack."

She turned her hands over in her lap. They were chapped, and in places blistered and raw. I suddenly felt sad; they had once been so smooth.

"I met your mother this morning as she was passing by," she said. "She told me you'd gone back for the food. I was afraid you'd get shot."

I didn't respond, and we fell silent. A breeze had started up, and I pulled my chupa around me.

"And you?" she asked after awhile, "your father . . . ?"

"Dead," I said. "His heart was broken, as much as anything."

I stopped for a moment. A rush of feelings, unexpected. I fingered my Mani beads.

"After he died I had to organize our people, but inside I was numb. It doesn't seem real. . . ."

"I know," she said. "My father died too. We were separated when we fled. Mama and I had to leave before we could find him. Several months later, we heard he was killed."

We sat for a moment in silence.

What has happened? I wondered. What fury unloosed?

"In the name of Papa," I said, shaking the tears from my eyes, "I've vowed to fight. Even kill. The precepts say not to kill, but with times as they are, there is no other choice. Defending our country and teachings come first."

"Everyone has to fight until Tibet becomes free again," Dekyong said sadly, "to protect Buddha's teachings."

We talked for a time, telling what had happened in the years we were apart. We painted pictures of what the future might hold.

Dekyong saw a small hut in a glen with a stream flowing nearby. A time of quiet and contemplation, dipping deep into the secrets of her mind. I saw a rocky outcropping, vines and wet green things tangled over it, a cave with a small opening behind. A place to read the texts in silence, and listen to bird calls and crickets.

I rested my head back against a mound of earth, with my face toward the sun, letting my mind drift.

"Wolf and Sheep," Lhamo sang the name of our game over and over. "Wolf and Sheep. Wolf and Sheep." We arranged the stones in the mud by the edge of the water. She crouched for a moment and studied them, then leaped over one of my stones. "I got you," she cried in delight. "The wolf takes the sheep!"

The sound of gunfire brought us both to our feet.

"We can't stay here," I whispered urgently, "the Chinese are following us."

"The gunfire is on the other side of the hill," Dekyong said. "There are people posted to block their advance."

We looked in the direction of the sound. For a moment we wavered, unsure what to do.

"Remember Tibet," Dekyong said.

We both had the same response. "Fight!"

The others in our group had gone over the hill ahead, and the gunfire was coming from behind. We retraced our path until we came to a hill sloping up to the side. We dismounted, tied our horses to a bush out of sight, and hobbled their feet to keep them from fleeing if we fired our guns. Then we settled behind a boulder to wait.

Dorjee Phurba, I whispered. *Protect us.*

Several shots rang out on the upper part of the hill behind us. I tightened my fist.

"Our sentries, shooting at the Chinese lower down," Dekyong whispered.

At the far end of the valley, five men in yellow-green uniforms ran up the road in our direction. Dekyong gave me a nudge and pointed at them. She took a breath, and raised a pistol with a long barrel.

I reached into the front of my chupa and took out the short-barreled pistol that had been my father's. My hand was shaking. I knew it was good at short range, having fired it from the roof of our house, but I wasn't sure it could reach as far as the soldiers.

I sucked in my breath and nodded at Dekyong to go first.

Zap. Zing. Zap.

Dekyong's pistol sent one, two, three, four bullets down to the road. Dust sprayed up, two men fell. The other three turned and ran back down the road for cover. I shot, but the bullets fell short.

"You shot two!" I whispered in amazement to Dekyong. It didn't seem real, the sounds from her gun followed far away by two men falling.

"There aren't any more bullets in my gun," Dekyong whispered urgently. "Let's go!"

The Chinese had no horses; the soldiers hiding below wouldn't catch up. We untied our horses and leaped on, racing in the direction the others had gone.

That night, we caught up with them in Tri-pa. Our families, worried when we fell back, had sent one of the men back to look for us. When he rode into camp with us behind, there were sighs of relief.

We gathered around a low-burning fire to recount the events of the day. We told about the Chinese soldiers Dekyong had killed and the others we'd turned back. But because of the wounded and dead, spirits were low. Many were busy helping those who'd been hit, wrapping wounds with bits of cloth, dressing them with Tibetan herbs. They took little notice of what we were saying.

Later we learned that after the first attack, many had changed their mind and left to go home. Kunsang and her family were among them. Many others I knew left as well. They thought it better to return than risk death.

The rest of us continued to Shothalhosum on our way to Lhasa, where we believed there would be sanctuary. Unknown to us, Lhasa had already fallen to the Chinese and the Dalai Lama had fled to India. Because news traveled so slowly at that time, it wasn't until five years later that we learned details of those last days.

Only later I learned that in the beginning of March of that year, 1959, the Chinese had sent an invitation to His Holiness inviting him to attend a theatrical show in their camp. They insisted he not be accompanied by armed guards and that he keep his visit a secret.

When word got out that His Holiness was going unattended, a rumor spread through the people that the Chinese were planning to kidnap him. By the morning of March 10, nearly thirty thousand Tibetans had gathered outside Norbulinka Palace. The next several days they kept watch, making sure His Holiness didn't leave and the Chinese didn't enter.

By March 16, the situation had grown so intense that everyone became desperate, including the Chinese. When the sound of Chinese guns was heard outside the palace that afternoon, His Holiness was advised to leave the city immediately to avoid an impending massacre. Disguised in a Tibetan army uniform and fur cap, he walked unnoticed through the crowd to a boat waiting to ferry him, his family, and a small group of advisers down river. The party was met by a group of Khampa fighters. They set out across the mountains toward India.

Four days later, unaware he had left, the Chinese began shelling Norbulinka. The shelling continued throughout the day. Norbulinka, the Potala, several monasteries and schools, private buildings were seriously damaged. The death toll ran into the thousands.

Had we known at the time that our cherished destination had fallen into the hands of the Chinese and that our beloved leader had fled, we might have lost hope. As it was, our spirits were low. That day we lost many of our pack animals and most of our belongings. Men, women, even children from our village were killed. Chief Ogmatsang Rinnam, the ablest minister of Derge, was wounded.

As one of the most respected and trusted leaders in the group, Gongma Ranangtsang, lay dying, several men helped raise him to his feet. They lifted his arms in a gesture of defiance and victory.

That day, we were confronted by Chinese troops. We were defeated and separated, one from another. That was the beginning of our time in the hills.

7

Capture

The night was windless and still. In the distance, the faint rumbling of thunder drifted toward me. Or was it a plane? I turned over to stare at the sky. The stars were in a swarm overhead, and on the horizon a sliver of moon was beginning to rise.

I pulled the sheepskin tighter around me. Behind me, the crest of the hill curled, dark and inhospitable. The place seemed filled with sadness, and no matter how I turned or where I looked, a tangle of images drifted in front of my eyes. A hand on the ground, ripped off at the wrist. A face caved in. A child curled next to his mother.

A bird cried, and a dark shape passed overhead. I watched as its wings rose and fell, and listened to the whirring of air through its feathers. If only I could fly. Away from this wretched place to some other world. I lay staring at the sky. In the darkness, I thought I saw Gyalsay Rinpoche's face looking down at me, his eyes filled with tenderness. *Om Mani Peme Hum,* I prayed. *Blessed Rinpoche guide me on the path.*

"Yesterday many were killed." The sad voice of the Prince of Derge spread through the crowd. "We've seen the danger in traveling in such a large group. Despite our vow to stay together, we must break into smaller groups and go separate ways."

He gestured to several of the other leaders. "People from Lingkha Shipa will go via Zayul. People from Gonjo and Derge will go on to Pelbar in hopes of meeting Chushi Gangdruk. The Chinese are close behind us—we can't risk waiting. We will decide later whether to go on to Lhasa. Gather what belongings you have left, and set out now."

Confusion broke out as people began to move in every direction. Children called for their mothers, animals wandered lost. Dekyong pushed through the crowd. When she reached me I could see she was crying. She threw her arms around me. We held on to each other, but we knew there was nothing we could do. She had her family to look after, I had mine. We had to go with our separate groups—there was no possibility of staying together. It seemed a cruel fate to be parting so soon after reuniting.

"Ashe Pachen!" My mother gestured frantically to come.

I took a gold ring from my finger and slipped it onto Dekyong's. I held on to her hand as if it were a lifeline. We were both crying.

"Ashe!" My mother called again.

I squeezed her hand and, avoiding her face, ran toward my mother. I turned once and saw her standing where I'd left her, her face in pain. But people passed between us and she soon disappeared.

That day we traveled north toward Rewoche, a town near Chamdo. My throat was tight from holding back tears. I had to struggle to keep them from spilling down my face with each step Shindruk took; with each step, Dekyong's eyes were always in front of me.

As we continued toward Rewoche, I noticed the terrain was familiar. It was some consolation to know we were still traveling through Khampa land, land still part of my home. For some reason it made me less lonely.

Mostly we traveled at night so as not to be seen, but whenever it seemed safe to do so, we also traveled by day. Each time we got to a place where the direction was uncertain, we asked Khaley Rinpoche to cast a divination. Whatever he said, we followed without hesitation. Traveling in this way, we were able to avoid the Chinese, though we were never totally free from their presence.

"A massacre!" a man shouted.

In front of us, we saw the scene of an earlier battle. Tents ripped apart, bodies strewn over the ground.

As we approached I could see huge vultures picking over the dead, pieces of flesh in their beaks. On some of the bodies, the flesh was cleared to the bone. At the edge of the camp a few starving dogs ate limbs they had pulled to the side. Everywhere scraps of bloody clothing were blown by the wind.

Haunted by what we'd seen, we traveled much of the night. Tormented, hoping to forget, I closed my eyes and let Shindruk carry me. I soon fell asleep.

When I awoke the others were nowhere in sight.

The night was dark and windless, the moon already set. Nearby I heard the breaking of twigs. The figure of a soldier crouched down. I held my breath, but nothing moved. I looked closer; it was only a bush.

In the distance, the howling of wolves. I flicked the reins and urged Shindruk on. A shape loomed toward us and I saw glistening teeth, a foaming mouth. I jerked to the side. But the shape was merely a rock.

We stepped over branches strewn on the ground that looked like human limbs, passed rocks jutting out that looked like half-crazed dogs. Wherever we went, I couldn't erase the images of the day from my mind.

Luckily Shindruk sensed the direction the others had gone and moved ahead on his own. After a time we caught up. By then, I had calmed.

We joined the others at a small wooden bridge suspended over a gorge. It was short but unsteady, and hung like a frail web over a river far below. Following the others, I started across. With each step the bridge sprang up and down, on either side a dizzying view. Afraid of slipping underneath the handrail, I kept my eyes focused ahead.

When I was almost across, I heard the shriek of a horse. The bridge began buckling and rippling beneath my feet. I held the guardrail and glanced back to see that a mule had panicked and kicked the horse behind. The horse reared up, its pack coming loose. I watched the pack tumble through the air and crack open on rocks far below. Watching the pack's contents fly in every direction, I felt that was happening to my life: pieces tearing apart, scattering to the winds.

Off and on throughout the day I heard the shriek of the horse and saw the pack tumbling down. Slowly, slowly. Cracking open, flying apart.

* * *

That night, eager to reach our goal as quickly as possible, we pressed on toward the plains of Shothalhosum halfway between Chamdo and Lhasa. At one point, the night was so dark we had to get off our horses and feel with our feet, sliding them along the ground to be sure we were still on the trail. It lightened a bit as we came into a clearing, and from the sound of gurgling water, we could tell we were near a small stream. We stopped to stretch for a moment, exhausted. Several young boys went in search of wood for a fire.

Just as we'd finished our meal, we heard the sound of an airplane not far away. "The Chinese," Thupten whispered, "searching for us!"

"Quick!" someone called. "Put out the fire!" A man came running with a pot of water from the river and threw it onto the flames. They hissed and flickered, then went out. We sat, not daring to move. The air had a damp, burned smell, and mixed with the chill of the night, it made my stomach churn.

After a few moments when the plane had passed, we took the reins of our horses and continued up a narrow valley, one foot sliding after another in the darkness. All night we crept slowly through the hills. By daybreak I was so exhausted I could barely see straight. But intent on getting Mama, Ani Rigzin, and Granny to the safety of a larger group, I kept walking.

As we crossed the last hill and rode down toward the plains of Shothalhosum, we could see several thousand people spread out across a vast area. By midmorning we reached the first group of tents and learned that the plane we'd heard in the night was American, not Chinese. "There is no need to escape to India," a young man told us. "American troops have come to help take back our country!" We were overjoyed at the news. "Perhaps now we will be able to go home," Mama said. The thought was in all of our minds, but no one else dared say it. There was still much to overcome.

We soon got used to the sound of planes overhead. Each night air drops were made in the middle of the night, before we went to sleep. First a red light appeared far away in the sky. Then we heard the humming sound we'd heard the night before. Several men marked a place with many small fires to indicate where we were.

Dark shapes fell out of the sky. They floated down, suspended from large pieces of cloth. There were thirteen men, and box after box of weapons, clothing, gold coins, and food. "Stay away from the boxes," we were told. "They are being taken to the center of camp."

The men who fell from the sky were Tibetans who had been taken by the CIA to be trained in America. A couple of them were from Amdo, but the majority came from Kham. I later found that I knew some of them. Sey Donyo, Raru Yeshe, and Buchay of Derge, Yeshi Raru and Yeshi Wangyal from Markham, Bugyal from Dugur. Also men from the households of Phurba Tsang and Drakpa Lama in Markham.

The day after the first drop, three of these men called a meeting. They distributed arms to each of our groups. "Take as many as you can use," one said, "enough for each able-bodied man in your family."

So many weapons came down that those left over were stockpiled. There were eight-rounders, or M1s as they called them, pistols, grenades, and radio sets. We already had two kinds of Tibetan guns: a Bura, which could take one bullet at a time, and a Kha-dum, which had a short muzzle. With the additional American weapons, we were well equipped.

I took two eight-rounders. I gave one to a man from Gonjo and put the other one on the side of my saddle. I carried my pistol tucked into the belt of my chupa.

The air drops happened perhaps eight or nine times over the next several months. After each drop there were distributions of food and meetings to plan strategies.

A distant cousin from Markham was among the men parachuted in. He often came to talk with my mother and me, but never about the training or their mission. "We are not allowed to tell what we know," he told me. "That way, if you're caught, you'll have nothing to tell. Everything is strictly confidential." I nodded my head and asked him no questions.

From time to time, I would see him go to the top of the hill and set up a wireless radio. I never knew what he heard or said, but suspected it had something to do with the air drops, for he always seemed to know when they were about to happen.

For the next four months thousands of us lived scattered through the area of Shothalhosum surrounding the village of Pelbar. Some were camped in the valley, some in the open land. Though we received provisions from the air drops, food was still scarce. Rice and vegetables were particularly difficult to get. Horses didn't have fodder, and at times we had to feed them bushes usually used for incense. Since there wasn't enough food or grass for the animals in any one place, we had to keep moving.

At first my family stayed in the house of a friend in Pelbar, but soon food in that area ran out and we rode to an area not far away, called Dadho. We stayed at each place for over three months. During that time, people continued to arrive almost daily from the towns of Gapa, Nangchen, Karu, and Naru.

One day I recognized a few familiar faces in a group that had just arrived into camp. As I approached to welcome them, I saw that one of them was Lhamo. A young girl clutched at her chupa, and when I reached her I realized the young girl was her daughter, transformed from the infant I'd held several years before into a toddler. I felt sad to see how Lhamo's face had aged in the years we'd been apart. The skin around her eyes was puffed, as if she hadn't had much sleep. Her body, once lean, had widened, and her belly seemed unusually round.

"It's been a long time," I said. "Your child is already walking."

"And a second one is coming," she replied. She gestured around and shrugged her shoulders, as if to say, *Can you imagine . . .*

As we stood talking, her little daughter came up to me and held out her hand. I remembered the crying baby and my frustrated attempts to calm her, but now she had grown and her face was smiling and cheerful. I looked into her outstretched hand and saw a small beetle crawling across her palm.

"For me?" I asked. She nodded and looked up with trusting and innocent eyes. At that moment she won my heart.

After that, each day when she saw me coming, she ran toward me with her arms held up. "Pema," I'd say, bending down to rub her forehead, "look what I've brought." Swooping her up, I'd let her reach into the front of my chupa for treats I'd hidden inside. Once a small frog. Sometimes a piece of sweet cheese.

The days settled into a routine. There was much conversation around the fire. Some, like me, spent time chanting prayers; others played games with sho dice. Always there was a search for food; occasionally messengers arrived with news.

One day a young man arrived who had been part of Chushi Gangdruk, with news that Chushi Gangdruk had been defeated and most of its forces fled to India. We gathered around him, eager to hear what had happened.

"A year ago, we were a force to be recokened with," he said, gesturing proudly. "One of our fiercest battles, on the banks of the River Nyemo, lasted three days. At the time, the nearby fields and houses were swarming with Chinese armed with cannons, automatic weapons, and grenades. As the buglers in our camp sounded the signal to attack, our leader, Tashi Andruktsang, led seventy horsemen onto the field. Galloping at full speed we charged the enemy like wild animals, fighting them hand to hand. The Chinese were unable to resist our attack and withdrew to a nearby village. We shot the doors and windows of the houses. We eventually burned them down. It was the only way we could destroy the Chinese.

"But not long after that, losses began to happen," he said, looking down at the ground with saddness. "The loss of Tsona, our main base, was particularly difficult. The will to continue weakened. It was then that we realized the current situation was impossible. We decided to save ourselves for a future struggle and retreat for the time to India. It was with great sadness that our leader Tashi Andruktsang handed over our weapons to the Indian authorities and went into exile."

We were despondent after hearing the story, and wondered if we should follow them to India.

Several days later, the Chinese attacked from every direction. There wasn't even time to open boxes from the last air drop, the attack was so unexpected.

*   *   *

It was early morning. I was on my way to the pastures to check on the animals when I heard shooting in the camp below. Whirling around, I ran back toward our camp. As I came into it soldiers ran toward us from the camp below.

I called, "Mama! Granny! Ani Rigzin!" We grabbed our horses and began to run. Ahead of us I could see Lhamo holding Pema in her arms and struggling to run. Suddenly I heard her cry. Pema was hit. Dropping the reins of my horse, I rushed over and helped her open the little girl's robes. The bullet had torn open her chest and blood was pouring out. She was moaning with pain and I could see she was dying. Lhamo stood paralyzed, her eyes large and clouding over. "Come!" I begged, but she didn't move. She stood with her eyes fixed on a distant point, her face growing pale. I tried to pull her after me, but she slumped to the ground, a trickle of blood seeping out of her mouth. From the look in her eyes I knew she was dying.

I heard shouts of the soldiers behind and looked frantically for Mama, Ani Rigzin, and Granny. They were running just ahead. I had no other choice but to follow. I felt a terrible sadness as I left.

We took refuge in the thick forest in the hills beyond camp with eight others from Lemdha. We crouched behind trees, our hearts still racing, and waited for night.

I leaned against the trunk of a fir tree and prayed. *Om Mani Peme Hum. Om Mani Peme Hum.*

As I prayed, Lhamo's face hovered before me. No matter where I turned, I couldn't get away from her eyes.   One moment they were looking at me, the next moment they were blank. It happened so fast.

All night it haunted me. It was as if she had been part of my body, as if a part of my being had died. Later, when the Chinese fired flares into the sky from an opposite hill, lighting the whole area as bright as day, I thought for a moment that her spirit had followed us. "What is it?" Mama whispered as the lights shot into the sky. "It's

Lhamo," I said. She looked at me quizzically but didn't say anything. We pressed our bodies flat into the earth and waited for darkness.

Several days later, after we had fled farther into the hills, we heard that the fighting had gone on for three days and at the end the Chinese had taken possession of Pelbar and the surrounding area of Shothalhosum.

For the next twenty-five days we headed toward India. We planned to go south by Nyulcu, cross the river into Jangthang, then on to India. I worried that if we were caught we'd be killed, but there was never any question in my mind of surrendering. Though our clothing was torn and we were weak from hunger, it seemed far better to die free than to surrender and live under the Chinese.

We traveled by night and took cover during the day. After three days we came upon a group of three hundred who were also headed for India, and joined them. Fear always followed us: fear of being captured, fear of being killed. At times the fear had no object, but floated like a vapor around us.

One night, as we moved farther into the hills, the track narrowed and we had to go one by one. I was walking at the end when I heard a voice speaking Chinese. "Who's there?" I called out. No one answered. I turned my head; no one there. But I smelled a strange pungent scent. The people ahead didn't notice.

Afterward I wondered if it might have been a ghost.

Later that night we reached a steep incline filled with rocks. Our horses had weakened considerably from the hard riding and scarcity of food, and the path was too steep for them to carry us. Dismounting, I gave my reins to Ani Rigzin and put my grandmother on my back; Ani Rigzin led her horse and mine. Using both my hands and my feet, I was able to climb slowly up, but the weight of Granny on my back left me winded.

Each time the path became too steep I carried my grandmother like that, on my back. When it leveled out, she was able to ride.

On the twenty-fourth day we reached the base of one of the highest passes. Climbing all night, we ascended to 6,000 meters. It was bitter cold, and with each step we sank up to our knees in freshly fallen snow. At times when the sky cleared, the moon was so bright on the snow we had to shield our eyes. We were worried that our dark figures might stand out against the white banks and be seen.

At dawn we descended into a valley. Granny was weakened from hunger and cold, and the rest of us were too tired to walk farther. Some decided to continue on, but many of us stopped. The ground was rocky. No trees, just a few thorny bushes. I found a place where the ground curved in and set Granny down. I put some branches under her for insulation, then lay down beside her and fell asleep.

I awoke to the cracking of gunfire nearby. A man was running down the hill toward us. "The Chinese have captured the group ahead and are coming in this direction," he shouted. "Prepare to fight, or flee."

Others were up and we crowded together. "Fight!" some said. "Flee!" others cried. Mama and Ani Rigzin were adamant. "Leave us here, and run," they urged. "We're old, but you can get away."

"We're staying together," I said.

Some grabbed their things and ran in the direction we'd come from, others toward the forest farther down. Those of us who stayed rejected the idea of fighting because of the number of small children and older people like Granny. Resolved to stay, we broke into small groups and waited. Mama, Granny, Ani Rigzin, and I sat huddled together, our arms intertwined.

The freeze of the night had gone. The warmth of the sun made me drowsy. I closed my eyes and for a moment forgot where I was.

The water curls around me. It is cool underneath, but the sun on my face is warm. Sonam, Lhamo, and I are floating on our backs. We close our eyes and pretend we are floating on clouds. "They are tickling," I laugh, and open my eyes.

Five Chinese soldiers were coming toward us with their guns raised. I looked to the side; three more were closing in. To the back. To the other side. Scores of soldiers, their rifles raised, walking slowly toward us. I reached for my pistol and frantically dug in the snow by my feet, trying to hide it.

As I was digging, I looked up. A soldier was a few feet away from me. I remember thinking how young he was, his face soft as a boy's. But as he came closer, I could see his eyes were like steel.

He grabbed my arm and pulled me to my feet. Granny cried out as she too was pulled to her feet. Another soldier came up and held my arms behind my back. The first raised his hands to my chest. As he touched me, a small shock ran down my shoulders to my feet, and I moved away. He grabbed at my arm, put his face against mine and said words I couldn't understand.

He moved his hands over my body, up and down. He felt a lump in the pouch of my chupa between my breasts and reached in for it. A few precious pieces of jewelry, some blessed strings, and amulets I'd managed to save.

He pulled them out, tossed them to a soldier a few feet away, then pushed me forward. Around me the same thing was happening. The children were crying. A soldier slapped one of the women for pulling away.

As the soldiers pushed us forward, I heard more shots being fired. A horse ran past us down the hill; he'd been hit under the belly and his guts were coming out. He ran into a cluster of bushes below us and fell, his feet quivering up in the air as he died.

Farther down, a small girl lay limp at the side of the road. Beyond, a snake curled, slit in half. We came to a river. The swollen body of a man floated by; after him several others, along with the bodies of horses. I had no idea where the river came from or where it was going.

At that time none of us knew what would happen. We couldn't begin to imagine.

We walked for a day, the soldiers at our side. There were a hundred of us, men, women, and children. Some children cried the whole way. A soldier poked at one with his gun, but the boy only cried louder.

At the end of the day we arrived in the village of Rok. A large house was being used to hold prisoners. When we arrived in its courtyard the soldiers took whatever belongings were left, our weapons, our saddles, our horses.

A soldier took Shindruk's reins in his hands and began to lead him away. I broke from the line. When I reached him, I pulled his head down, stood on my toes and touched my forehead to his. "Good friend," I whispered. "Good Shindruk. You'll be all right."

The soldier cried out and pushed me, another took my arm and yanked me back into line. As Shindruk was led into the stable he turned his head to look at me, but the soldier snapped his reins, and he was taken away. I watched him disappear into the building. I bit my lip, hit my fist in my hand, and looked down.

Two soldiers came over to me and patted up and down my body. I stood numb, staring in the direction Shindruk had gone. He was so kind to me, I thought, he doesn't deserve to be taken away. My eyes began to tear, but I willed myself to stop. I didn't want to give the Chinese the satisfaction of seeing me cry.

Two soldiers led Mama, Ani Rigzin, Granny, and me into a large bare room in a vacant house. Three women and two children were crouched inside on the floor. The soldiers locked the door behind us. In a way it was a relief to be closed in, finally away from the soldiers. I lay down on the hard wooden floor, my head on my arms, and pulled my chupa over my feet. The room was damp and musty. I tried to sleep, but the crying of a small girl in the corner kept me awake.

In the dark I saw Shindruk.

A little white colt nuzzles its mother's leg. It is several days old, and still wobbling on tiny legs.

I wondered if the rumor was true, that the Chinese eat horses.

A tall officer with four red stars on his uniform stood on a raised platform in front of us. His words spewed out like machine-gun fire, while a young Tibetan standing stiffly at his side translated. I was soon to become used to this form of address. The rapid harsh words in Chinese, the monotone Tibetan translation.

"As a punishment for killing the soldiers who have come from China to help you, you must turn over all your possessions, the ones you have with you, the ones in your home. . . . The officer's words sounded mismatched as they came through the translator. "If you do this, you will be free to go. If you refuse,"—he raised his hand with his fist clenched above him—"you will be imprisoned, with serious punishment."

Suspecting they had no intention of releasing us, no one agreed.

For the next month we were kept in the house. Soldiers guarded the outside, but inside we were free to talk as we wanted. Every day more people arrived. Many had been in the hills fighting like us, or fleeing to India. Each day at least four new ones arrived. We were given a small cup of tsampa in the morning and watery rice porridge at night. For the first two weeks the days settled down, and free from the fear of capture, we were relatively calm. But after two weeks, the interrogations started.

I heard footsteps far down the hallway, tapping briskly on the floor, coming in our direction. They stopped outside the door to our room. The door flung open and two soldiers entered, their guns raised.

They peered through the dim light, as if looking for someone in particular, then walked over to me. One jabbed his boot in my side, the other motioned me to get up and follow. They led me down the corridor, up a narrow stairway, to a small damp room.

The officer with red stars was sitting behind a small table at the center of the room. On one side the Tibetan translator, on the other two soldiers. The officer gestured me in front of him and began to speak. His face was pale and shiny, his hair slicked back, his eyes bulged as he spoke. Beads of spit sprayed through his lips when he raised his voice, his hand moved in short jerking movements as if hitting the air.

"You are a commander of enemy forces, trying to ruin the work of the Motherland. You are responsible for the crimes you have committed, and the crimes of your father. We have a report he killed a Tibetan interpreter and you will be punished for his crime. But, if you admit all your faults, we will agree to spare your life." The words rolled from the mouth of the Tibetan with no intonation.

I felt angered at the mention of my father's name, and before I had time to think, I responded.

"My father didn't kill your interpreter. The man was passing through our area on his way to Samye with food for your troops when he was shot. No one ever found out who did shoot him, but it wasn't my father." Realizing I should have stayed silent, I closed my mouth. But too late.

The officer leaned toward me, his eyes bulging even further, and spit out more words.

"Which hometown are you from? How many men were fighting under you? Who were the men who were dropped from the plane? What hometown were they from?"

The questions came at me so quickly, I felt dizzy. I didn't know what to say.

"Do you know Yeshe Rushodtshang, the Tibetan who was dropped from the plane? Who did he meet? What did he tell you? What are his plans?"

I looked down at my hands in my lap, not opening my mouth. I knew Yeshe Rushodtshang had been on a secret mission. Even if I'd wanted to, I had nothing to say.

My silence angered the officer and he shouted to the soldiers sitting at his side. Each stood up and took willow sticks from a bucket of water at the side of the room. They came toward me around either side of the table, waving the willow sticks in front of them as they walked. Before they reached me I felt the drops of water flicking off the sticks. Then they were on me. They lashed my face, my hands, my back, my feet, my head. *Om Mani Peme Hum,* I whispered under my breath. *Guru Rinpoche.*

"What was your connection with the American planes? What were the names of the men? What did they tell you?" The questions were spat out.

"I had no connection with the American planes," I whispered, barely audible. "I have nothing to say."

My ears were beginning to ring, and my face was burning. My previous karma, I thought. The pain will eliminate my sins. The soldiers grabbed at my hands and pulled me to my feet. I stood unsteadily as they tied my hands behind my back.

"What were their names? What did they tell you?"

I swayed, but didn't answer. The men tossed the rope up over the wooden beams running across the ceiling.

"Answer! What were their names?"

I was mute. The men gave a sharp tug on the rope and my arms yanked behind me and twisted up. Pain like a burning iron shot through my shoulders. A bitter liquid came out of my mouth.

I hung, suspended by my wrists. They hit my face with a board, and the room became dark.

Cold water ran over my head. I was lying on the floor. The first thing I thought was that my eyes were going to come out of my head, there was such a pressure behind them. My shoulders throbbed with pain, and my wrists were burning.

"The soldiers will take you back to your room," the interpreter said, his voice even flatter. "We will see if your memory is better tomorrow."

Two soldiers dragged me back to our room and dropped me inside the door. Mama and Ani Rigzin let out a cry when they saw me.

"We never lifted a finger against you!" Mama cried. "Look what they've done!"

They rushed over to me. Mama took my head in her lap, Ani Rigzin tore off part of her chupa and began to wipe blood from my face.

Mama was beside herself, and cried through the night. She held me in her arms, rocking me from side to side. Ani Rigzin sat beside us and prayed. My nose bled for quite a long time. Except for the pain, I felt numb. But it broke their hearts.

*   *   *

Every day for the next seven days the soldiers came to my room. They came after breakfast and the questioning went on until lunch. There was a half-hour break, then again the questions continued until evening. They tied my hands and hoisted me into the air, then beat me. There was no part of my body they didn't beat. When I lost consciousness, they poured water over me to wake me. And every day, Mama and Ani Rigzin cried.

Even if I had wanted to talk, I couldn't. My mouth, my nose, my eyes were swollen shut. I soon learned it was better to be kicked than hit, but the times they hoisted me into the air were the worst. My wrists and shoulders hurt so badly that I wished they would kill me instead of continuing the torture. But I knew if they did I would be reborn with the same sins in front of me. It was better to suffer and hope for a higher rebirth.

After a while I no longer felt anxiety when I heard the steps on the walk, no longer cared what they did. At times I saw my body lying on the floor, but my spirit was somewhere else.

In the moments I was able to think, I thought of the terrible karma I must have had in a previous life to be beaten like that, and prayed that the pain I was feeling would eliminate all sins that had been built up. I prayed to the Three Jewels. *Guide me. Om Mani Peme Hum.*

We remained in the makeshift prison for several more weeks. I was frightened much of the time, and felt an anger I couldn't erase, no matter how much I prayed. I had fallen into the hands of the Chinese.

I was worried what would happen to Mama and the others. I felt helpless; there was nothing I could do to make their lives better. At times I thought of escaping, breaking through the window in our room, and running free. But across the way was a small house with a dog who might bark, and below several soldiers guarding the house. Even if I could get beyond all that, there was no way of taking the others.

After a month, the Chinese released all the women, children, and old people. "You are free to go where you want," the soldiers said. Each person was given a permit to return to their hometown if they wished. The others of us who were "guilty of crimes" were detained.

Two days later, those remaining were summoned to a meeting, several hundred of us, but I was the only woman. Once again, the four-star officer stood on a platform in front of us. He told us we were being taken to Chamdo and must do whatever the soldiers told us to do.

"Sit when we say sit. Walk when you're told to walk. Eat when we give you food. If you try to escape you'll be shot."

We were tied hand to hand like a flock of sheep and made to line up into a straight line, one behind the other. Soldiers behind, soldiers in front, and soldiers on each side. I was somewhere near the end. We began to walk.

It was a clear day, but cold. The ropes felt like ice on my wrist, and however I turned they bit into my skin. Chime Gonpo was in front of me, Anak Pon was behind, and with our hands tied together, each time one moved it affected the other.

"Face front!" we were ordered. "Stand still!" But the ropes between us threw us off balance. Our shuffling angered the soldiers. They prodded us with the ends of their rifles. "Move!"

As we began to walk through the gate, I saw my mother standing at the side of the road. Ani Rigzin and Granny were standing a few feet behind her. Seeing them, I felt saddened, for the last few months had taken a toll. They looked like three beggars wanting food. Their hair was disheveled, their chupas torn. Mama's face was lined with dirt. Granny leaned on Ani Rigzin, barely able to stand.

"Mama." The word rose in my throat, but disappeared before I spoke it out loud. Why are you still here? I wondered. Why haven't you started toward home?

When she saw me, Mama ran toward me. "Stay away!" I whispered frantically. But she kept coming. She reached a soldier in front, and he put up his rifle to stop her. "Please," she begged, grasping at the soldiers arm. "Please don't take my daughter away . . . if you take her away we will die of starvation."

Ani Rigzin and Granny came after her. They were also crying. "If you take her, take us too," Ani Rigzin cried. "Take us to prison with her, we're no good if she leaves." The soldier shoved them back with his rifle.

I tried to reach for a soldier who was walking at my side. "Please, please, let me speak to them. I will tell them to leave. They are old, they don't understand." But the soldier walked ahead as if he hadn't heard me, perhaps because I couldn't speak Chinese.

Once more Mama reached for the soldier's arm. He turned and struck her down. As we started walking away up the road, I heard her calling, "Ashe, Ashe . . ." I turned to look. The soldier struck, then kicked her. Ani Rigzin fell on his back trying to pull him off.

When we were almost out of sight, I looked one last time. Mama and Ani Rigzin were standing. Granny had fallen in the road. As we rounded a bend in the road, I could still hear them calling to me.

It took us three days to walk to Lhodzong. They were the only thing on my mind, all through the walk. Wherever I looked, they were always in front of me.

~

In Lhodzong, I found several of the chieftains and a large number from the entourage of the Prince of Derge. They had been captured before us and were being held in an animal shelter that was serving as a makeshift prison. It was a relief to see so many familiar faces. I wanted to ask them about Gosay Tsering, Shamo Chemi, Thupten, and so many others. But we weren't allowed to speak to one another and only exchanged glances.

Lhodzong was a collection center. From there people were taken to Chamdo. The prisoners with the most serious "crimes" were put on the top floor of a big house being used as a prison. I was put in a room with one other woman. Her name was Jamyang and she was from Shothalhosum.

Every morning we were given a small cup of rice porridge, and in the night the same thing. One of the guards gave me scissors to cut my hair, and a needle and thread to mend some of the holes in my chupa. He was one of the kinder ones.

Many hours passed with nothing to do. I wanted to do my practices, but the Chinese had banned all prayer. It was "blind belief," they said, and if they saw our lips moving, they threatened to beat us. But whenever I could I would pray silently in my mind. I was kept there for a month.

From Lhodzong, we walked to Nyulchu. Some were chained together, some bound with ropes which became tighter as they got wet. The only time we were untied was to go to the bathroom. We had to raise our hand and say "bako," then we were allowed to go to a nearby bush. We had no bedding to sleep on, and our only clothes were the ones we had on. We crossed several steep passes and many rivers. There was no relief.

The morning was biting cold. A wind had come up from the north and was funneling down the deep ravine between the rocks on either side of us. Even the sun, which was rising over the peak ahead, seemed frozen in the sky and gave off no warmth. In the icy air, there was no sound except the scraping of feet on the path.

My hands were numb from the cold. The ropes had tightened and were slowing my circulation. I tried to shift my mind from the pain, but it always turned to the image of Mama lying on the ground, the rifle coming down on her back, her hand stretched toward me, her voice crying "Ashe" over and over.

I looked desperately for some place to turn my attention. In the distance a rock hung out over the path, and I fixed my eyes on its rounded tip, not allowing them to waver. Like the Lung-gom yogi who glide effortlessly at great speed with their eyes fixed on a distant point, I tried to bring my attention into such focus that I could move swiftly, at least in my mind. With my eyes not wavering from the spot, I was able to move far ahead, beyond the pain in my hands, the image of my mother, and the soldiers walking sullenly at my side.

When we got to a place where the path led steeply up, Tanag Tulku, an elderly lama, slipped and couldn't get up. His will to continue seemed gone. Two Chinese soldiers walked up to him and poked at him with their rifles. When he still didn't move, they each took an arm and dragged him over the sharp rocks.

Farther on, another elderly man slumped to the side of the trail unable to go on. A soldier hit him on his back with a rifle until he struggled back onto his feet.

The same thing happened again and again. Each time someone stopped, he was beaten. In this way we crossed several high passes and walked down into Nyulchu.

At Nyulchu, 250 trucks waited to take us over the road that had been recently completed leading to Chamdo. The soldiers crowded thirty prisoners into each truck. We were bound together and guarded by four soldiers with bayonets on the end of their rifles. Throughout the whole trip, they kept the rifles pointed at us, as if we might try to escape.

The road was full of rocks and holes. The truck bumped up and down so much I was sick. I was the only woman, and the only one who got sick. Everyone's eyes on me, even the soldiers; I imagined the others thought that because I was a woman my stomach couldn't handle the ride, but it was my first time in a truck and I couldn't get used to its strange wavering motion. The sight of the land rushing by so fast made me dizzy. And with the bitter smell of smoke sputtering out underneath, it was difficult to breathe.

"Please sit down," the Chinese officer said softly, gesturing to the richly colored carpets. We were seated on the floor in a storeroom of Chamdo Monastery. All the best monastic carpets had been taken from other places and carefully laid out. When I saw them I wondered why they were trying to impress us, but I never figured it out. The officer's voice was so courteous and respectful, I imagined we might soon be released.

"You will stay here and rest from your long trip," he said. His voice was disturbingly sweet. "Later, we will ask a few questions." The word "question" should have alerted me to his intention, but tired and happy to be inside the monastery, I let it pass without much thought.

In the late afternoon, we were taken down to the deity hall in groups of ten. The hall had been stripped of all its statues and

Thangkas. The sight of it bare and filled with soldiers brought me back to reality.

On the sides of the room soldiers stood in a line watching us, their rifles pointed toward us. Two soldiers searched our bodies, they even searched the looped buttonholes of our shirts. The strips we used to tie our boots and the rope to tie our chupas were taken away to prevent us from hanging ourselves. They tore off our charm boxes and blessed strings, and left us with our tattered clothes.

After we had been searched, we were led down the corridor to Sheja Hall, the huge main assembly hall. We were no longer treated with courtesy, but pushed and shoved by the soldiers who were leading us. Inside the hall, more than two thousand of us sat in lines, as if we were a congregation of lamas. We had to sleep in the space we were seated in. At times I was able to curl on the bare floor using my boot as a pillow. At other times, when more were added, it was so congested we had to sleep sitting, back to back.

In the crowded conditions, without even a palmful of water to wash our face, we were soon infested with lice. The lice were so bad that I could see them crawling all over the heads in front of me. So thick I could sweep them off with my hand and not make a difference in their numbers.

For the next ten months we lived like this. Lamas, tulkus, abbots, kings, chieftains, commanders, and other leaders of the Khampa resistance, treated worse than dogs. Except for the daughter of one of the prisoners, who was allowed to go in and out to care for her ailing father, I was the only woman.

"Come get your food!" Two prisoners arrived at the door carrying buckets balanced at each end of a stick. The cooks, prisoners with minor "offenses," followed behind and distributed the food. The supply was meager, two fistfuls when I finished kneading it. Normally it would take more than ten to feel full. In the evening we got a watery rice porridge.

Because of the scarcity of food, people began to deteriorate. I rationed whatever tsampa I had, taking as little as I could, and saving the rest for elders who were beginning to weaken. Khaley Tulku was one of those whose health wasn't good, and every day I made sure to give him a small ball.

After a while, I became known for giving away part of my food. Men turned when they saw me coming. They whispered, "Pachen, Pachen, give me some tsampa." I began to feel severe pangs of hunger, but I was happy I was able to help them.

My meager addition wasn't enough to do any real good, and after a few months a few of the older men had difficulty getting up. When they tried to get up they often fell down, and they had to be supported when they went to urinate.

Whenever someone had to urinate, he would be forced to do it in a huge container by the front door to the hall, in front of a whole room of people, both Tibetans and Chinese soldiers. I was given a smaller container which I was able to put under my chupa and squat over, but it was still in sight of the others. Once a day we were taken two at a time to do bowel movements. Other than that there was no chance for relief.

When the container of urine was full, two people were ordered to carry it out. A stick was put under the handle, and we had to lift it up and carry it on our shoulders. Two soldiers followed outside to the place where we were told to dump it, to be sure we went no farther. I volunteered several times to help carry the bucket. It was the only time I could breathe fresh air.

"The time has come," the officer said through a Tibetan interpreter, "to confess your crimes. How you fought the Chinese army. Your plans, your organizations, your alliances."

He was a short, round man. His face reminded me of a rat; his eyes, tiny, thin slits. He was rumored to be an important official, "one of the top," someone told me.

"If you cooperate by confessing and handing over your possessions," he continued, his voice coming out in sharp little squeaks, "amnesty will be granted. No punishment will be inflicted.

"However—" He stopped even after the translator had spoken. I leaned forward to hear what he would say next. "However," he said again, seeming to enjoy the suspense, "if you refuse"—he paused,

and for a moment his eyes widened—"there is no option but death."
He shot the last words out, then turned and left.

The day after the officer addressed us we were divided into sections, or "tsugs" as the Chinese called them. Section one, section two, section three. Each section was composed of ten or twenty people, and each was told to form a circle, with one Chinese official sitting on a chair, conducting questions. One Tibetan was ordered to draw up a list of "confessions," which was handed to the official. After scrutinizing the list, the official sent those with the highest "crimes" to a room upstairs, and the sessions began once again.

Again, the questions were spat out. "What guns did you use?" "How many did you have?" "Who was involved?" "What help did you give Lingkha Shipa and Derge?" Again I was beaten.

"How long do you think we will be here?" I whispered one day when no one was looking. A young man who had come with the Prince of Derge to our village a year ago was sitting next to me. His name was Sogmo Gega.

Sogmo shook his head, "If you think it's going to be easy to leave," he replied, "you're wrong. They will keep us at least a year, probably more." He lowered his voice. "You haven't seen anything yet."

"If that is true," I replied, "we'll all probably die. Some are already starving." And in truth, some were so hungry that they contemplated eating their feces.

In the daytime there was nothing to do but sit in silence. In a way, I began to look forward to the time when I was awake and not being questioned or beaten, for my mind was then free.

Light poured down from the windows high up near the ceiling. In the quiet, my mind floated freely and words from the sacred texts came back, offering their support.

> Rest in natural great peace, this exhausted mind. Beaten helpless by karma and thought, like the relentless fury of the pounding waves, in the infinite Ocean of Samsara. Rest in natural peace.

And so I said my prayers each day, did my practices in my mind, even prostrated one hundred thousand times, in an invisible corner. I was never able to free myself completely of the desire to be released, but at least I achieved a small inner peace.

After ten months in the great assembly hall of Chamdo, I was transferred to another part of the monastery. I felt sad leaving the men I'd been with for so many months. Leaving them was like leaving a family, but I had no choice. My name was called and I had to go.

I was taken to a part of the monastery called Deyong Nang. It was there, and in the prison after, that I suffered some of the worst days of imprisonment.

8

Prison I: 1960–1965

The soldier pushed me into the room and closed the door, the metal latch making a hollow clank as it slid across. Footsteps tapped down the hall, growing fainter and fainter until they disappeared.

As my eyes became accustomed to the dim light I saw the room was small, and had once been used to keep animals. The floor was dirt, the walls rough and wooden. Sitting around its edges were women and children.

"Ashe Pachen," a voice from the corner whispered. As I turned to see who it was, a short, stout form stood up. Instantly I recognized the face of Tamdin Choekyi, wife of Chime Gonpo, the minister of Derge.

She took my hands and bowed her head, then held a finger up to her mouth: "Shh." A guard might be nearby. Her face was red, perhaps from bruising; in the low light it was difficult to tell. When she smiled, I noticed many of her teeth were gone.

Tamdin gestured around the room, and I saw many familiar faces. Her daughter, Soyang, who must have been twenty-one; her son, Asong, probably eight or nine. Wangzin and her four daughters, Nanchen, and two others, a mother and daughter, whom I didn't recognize. Except for the last two, the rest had been captured in the same area as us.

Tamdin Choekyi kept her hand in front of her mouth, motioning that there might be a guard outside our door. "If the guards hear us talking," she whispered, "they'll think we're planning an escape; their questions will be unending." She peered through a crack in the door. When she signaled there was no one nearby, we all began to talk.

I took Tamdin's hands. She was like a part of my family. Her husband and my father had taken an oath to help one another in times of need, even to die for each other if necessary. "He hasn't been arrested yet," she said when I asked. "He's still up in the hills helping to attack the Chinese."

I was happy to hear that there were still people fighting to free Tibet.

Several days after I arrived, Tamdin Choekyi and I were called. "Lemdha Pachen, Tamdin Choekyi, come out!" When we heard our names we stiffened, for we knew what to expect. Two soldiers arrived and gestured us out of the room. We were taken upstairs to a small room that had once been a monk's. It smelled of stale cigarettes and mold.

At its center, a Chinese leader sat at a small makeshift table, with an interpreter beside him. At the door there were two additional soldiers. The leader waved his hand brusquely for us to come before him. He put out one cigarette, lit another, and took a few puffs before he spoke.

"Neither of you have confessed your crimes against the Motherland. Unfortunately," he said, narrowing his eyes and slowly inhaling, "if you don't confess immediately, there is no possibility of release." His words poured out surrounded by smoke.

As he was speaking, one of the soldiers brought a long iron bar and threw it on the floor in front of us. It was a long flat metal bar, stretched between two round bands. As it hit the stone floor the metal made a sharp clank, and for a moment there was no other sound except its echo and the barely audible inhaling and exhaling of smoke.

"If you don't confess," he continued after he was sure we had time to study the irons, "you will wear these leg irons until you change your mind."

"Now," he said leaning forward toward us, "shall we begin?"

"Have you known Tamdin Choekyi before?" he asked me.

"She is famous for her bravery," I said somewhat curtly. "Of course I have heard of her."

The officer scowled, but continued.

"Who else was with you in Shothalhosum?"

"My mother," I said stubbornly, not wanting to give other names, "and my two elder relatives."

The officer looked annoyed. Without changing his expression he snapped his fingers at one of the soldiers by the door. The soldier stepped forward. I saw his hand rise above me. Whack! The palm of his hand burned my face, and my head jerked back. One, two, three times he hit.

"Perhaps your memory is better?" the officer said with a slight smile, when the soldier was done.

"I have answered your question, there is nothing else to say."

His face reddened, and in frustration he turned to Tamdin Choekyi. "Where is your husband hiding?" he asked.

"My husband is not hiding," she answered defiantly, "he is away on business." She too was hit.

The leader put his cigarette out in anger. He gestured to the leg irons. The soldiers by the door came over and snapped them around our ankles. The metal was cold. It was difficult to stand with my legs held apart, and for a moment I almost fell forward, but determined not to give them the pleasure of seeing me fall, I tensed my knees and stood still.

"Until you confess," the leader said as he got up to leave, "you will remain as you are, with your legs hobbled, like dumb animals."

Tamdin Choekyi took several awkward steps toward him. Raising her head in the air, she said, "What a powerful country you belong to, chaining two helpless women." She flapped her chupa at him with her hands. "Ha, ha, ha," and turned and walked toward the door. The iron bar clanked on the floor as it dragged between her feet.

The leader couldn't have realized that the flapping of a chupa was an expression of disgust and would bring him ill luck. Nonetheless the gesture made him angry. He waved us away, spun on his heels, and strode out the door. Tamdin Choekyi hobbled between the two guards after him, her head held high. I walked slowly behind.

At that time, I had no way of knowing we would wear the irons for more than a year.

After that, we were subjected to continual "struggle sessions." Each time, several guards came to our room and made Tamdin Choekyi and me kneel before them. The others in the room were told to surround us, and were ordered to taunt us, even beat us. Their goal was to elicit a confession, and a favorite method seemed to be turning the prisoners against each other. One or two of the women invented something of little consequence and pretended to hit us with their sleeves. Then the questions began.

"Who is the best man in your organization?" "How did you collect your men?" "Where did you hide your wealth?"

When forced, I responded with an answer that had already been given; they were never able to get anything new. As they beat me I jerked to the side so forcefully I often hit their legs with my head. The movement only angered them more.

Their rods came down on our backs. We knelt impassively, letting them beat us until they were satisfied. What worse could possibly happen, I thought. They have taken our wealth and ruined our lives, they have beaten and killed our people. What worse could happen? They were not worth begging for forgiveness. And while I felt physical pain, I didn't feel emotional suffering. All the time, my mind was elsewhere. I was thinking about what had happened to my mother, my grandmother, and my aunt.

At the end of the sessions when the guards left, the women praised us for not uttering a single sound during the beatings. They were afraid to hold us for we weren't allowed to have physical contact, but they did their best to comfort us with their whispers. "Don't worry," they said. "One day you both will be free."

I had bruises all over my face and body. The beatings made me angry, but I turned my anger to prayer. I prayed to take on the pain of all who had been inflicted with so much suffering. *Let me carry their pain. Let me be the one to suffer, instead of them.*

I was at Deyong Nang from 1961 to 1963. During those years there was a great famine throughout China and Tibet. We heard news in prison that the harvests were poor, and the "Great Leap Forward" had led to a split with countries that supplied grain to China. As a result, we were told, grain from Tibet was taken away from the Tibetan people and fed to the Chinese armies or shipped to China. Millions were said to have died of starvation across China, and tens of thousands starved in Tibet.

The famine affected the prisons as well. The temple next to Deyong had more than five hundred Tibetans imprisoned inside, and over the next two years, five or six prisoners died every day.

I later learned that the bodies of the dead were dumped in a ravine behind the monastery. The ravine became so filled that the Chinese started throwing the dead bodies into the Zachu and Ngomchu Rivers. The vultures and the dogs were not able to eat all the bodies remaining in the ravine, and soon the carcasses began to rot. The stench of decomposing bodies was so powerful that for years people could not go near the ravine.

As the time passed, I got used to the routine at Deyong. I learned to move with the iron between my legs. I stuffed pieces of cloth between the metal and my ankles to ease the cold and rubbing and shuffled along slowly, one foot then the other. Though we continued to have struggle sessions, we were given a little more freedom and were able to go outside to the toilet on our own.

The toilet was a small wooden shack with planks laid over a pit. The only time we had a chance to see others who were not in our room was on our way to and from the toilet. We lingered outside the building, and when we were sure that no guards were looking, we would exchange a few words.

One day on my way to the toilet, I saw a young man whose face was swollen so badly that I couldn't see his eyes. His legs looked as if they were filled with water. As I passed him, he called, "Ashe." There was something about the voice that was familiar, but his face was unrecognizable.

"Who are you?" I asked, "Do I know you?"

"I am Phurba," he said.

The Phurba I knew was from my hometown. He was as handsome and smart as a leopard. This man bore no resemblance to the Phurba I knew. "What has happened?" I gasped.

"I haven't been able to sleep," he said, having difficulty forming the words with his swollen lips. "I can't see very well and there is a constant loud rushing noise in my ears."

"It is wind disorder," I said, knowing the symptoms well. "It's from not getting enough to eat." I wanted to give him something, but having nothing to give, I reached out and briefly touched his arm.

The next day, when I came to the toilet, he wasn't there. "Phurba's been taken to the clinic," someone told me. I knew that the people who were sent there were near death, and I felt desperate to find him some food.

That night, I approached a woman who worked in a mill outside. I offered her a small Dzi stone, one of several I'd been able to hide on my body, and asked her to try to get some meat the next time she went outside.

Several nights later, when she returned, she took me to the side and gave me a small piece of meat. "It is all I could get," she said. "I was able to bribe one of the workers."

Pretending to go to the toilet, I went instead to the clinic and asked one of the prisoners who was working there to give the meat to Phurba. From the doorway, I could hear Phurba groaning in pain. Several days later, I was told he passed away. His body was thrown behind the clinic with the other dead bodies. The next day a truck came and took it away. Two other young men from Lemdha died in the same way. From one neighborhood, all three died.

Toward the end of my stay in Deyong Nang, I saw Dekyong once again. It was at night, and I was on my way back from the toilet when I saw two guards walking toward me with a group of women and children. As they came closer, I made out Dekyong and her mother among them. Their chupas were ragged and falling apart, their faces were burned and bluish from having been exposed to the sun. The charisma that they had both had was gone. They looked like common beggars.

I couldn't say anything as they passed by me because of the presence of the guards. When Dekyong saw me she let out a little cry, but continued walking, and they soon disappeared into the next building.

The next day I ran into her as I was going to the toilet. We were afraid to embrace, but our eyes conveyed how we felt just the same.

"We were on our way to India when we were caught," she whispered. "We had reached the village of Zayul, and from the top of the pass we could see the Indian armies walking along the border. As we were descending, we were spotted and caught by the Chinese. We were that close, but we couldn't get down."

"At the time, we thought it was better to be arrested than to die of starvation," she continued. "We were weak from hunger, we had eaten nothing for weeks. Several days before our arrest, we had come across a dead man, and ate a piece of his flesh. We had no other choice."

For the next month Dekyong and I met in this manner and were able to catch short snatches of conversation when no one was nearby. We talked about our different experiences fleeing, we talked about the places in prison we had suffered the most.

"Had we remained outside," Dekyong said, "we would have suffered the same. If we ever get back to our homeland, I have a sense that the Chinese will torture us. I'm afraid of their torture," she said, "but I'm not afraid of death."

A month later the guards called us all outside. All the people from the east side of the Yangtze River were told they were being sent to a prison on that side of the river. Dekyong's name was called, as was her mother's.

It happened so suddenly.

She was standing two rows in front of me. When she heard her name she turned, her eyes frantic with fright. A guard stepped forward and took her arm. I could see she was crying. "Dekyong," I called out. The guard shoved her forward. She stumbled; he shoved her again.

I pushed through the others in front of me, trying to reach her. A guard saw me and stepped forward to block my way. I tried to push past, but he held me back. I was close, but I couldn't touch her.

She turned and called out, "We will meet again. Don't lose hope."

Later, I heard they weren't sent to prison but were taken from place to place. They were subjected to severe struggle sessions, taunted, and beaten. Months later, they died of starvation.

I never saw her again.

∽

In the days after Dekyong's departure I spent much of my time in prayer. I prayed for Dekyong and her mother. I prayed for Mama, Granny, and Ani Rigzin. I prayed for all sentient beings, that none of them suffer.

> *Protect the living beings from evil,*
> *Free them from the dangerous passes,*
> *Hold them back from the lower realms,*
> *Take them to the land of liberation.*

I thought of all the suffering and death that surrounded me, and of all the things I had seen. And I remembered Gyalsay Rinpoche's words, "At the moment of death, the only protection is the force of one's own goodness."

The hunger continued. I thought often of Mama's food. Thick, rich soups, shining noodles, potatoes covered with pieces of sausage, steamed dumplings, sweet bread. I thought of all the wealth we once had, the silver, the gold, the jewels. I knew, at that moment, if I were given a houseful of riches I would trade it for something to eat.

Months went on in the same way. With struggle sessions, with hunger. Many of my friends had bodies that were bruised. Many of them died.

One day a soldier arrived at the door to our room. "Pachen Dolma, Tamdin Choekyi, prepare to leave." Tamdin Choekyi's children started to cry. They ran to their mother and held her. A guard took her arm and pulled her away.

"Mama, Mama," her little son cried. He pulled at her chupa, trying to hold her back. But the soldiers turned and pushed him aside. I could still hear his cries as we went through the gate.

The image of Mama flashed into my mind. I put it aside and kept walking.

A huge open truck waited outside the gate. A soldier lowered a wooden board and gestured for us to walk up. Its angle was steep, and as I inched up it, the metal of the irons dug into my ankles. They were heavy, and I stumbled trying to climb. With the help of a prisoner inside, I was able to get up.

Many of the leaders and lamas whom I had left in the assembly hall were inside the truck. I was happy to see them again, and it eased the parting for me. But Tamdin Choekyi was silent, and I knew for her it was different.

Silthog Thang was a secured prison, where those who were considered guilty of the most serious crimes were sent. It was located across from the monastery on the other side of the river bank, between the Zachu and Ngomchu Rivers. As we drove up, there were people standing behind the wire fencing.

When we got closer I could see that they had barely any flesh on their bodies. The skin of their faces was pulled tight, their eyes sunk deep in the sockets, their cheeks almost bone, like a skull. But it was their arms and hands that caught my attention. Thin like sticks, hanging limply at their sides. One man raised his head and looked at me. When I looked into his eyes, I felt a shock, for his eyes were completely blank, as if nothing but hollows on either side of his face. Others had eyes so large and liquid, it seemed the only part of them still alive.

Beyond the high fence there weren't any buildings, only tents. Row after row. Tamdin Choekyi and I were taken to a tent with ten other women. There was a woman from Chamdo Thel, and others who had been caught fleeing from Lhasa.

No one else in the tent had leg irons like we did, though many of the men in other sections were chained. So many, in fact, that as the irons scraped over the ground, they made such a clinking noise it filled the whole area with their sound.

Silthog Thang was damp and cold. It was winter when we first got there, and the sun remained only a short time in the morning before sinking below the hills. Cold air rose up from the nearby river and hung over the tents.

That first night it was already freezing as I climbed onto the wooden plank I was sharing with Tamdin. It was narrow, and we had just enough room to lie side by side. The tent was full of holes and all night the wind blew from all directions. It got colder and colder until I thought that there could be no other place as cold. I was wearing the chupa I had on when arrested three and a half years earlier, and by then it was worn almost bare.

As the night wore on the iron on my ankles was like ice, and after a while it began to burn as if flaming hot. I tried to twist to the left, or to the right, thinking one side would keep me warmer than the other, but with my legs in the irons, and Tamdin squeezed at my side, there was no possibility of turning over. The only part of my body that felt a small sense of warmth was the part next to Tamdin. The rest was unbearably cold.

Throughout the night I tried to pray. *Blessed Rinpoche, look with love, mercy, and compassion upon the beings without refuge or protection. Keep them safe, and guide them to freedom.*

"Pachen Dolma! Tamdin Choekyi! Come out!" It was still early morning and no one was up. My legs were stiff from the night, and I had difficulty moving.

"Come out! Come out!" There was a rustling at the tent flap and a guard peered in. "Pachen Dolma, Tamdin Choekyi, you are wanted outside."

Still drifting on the expanse of the night, I felt loose and unformed. I tried to pull my strength around me as a shield for what I knew was to come. *Om Mani Peme Hum,* I whispered as I moved into a sitting position. But however I tried, I couldn't gather myself.

I looked over at Tamdin Choekyi sitting beside me. We exchanged glances as if to say, *What more can they do?* Still trying to shake the fog from my mind, I awkwardly slid off the bed.

The guard took us across the grounds, between the rows of tents, to a small cement building. I took a deep breath and closed my eyes before following him inside. *Let my pain take the place of others' suffering,* I said to myself.

Inside, a Chinese soldier sat behind a small table. Two others stood on either side. But this time there was no translator, at least none I could see.

The man at the table pointed to us. The soldiers walked slowly around the table. They bent down and reached for my feet. *Om Mani Peme Hum*. I took a deep breath.

I tensed as I felt their hands on my ankles, tugging at the iron. I waited to be yanked, to be kicked, to be hit in the stomach. But then the sound of metal, like a key in a lock, and my ankle cuffs loosened.

When they finished with mine, they did the same to Tamdin Choekyi. I waited for something more to happen. But the man at the table merely pointed to the door, and we were taken outside.

After a year with irons restricting my legs, I didn't know how to walk without them. It was a frightening sensation, as if some part of my body were missing. With each step I took I expected to feel the familiar draw on my leg, but instead my leg sprang forward as if it had a life of its own. Several times I was thrown off balance, and was reluctant to walk too far for fear I would fall.

When we got back to our tent I felt a surge of joy, like a bird flying free from a cage. We hadn't confessed anything, and nothing was said to explain why the irons were released. The only thing I could think was that it was somehow because of my previous karma. Perhaps I had suffered enough to wipe away some of my sins.

At the same time I prayed that the suffering I had gone through would keep others from suffering any more. I prayed to God that no one in this universe, including those in snow-clad Tibet, would ever again have to suffer the way that I had. With those prayers, my mind came slowly to peace.

After the irons were removed, Tamdin Choekyi and I were made to accompany the other women to work. At the corner of the compound there was a laundry site. Wooden planks were laid across to make a place for washing, and nearby there was a big earthen hearth where the clothes were boiled.

We began work as soon as we'd finished our morning breakfast of two small dumplings. We arrived at the laundry site as the sun was coming up. Sometimes it was very cold at that time. We would work until dark. Though the guards were strict, when they weren't nearby we'd sit down for a moment. Otherwise, except during mealtime, we were on our feet.

Each day, guards gave us the clothes of the Chinese soldiers to wash. Occasionally they gave us clothes of the prisoners as well. There were so many lice in the clothes of the prisoners we had to sweep them off with a brush. We swept them onto the ground to keep from boiling them and taking another life, careful not to catch the guards' attention, for if they spotted us they would blame us for being religious. When we couldn't brush them off, they boiled, turning red and floating on top of the water. When that happened, the image stayed with me for days.

In a nearby section of Silthog Thang there were prisoners whom the Chinese accused of not "correcting" themselves enough. This meant that they remained faithful to the Dalai Lama, spreading word that he would one day return to Tibet, that Tibet would be free again, and the Chinese would be forced to leave.

Others, who expressed faith in communist China, were rewarded with toothbrushes, towels, and small red books by Chairman Mao. For some who seemed truly converted, prison terms were reduced by several years. For those who didn't correct themselves, execution was the punishment.

One day we were all called into the courtyard. Six prisoners were brought onto a platform before us. A young lama named Gyalwa Yungdrung was among them. I had met him in the hills of Naru when I was fleeing, and was struck by his eloquence and his passion in defending our country.

But it wasn't until his name was called out that I realized who he was; his face was black and blue from beating. He was told to stand in front of us, without speaking or looking up. An officer stood beside him. "He is a traitor." The officer coughed the words out in a guttural voice. "He is an imperialist spy. He is a tool of the revisionist forces."

As the officer was speaking, Gyalwa Yungdrung raised his head with effort, and thrusting one arm in the air he shouted, "May I take on the suffering of all prisoners! Long life to the Dalai Lama! There is a free Tibet!"

The officer leaped at him and stuffed a cloth in his mouth. Two soldiers walked up to him. They raised their guns. Gyalwa Yungdrung looked straight ahead. His eyes gazed far away. I thought I saw his lips moving in prayer. "Pray to Lord Buddha," I said under my breath. Two shots rang out. Gyalwa Yungdrung slumped to one side. Pieces of his brain splashed onto the prisoner beside him. I closed my eyes.

Gyalsay Rinpoche's face appeared before me, soft with compassion. He bent toward me and looked into my eyes with eyes that were tender and filled with light.

With my eyes closed, I heard the sound of a body dragged down the steps of the platform. Its feet made a hollow sound on the wood as they hit each step. I heard the sound of a truck driving away, and the voice of the officer: "This will be the fate of each of you, if you don't correct."

Several weeks later, Tamdin Choekyi was released. Some say that she was freed because her husband was caught in the hills, and it was he, not she, they were after. But they continued to hold me. "You were a commander in chief," I was told.

In truth, I was being held more for my father's role in organizing the resistance, and for the plans he laid out before he died, than for what I myself did. I merely tried to carry out some of his plans. But after a while, the Chinese blurred the two, and out of duty to him, and my country, I bore the responsibility as if it were my own.

I was moved into a section of Silthog Thang called Lokheschu. Rows of brick buildings faced each other on either side of a courtyard. The walls of the buildings were covered with plaster. Each building consisted of a series of rooms, one after another in a line, and each room housed fifteen prisoners. The beds were made from earth, slightly elevated from the floor, and at the back of each room was a small window. The toilet was outside the main door. As in the tents, there was no bedding, only the clothes that we wore.

The women in my room were assigned to a work unit. Every morning we walked in a single line out the gates. Some of us carried earth and stones to clear the field. Some worked with mud to make bricks. Some built more cells.

The work was difficult. There wasn't enough food to fill our stomachs, and as they worked many dug through the fields for small worms or insects. Occasionally I came across the root of a plant as I was digging and hid it in my chupa until I was back in the room and could eat it.

One night, after watering the fields, a prisoner came across the carcass of a horse. Not having a knife, he began hacking at it with a rock. As soon as he had cut a hole big enough for his hand, he began to eat whatever he could grab. It was only after he had eaten his fill that he began to recognize the foul stench of animal feces. But he was so hungry that he continued to eat all the innards he could pull out. The next day he became ill, and several days later he died.

Every year for a month or two the Chinese conducted a program called *"Guntod Lobjong,"* or "Early Winter Education." When a guard announced the program was about to begin, the women in my room said, "When Guntod Lobjong starts we'll have to suffer so." As the day drew near they worried more and more: Who would be taken away, who would be punished, who would be killed?

The program started early in the morning. Prisoners from different cells were brought together into the courtyard. Four Chinese leaders sat in front of us on chairs. Behind us soldiers held guns, guarding us.

A short, fat officer with a cap pulled low on his forehead stood up. "The purpose of the Early Winter Education is to help you to see the reality of your situation, and change your ways." He took a few steps toward us and said, "Many of you continue to stubbornly cling to your empty beliefs, but what has your religion done for you?

Where are you gods and spirits now? And where is the Dalai Lama? He has fled with his tail between his legs, and left you. He and other Tibetans in India are in disagreement with each other. They have fallen on each other like dogs."

Hearing the Dalai Lama being called such names, I wanted to leap up and hit the officer in his round ugly face. I started to move. Wangzin put her hand on my arm. I sat back and spit on the ground.

"First," the officer continued, "we are going to give you a chance to confess a crime you have not already confessed. What empty hopes are you clinging to? What superstitious practices are you involved with? Which rules have you not adhered to? What rumors have you spread against the Motherland?" He walked back and forth in front of us as he spoke, pointing to one prisoner, then another, for effect.

"First you must confess your own crimes. Then you must speak about others. What crimes did you see them commit? Were they hoping for the revival of the old Tibet? If you don't have at least a word or two to say about others"—he stopped and narrowed his eyes—"then that, in itself, will be considered a crime."

After he had finished speaking we were sent back to our respective rooms and made to sit in a circle. Then the struggle sessions began. First they asked for confessions. "I confess I took an extra ball of tsampa." "I confess I carried less than my share of stones."

Then the discipline. The taunting, the beating.

I was careful not to say anything about anyone else. I was able to endure being beaten, but to speak about someone else was something I couldn't do. I was silent when asked to accuse others, even when it meant more beating. Most people from Kham were like that. Tough. Honorable. Proud.

When the sessions were done they gave us a copy of the newspaper *Tibet Daily*. "Do you have any suggestions or complaints?" they asked. "Read the article about America, and how it exploits the masses. They are ruthless imperialists. It is they whom the Dalai Lama has gone to for help."

Afterward they taught us songs. "Imperial America . . . a tail was born . . . and ran away . . ."

Like me, many of the prisoners were sustained by religion. We had faith that the Dalai Lama and the exile community were united and would one day return to Tibet. So, when asked to confess, we never mentioned the Dalai Lama or Tibet, but instead picked an insignificant rule and confessed to breaking it.

One of the programs during Early Winter Education was "destruction of old and establishment of new," which meant destroying everything that had to do with old civilization and establishing policies of communist China.

They singled me out during this program, accusing me of not changing my beliefs and faith, of being stubborn and "old minded." They accused me of "suppressing the progressive forces of the country," which meant I was critical of those Tibetans who were working for the Chinese. But no matter what they did, I refused to say what they wanted me to. I wouldn't be like the insect Bu Nyima, who always turned his head in the direction of the sun, in whichever way was most comfortable.

"How can you call this education?" I shouted one day as they were taunting me. "We can't receive education in prison. It is indoctrination, not education!"

That day, the beatings were more severe than usual. After the "teachers" finished beating me, they brought out an iron clamp for my feet and threw it in front of me. I thought they were going to chain me again, but they didn't. "Your prison term has been increased by three years," the short, fat officer told me, "and you will spend the next nine months in isolation."

They opened a small wooden door and threw me into the room. I fell onto my hands in the darkness and felt the dirt of an earthen floor. Behind me I heard the door close. There was a dull scraping as the key turned in the lock. I lifted myself onto my knees trying to see where I was, but I could see nothing but black all around me.

My knees were damp. As the moisture seeped through my chupa, I took off my shirt and put it under me. I felt with my hands for the wall. It was close around me on all sides, only a bit larger than the size of my body.

Several times I felt the wall with my hand, like a blind man trying to locate himself in a new surrounding. Down one side, across, up the other. It was rough cement, damp, though not as damp as the floor. In places there were small indentations where pieces had fallen away, in others, cracks running up to the ceiling.

I stood up slowly so as not to hit my head and found that the room was just high enough to stand. I sat down, then stood up again. I walked several steps back, then forward. Small red lines curved in front of my eyes; I heard a noise like the wind in my ears.

When I turned to look in the other direction, the lines followed, the noise got louder. The walls seemed to move closer. The ceiling seemed to have dropped. In a panic I brought my hands to my mouth. "Guru Rinpoche, help me!" I called out.

I fell to my knees and began to sob. "Mama," "Papa," "Ani Rigzin." I cried for my family, I cried for my home, I cried for Gyalsay Rinpoche. After I could cry no longer, I prayed.

> *Beloved teacher, like a great ship crossing the perilous ocean to the dry land of liberation, dispel the darkness of ignorance. . . . Like a father and mother, give your love to all sentient beings. . . . Like a river of compassion, soothe the torments of those caught in the cycle of worldly existence. . . . Release the beings in all realms. May they attain Freedom.*

The next day I found that the cell was just large enough to do prostrations. As soon as the guard left my breakfast and I heard the keys turn in the lock, I began.

I put my feet against the back wall, brought my hands above my head, to my mouth, my chest, then bent to the ground, stretching out the length of the room, my hands joined above my head.

"In reverence, I prostrate with my body, speech, and mind," I whispered.

Over and over I raised my hands, I stretched out over the ground. I prayed that the bad karma from many lifetimes that was causing this suffering would be washed away by prayer. To accomplish that, I vowed to prostrate one hundred thousand times.

Every two days the guard brought me food. I portioned it out, giving myself a level scoopful of tsampa in the morning, the same in the evening, and in the afternoon a few boiled vegetables and a nugget of dumpling. Each meal lasted only two mouthfuls, though some days, inexplicably, there was more, and then it lasted three.

The days were completely dark. I could only separate them from the nights by the sound of the birds. As soon as I heard the birds begin to sing outside, I knew a new day was beginning. The only way I could tell the level of tea in my cup was to dip in my finger.

My only interactions were with the Chinese, mainly a guard who brought food to my door, but then it was only a glimpse of his hand as the bowl was laid on the floor. And every so often one of the Chinese officials, a man named Tra Thang Dangiya, came to the door with a translator. He was a tall, thin man with glasses, and always had an expression of impatience.

"Are you ready to accept your crimes?" he said each time he came, tapping his foot on the floor outside my room. "If you are ready to make a confession, you will be let out sooner. If not, you'll have to remain." At the end of his speech, he stamped his foot to show he was serious. But I never responded.

"You will be chained in this dark room and will never come out!" he shouted, his face trembling with anger. "You are a reactionary fool!" He spat the words out. "You have an opportunity to redeem yourself and liberate yourself from the old and evil ways, but you throw it away. You are like a swine who only eats garbage, instead of real food!"

Each time, after threatening and scolding me, he turned abruptly and left, and I was alone again for a month. After those meetings, my food was reduced for several days.

As the months went on, I grew more depressed. During the day when I was prostrating there was nothing on my mind. But afterward, with my body sore from scraping the ground and nothing but darkness around me, I began to think of my home. At those times, the sadness from missing my family came as a physical pain in my heart, as if a cold hand were squeezing it tight. All I wanted was to feel human touch. I imagined Mama's soft skin against mine, Papa's hand on my head. Several times I had images as clear as if they were real.

"She will need the water treatment," the doctor had said after diagnosing my chicken pox.

When he left, Mama and Papa spread a yak skin on the ground, took off my clothes, and laid me on top. Mama put a woolen cloth over my face, Papa stood above me with a bucket of water. Just as he was about to pour, my uncle rushed into the room. "No, No," he shouted. "You are all witches. You are trying to kill my niece!"

Thupten and Tashi wrestled him to the floor and locked him into the pantry. I heard the crashing of silverware thrown on the floor, pots and pans hurled at the wall. "They are trying to kill my niece!" my uncle cried above the clatter. As I listened to his shouts, cold water splashed onto me from above, slapping against my skin, stinging like needles in each little bump. I felt cold and alone.

Just then my uncle appeared at my side. Having broken through the door, he lifted me up off the floor and wiped the water away with his hand. Opening the front of his chupa, he gently tucked me inside. "There, there, little one," he whispered, rocking me in his arms, "don't cry."

"There, there, you are safe."

In the darkness, strange shapes appeared, then drifted away. Monsters with many heads, their tongues hanging out, blood dripping from their lips. Beings with finger-sized claws, pointed and sharp. Winged serpents, fire flowing out of their mouths. Leopard-sized birds with pointed beaks and wings of steel.

Dorjee Phurba, I called to my protector deity. *Come battle these demons, protect me.* I imagined him in the air in front of me, his three heads, his six hands, his magnificent golden wings, molten rays flowing out of his heart. Bodies of those who tried to destroy him lay defeated at his feet. And I heard the words of Khaley Rinpoche.

"As you are watching, this wrathful and ferocious being enters your body, filling you with the force of his power, enabling you to annihilate all obstacles standing in the way of your freedom. Merge yourself with his strength and power. He is now, and always will be, your protector."

As I saw him, the other creatures disappeared. His luminous presence hung before me, suspended in the air, and with the sight of him standing in front of me I was no longer afraid. That night I slept particularly well.

Halfway through my nine-month confinement, I started to worry that I might not be able to finish the one hundred thousand prostrations I had vowed to complete. Therefore, each day before my prostrations, I prayed that I would not be removed from the cell until I had reached that number. And each day, I pushed myself to do more.

Because of the small amount of food I was consuming, I began to weaken. One day as I was prostrating I suddenly became dizzy. The room was hot; I couldn't get enough air to breathe. I wavered to the side, then fell forward. When I came back to my senses, I was lying on top of the toilet pot. The pot, emptied every two weeks, was swarming with worms. My clothes, my body, and the entire floor were covered with its contents.

That night when they brought me tea, I had just enough to wash my hands in it, but I couldn't wash the rest until months later when I was finally released. For days, flies flew around my head and crawled on my body. I took consolation from the fact that I was able to continue with my prostrations. I considered my suffering an atonement for the evil that had befallen all of Tibet.

When I wasn't praying and prostrating, I was depressed. When I wasn't depressed, I was angry. To deal with the anger, I began to visualize. I remembered Gyalsay Rinpoche's words: *"There is no distinction between friend and foe. It is important to treat them the same. Your enemy is your teacher."*

I visualized my father on my right side, my mother on my left, and our great enemy, Chairman Mao Tse-tung in front of me. My father was there to give me strength and courage, my mother to give me tenderness and caring. Mao Tse-tung was there because in all the world, I could think of no one more sinful. He had caused thousands of temples to be destroyed through his policies; thousands of lamas lost their lives. Tens of thousands of Tibetans had been starved, beaten, killed. What huge karmic sin he gathered to act as he did. With him before me, I prayed for his sins to be cleared. But I was never able to be free of my anger; as soon as I stopped, it came back.

One day, nine months after I'd been put in the cell, a guard came to my door and I was released. When I heard his key in the door I expected to see his hand reaching in to put a bowl of food on the floor. Instead, the door opened wide and he walked in. He grabbed my arm and pulled me up. He shoved me out the door. The corridor was dimly lit, but still the light was too bright for my eyes. The walls began to spin; I heard a ringing noise and started to fall. I felt as if I were floating and falling down at the same time.

The guard caught my arm and, half-pulling, half-pushing me, guided me down the corridor to a bench outside. The light hit my eyes like sparks of fire. Everywhere I looked the buildings were red and distorted.

For some time I sat on the bench. But soon other guards came. "Go, go, go," they said, and I had to move. When I got back to my old prison room, the others were out working. I lay down on my bed and gazed at the space surrounding it. My eyes had difficulty focusing and I let them float on the air and the light. I was so dazed that I hadn't thought to question my release. My mind accepted the change as if it were natural. I had been isolated and now I was released. As simple as that.

At the noonday meal, I was called to get into line with the others who'd come from the field. I walked through the line as if in a dream. Each pot of food was radiating light, each person surrounded by rainbows. They all had an otherworldly glow.

Two of the women from my room took me aside when the guards

were out of sight. They were overjoyed to see me. "We were so worried about you," Tsering Dolma said. "We were inspired by your bravery. Everyone admired your courage standing up to the Chinese." As they talked I saw that they had suffered as much as I. The only thing they hadn't gone through was living alone in the dark cell. Otherwise it had been equally bad for them.

Occasionally a letter was able to get through to us from outside. One day, several months after I was released from my cell, I received an envelope from a woman who had been in Silthog Thang with me. She had been transferred to a work camp and had news of my mother. "Your mother is alive," she wrote, "and living near Kongpo. She is working for a family, cooking and doing their laundry." This news had come so unexpectedly that it dazed me. I imagined Mama, Ani Rigzin, and Granny, all living together. For days all I could think was how I could get to them.

When I heard that some of the women in my section were being transferred to Kongpo, I appealed to the authorities. I told them that I had committed the same crime as the women being transferred, that I was a good worker, that they wouldn't be sorry. Over and over I begged, and finally they transferred me.

On the way to Kongpo we stopped for the night in a temple which was being used as a prison. It was late in the afternoon, and the air was still damp from a rain earlier in the day. A light breeze was blowing, and the smell of fresh grass and wet earth made me realize it must be spring. It was the first time in many months I'd thought of the seasons, and for a moment I stood outside the truck, savoring the breeze on my face.

I stood by the steps of the monastery and watched a group of men returning from work in the fields. As they passed, one caught my eye. He looked much older, his shoulders bent over, but I could tell by the profile of his nose and chin that it was Khaley Rinpoche.

"Rinpoche!" I cried out before I could stop myself. He turned, and a shadow of recognition crossed his eyes. He lowered his head slightly in acknowledgment and walked on with the rest of the men.

Later, in the courtyard as I was leaving the evening meal, he came up to me. Aatop, my father's old manager, was with him. I could barely contain myself, but only looked into their eyes and nodded.

Looking at him square on, I saw that Khaley Rinpoche's face had been battered. A scar ran over one eye, through his eyebrow. The top of his lips were misshapen. It broke my heart to see him. My blessed Rinpoche in pants like a common Chinese, his face so broken.

"Have you seen my mother or the other two elders?" I whispered. Aatop looked down at the ground and shifted his weight from foot to foot. For a moment they both were silent. Then Khaley Rinpoche answered, "Your mother is well . . . but your aunt and your grandmother have died. They were poisoned and several days later they died."

The news was so abrupt, I felt stunned. I dropped my head in my hands and began to cry. Khaley Rinpoche put his hand on my shoulder. "We will all have to face death eventually," he said gently. "There is no reason to get upset, there is nothing we can do. When our time comes, each of us dies."

The next day we went on to Chundo Dzong in Powo. I was with eight women who had come from Silthog Thang, and the guards led us to a room in the monastery that had once been a monk's room. It was small but comfortable, and for the first time there were beds to sleep on.

"You have been brought here to clear the land," an officer told us. "Each day you will help clear the fields and plow them. Your work will contribute to the growing of barley and wheat for our troops." The thought of growing food for the Chinese angered me, but I held my tongue.

The day after our arrival I went to one of the staff. I had been told that there were a few guards who were kind and could be approached for assistance. The guard I spoke to was young and had a warm smile. When I asked him to locate my mother, he gave a slight nod of his head and put the piece of paper with her address from Khaley Rinpoche in his jacket pocket.

All that day I could barely keep my mind on the work. My hand trembled as I picked up each rock. My stomach churned with excitement. The thought that my mother was so close made me half crazed with anticipation. Several times I imagined I saw her crossing the field. But it was only a bush, or another prisoner. Nevertheless I kept looking into the distance for her. She's so close, I thought, I must be able to see her.

But for the next five days there was nothing. Each day I looked for the guard, but he was nowhere to be seen. Perhaps he's been transferred, I thought. Perhaps he has given my message to the authorities. Each day I grew more anxious. What had happened to him?

Then one morning as I was getting ready to leave for the field, there was a shout for me. "Ashe Pachen," one of the women called, "the young guard is looking for you."

I moved as fast as I could, almost running down the corridor of the temple. My heart was racing in my chest. I reached the gate of the temple and looked down the road, stretching empty as far as I could see, nettle bushes at each side.

Then I saw a movement behind one of the bushes. A woman peered out through the branches. Soon after, the young guard appeared with her at his side. Her clothes were in rags and she was wearing the kind of black chupa normally worn by Kongpo women, with no shirt underneath. Her hair was matted and unkempt. She was bent over, leaning on a stick. She looked at me with her eyes fixed on my face, as if she were trying to take in each part.

"Mama!" The word caught in my throat.

She broke from the officer and stumbled toward me. Her face had aged in the four years we'd been apart. "Mama," I murmured, barely audibly when she was in front of me. "Is it you?"

Her mouth curved up in a familiar half-smile. I threw myself into her arms and began to cry. She stroked my hair and held me tightly. "Don't cry," she whispered. "I've brought you some food."

The guard allowed us to sit on the temple steps and talk. At one point he came to tell her to leave, but she begged for more time and he reluctantly agreed. Over the course of the day, she told me what had happened since we had separated in Rok.

"The day you were sent away, we were left with other elders and small children," she began. "We were free, but we didn't know what to do. The others were going to the village of Tramo Dzong in Powo where they heard conditions were better, and not knowing what else to do, we joined them. We crossed Dungla pass during a snowfall, carrying whatever belongings we had on our backs. The pass was long and unforgiving.

"On the way up, the snow was so high it nearly covered the whole body, and your granny and I barely made it to the top. It wasn't so difficult for Ani Rigzin. We remained at the top for the night, and early the next morning we started down. But we could no longer walk, because our feet had been frozen in the night, and we had to roll and slide all the way down. Even in those hostile conditions, we were able to sustain ourselves and we didn't die.

"When we got to Tramo Dzong we couldn't sell our jewelry for fear of alerting the villagers and the Chinese that we were from noble families, and had to keep it strapped around our waist the whole time. We couldn't put on better clothes, even if we had them. We didn't want to draw attention to ourselves.

"We were taken in by the family of one we were traveling with. During harvest time, we helped to reap barley. We begged tsampa from others in the village. In this way, our life went on."

She paused and looked off for a moment, as if trying to compose herself. She wiped a tear on the back of her hand and continued.

"After a year, the Chinese found out we had come from a family of lords and bribed one Tibetan woman to turn against us. One day she came to us carrying nicely knitted dough of tsampa and butter. She asked us to take it. Grateful for whatever was given, we shared it among the three of us. As soon as we ate it, we felt terrible pains in our stomach. Our host saw we'd been poisoned and sent for a doctor.

"The doctor was able to bring us back to life from an unconscious state, though we weren't able to talk. Your father's mother remained two days, then passed away. Ani Rigzin was alive a little longer. Before she died, she talked about you constantly. She said if she could see you it would be as good as seeing your father.

"I was able to survive, but the others were less fortunate. A few days after they died, I summoned the strength to carry each one on my back to the river, and threw each in. No one else would do it, for fear of the Chinese."

I took her in my arms and held her as she cried, then the guard led her away.

That night I felt such an ache I couldn't sleep. Over and over, I saw the small stooped figure of my mother with Granny on her back. I saw Granny falling into the river, her body floating slowly away. I heard Ani Rigzin calling my name. "Ashe . . . Ashe . . ." I was heartsick I couldn't do anything for them. I couldn't even provide them one good meal.

Every Sunday my mother came to visit me. On other days when I was taken into the fields with the other women, I often saw her watching me from a distance with a basket on her back. She was always smiling whenever she saw me, though she didn't look much like the mother I'd known. Stooping to pick up animal dung for her basket, her clothes ragged, she looked like a common servant, a beggar.

After a year in Kongpo I was told I was being taken back to Chamdo. As usual, no reason was given. I begged the young guard to allow me to see my mother one last time.

I walked out the gate in a line of prisoners. My mother was nowhere in sight. Two Chinese soldiers were in front of me, two behind. As we started down the road, one of them pointed to bushes at the side. "What's that old woman doing over there?" he said. I looked and saw my mother peering around the bushes, watching us go.

I think the soldier felt sympathetic, for he motioned her over and allowed her to follow beside us as we walked to Dzonga. When we reached the place where the trucks were meeting us, the officer allowed us a few moments alone. Mama gave me a bag of tsampa and told me she had several large bags of barley stored for when I was released. I gave her a pair of shoes and some clothing I'd been able to gather from other prisoners.

"There will be a time," I said, "when I will get out of prison. I will come find you. And when I do, I will feed you and care for you. I will bring you the warmest clothes to wear. I will feed you the best food. You will never go hungry again."

I was crying as I spoke. When I finished, I could see Mama was trying not to cry. Her mouth trembled at the corners and she was blinking her eyes.

"Remember the time I took you to Gyalsay Rinpoche?" I asked, taking her hands in mine. "Remember the teachings he gave us? Don't think of things that don't matter. The most important thing is to have a clear state of mind. Think of the teachings, and practice them. Don't think of me."

My mother reached toward me. There were tears running down her cheeks. She took my breasts in her hand and kissed them. She lay her head gently on my chest, and we stood silent for a moment.

When she raised her head she looked so unhappy I had difficulty looking at her. She clung to my hands, then looked around as if trying to find something to give me. "I am going for some butter," she whispered, wiping her cheeks. "It will keep you strong." And before I could stop her, she left. I watched her small ragged shape disappear down the road.

A short time after she left, the truck arrived and the soldiers began loading us into it. "Wait," I said frantically, "my mother has gone for some butter. Please look for her. Tell her we're leaving."

But they wouldn't wait. The soldiers ordered me into the truck and we left. As we drove away, I strained to see out the back. There were several people walking by its side, but my mother wasn't among them.

I never saw her again.

9
Prison II: 1965–1980

- Wear only the clothes that are issued to you, nothing else. Head must be shaved.
- When talking to officers and guards, speak from a distance of five steps, never in front or close by.
- No prisoner is allowed to care for another prisoner. If such an incident occurs, report it to the Chinese officials.
- Work tools must be treated with care. Complete more than is required in your quota of work.
- Accept that Tibet is an integral part of China.
- Reform your thoughts.
- Obey the authorities.
- Follow these rules.

"Drapchi is the number one prison in the Tibet Autonomous Region," the officer continued after he had read off the list to us. He was a short man, his face pocked and sallow. "This is not like Chamdo or any other prison you have been in. This is a real prison." He brought the heels of his boots together in a sharp click, then turned and began to walk back and forth in front of us. His words droned on, but having heard about the virtues of the Motherland before, I lost interest and glanced cautiously around me.

The room was large, and except for a few tables and chairs, it was bare. Two round balls were suspended from the ceiling by wires, lighting the room like miniature suns. I had never seen anything like them, and I couldn't stop looking at them.

"The prison is divided into five divisions," the officer continued in his high, rasping voice. "The men will go to the second division, the women to the third. Each will then be assigned to a cell of eight people. You will be issued your uniforms and taken to your section."

Still marveling at the glowing balls above me, I was led with others out the door to a smaller room down the corridor.

* * *

The room was empty except for a table piled high with uniforms at the right of the door. An old Chinese woman was standing behind it. As I entered, she shoved a bundle of black into my hands and gestured to the side of the room. I walked to the farthest corner and stood motionless. The chupa I'd been arrested in five years before had grown on me almost like skin; I felt reluctant to remove it.

As I pulled my arm from one sleeve, the material clung to me. It was an odd sensation, as if discarding part of my body. The brown threads on the sleeve, once woven tight, had loosened and in places the wool was worn thin like a leaf. I rubbed it between my fingers as if it were a Mani bead. The feel of the fabric was still soft, almost as soft as when I first got it.

"Stand still, Lemdha Pachen." The tailor pulls at the hem of my chupa, but I wiggle my feet, then raise myself up on my toes. The tailor stands up and drops his hands in exasperation. Seeing his face dripping and red, I begin to giggle. "Ashe Pachen!" my mother calls from the back of the room. "You are twenty-three years old, stop acting like a small child." I lower my feet, but as soon as the tailor kneels down, I raise them again. And unable to contain myself, I break out in laughter.

Mama walks across the room until she is standing in front of me. "If you continue to behave this way," she says, looking up at me with a frown on her face, "you will have to keep wearing the same chupa you've worn the last six months. If you want something new, stop teasing Gedun Sonam and stand still."

I feel the soft brown wool on my fingers, and see the fresh dark folds running down to the floor. Remembering how good a new chupa feels, I lower myself onto my feet and try to stand still.

"Hurry up!" the woman at the table called out to me. "You need to move on to your cell." I slowly pulled the other sleeve off, and felt the chupa slide down my arm and onto the floor. I unfolded the bundle. Inside, two pieces, a shirt and pants. I put on the shirt; the material was stiff and the sleeves were too short. I couldn't bring myself to put on the pants.

"Hurry up!" the woman shouted again. "Get dressed." I put one foot into a pant leg and almost fell over trying to get my foot in the other.

The woman gestured me toward the door. When I started to walk, the pants rubbed my skin. I tried to walk with my legs apart, but however I held them the rough cloth touched my skin. Leg irons of cloth, I thought, as I walked awkwardly across the room. I vowed to change back to my chupa as soon as I could.

The woman's face was set like a statue, looking straight ahead. I scowled at her, wanting to take off the clothes and throw them back. Instead I walked out the door.

A guard was waiting outside the room, and he led the eight of us down a corridor and out into the yard. The day was just breaking, already the sky was gray and threatening rain. A cold wind blew from the mountains, and I pulled the cloth of my shirt around me. Unlike my chupa, which wrapped close to my body, the shirt gave no protection; however I pulled, the wind came through.

We walked behind the guard through another gate and entered the main compound. A path ran ahead between low cement buildings, each surrounded by walls. One of the women who had been there before pointed to the different buildings.

"At the end is the fifth division where all the important lamas and government officials are held. Over there," she said, pointing to the first of three buildings on the left, "is the first division, for prisoners serving life sentences. The second and fourth are for men, and there on the right is the third division, where all the women are kept." There were high walls around each division blocking all but the tops of the roofs from sight. What I could see looked cold and gray.

As we were about to walk through the wall surrounding our division, Tsering Dolma nudged my arm and gestured to my left. Beyond the concrete walls and wire fencing I saw glitters of gold in the distance, so faint that at first I thought they were clouds. I squinted and the shapes became more distinct. Golden spires rising up from a golden roof, and below, a faint patch of red. The Potala! I whispered. Tsering nodded. For a moment, I forgot where I was and stared toward the palace of His Holiness.

Ever since childhood I'd heard of Lhasa and the great Potala palace. "The Potala Palace," my father once said after returning from a visit to His Holiness, "is a sight to behold."

We crowd into my father's room to hear of his trip. "The great Potala rises up from the valley of Lhasa like a mountain with over a thousand rooms," he began when we had settled on mattresses around him. "So immense are the stones that one must take several paces to reach the next step on its endless stairway. We climbed, stopping every so often to look out at the valley below, then continued, climbing higher.

"At the top, we crossed the threshold and walked through long winding corridors, the walls covered with paintings of the life of Lord Buddha, bodhisattvas, and deities. All the woodwork was carved and painted, not an inch was left untouched. After walking for some time we came to the tomb of the Fifth Dalai Lama, a chorten three stories high.

"Thick slabs of gold covered the chorten from top to bottom. Jade, turquoise, rubies, and coral were studded throughout. Its top was adorned with an immense necklace of jade and coral. Small trees of coral, images of the purest jade, Buddha lamps of the finest gold and silver lined the altar. And on the floor in front of them were golden butter lamps standing as high as my waist, large enough to burn butter for three months."

Our cell housed eight people. Inside, narrow beds of dried earth filled the room, a thin cotton bedding roll on each. The floor was hard and cold, the walls were rough. At least there's bedding, I thought when I saw it.

A row of cells ran down the corridor outside, one after another. At the end, a small room for the toilet. A concrete wall surrounded the building, with a narrow yard of dirt between the two. The place had no color, nothing green or growing anywhere in sight. But in time I got used to it.

It was my home for the next eleven years.

*   *   *

The next day we were called to assemble for work at the gate of our compound. We were told to get into a single line, with soldiers at the front and back. A Chinese woman named Chungla was standing at the gate, inspecting us as we went through. As we approached her, she stepped into the middle of the path and stopped us.

"What is this?" she said sharply, pointing at the chupas several of us were wearing. "We have given you clothes to wear, why aren't you wearing them?" The Tibetan who was translating looked down at the ground as he repeated her words. "What makes you carry an old brain?" Her words were shrill and her face narrowed into a frown as she spoke. "Take off these Tibetan rags, put on what we have given you. They are better to work in."

Her voice rose as she spoke and the vein on her neck stood out. I wanted to leap, put my hands on her throat, and shake her. I wanted to hit her face with the back of my hand. Instead I stood still and looked at the ground.

"Ha!" she continued. "You are not ashamed to protest, so why are you suddenly ashamed to wear a good pair of clothes? Go back! Change and come out. Otherwise you will all be punished."

We returned to our room, took off our Tibetan clothes, and put on the Chinese uniform. I was ashamed when I walked into the yard and didn't want to be seen by others. I felt I was betraying my country and His Holiness, felt stripped of my culture. I was convinced the Chinese had given us black to wear because they knew black was the color Tibetans liked least. Their aim was to destroy Tibet and our loyalty to His Holiness. Destroying our customs, our spiritual practices, even our clothing were the methods they used.

For the first few days the rough cloth rubbing on my legs felt unbearable, but as time went by I got used to it. After a while, those of us with Tibetan dresses tore them up and used them to stuff our bedding.

～

I arrived at Drapchi in 1965, and for the next several years the routine was the same. Every morning we were awakened early to exercise. We were ordered to run back and forth in the "yard." After exercise we were taken to work in the brickyards near Sera Monastery, one of the three great monasteries of Lhasa.

Some worked digging earth, some mixed the earth with water to make clay, some heated the clay to make bricks. After the bricks were dried, we carried them back to Drapchi. We each had to carry ten bricks at a time; when we tried carrying less, we were punished. We worked long hours, with little food to keep us going. Gradually over time our bodies weakened.

One day, during exercise period, I fainted. When I regained consciousness a guard was standing over me. "Get up," he said, "keep running." From then on, I began to feel ill. Water formed in the lower part of my body. The inside of my thighs rubbed together as I walked, and I couldn't keep up with the rest. The guards pointed to me when I began to lag behind. "Go! Go!" they shouted. As I weakened I could only carry one or two bricks at a time, but the guards wouldn't let me stop or sit down. When I felt I couldn't continue any longer, I asked permission to go to the hospital. To my surprise, they granted my request.

The doctor at the hospital was a Chinese woman. She was kind to me. "Your illness is severe," she said, "you should stay in the hospital. You have a congested heart." She gave me a letter to take to my leader.

When I gave it to him, he snatched it away and scolded me. "Why did you go to the hospital for such a minor illness?" he said. I didn't say anything, and turned to go back to work. After a short time he came over to me. "Get your clothes and go to the hospital." He spoke as if the thought had been his.

The hospital was small. For most of the time I was there, I lay in my bed and looked at the walls. At first I was too weak to do anything but stare. A long crack ran across the ceiling, and at times I thought I saw the hand of a deity reaching out. The hand was small and black, covered with hair. It reached only a little way out, then quickly retreated. I wondered if it was looking for food.

"Turn over and get your injection," the prisoner said. He was an assistant to the doctors and also a favorite of the guards. Instead of doing hard manual work, he was allowed to work in the hospital. Whenever he came to my bed I stared into his eyes and pursed my lips. "Traitor," I whispered under my breath. "Turn over," he replied, pushing my shoulder. With a scowl, I turned on my side.

Many of the prisoners in the room were suffering from heart ailments, but there were also many whose minds had been lost. A woman two beds away whimpered all day and night. At times she sat up in her bed and shouted, "Don't hit my child." Another across the room laughed uncontrollably and occasionally let out a shriek. The doctor was patient and never lost her temper, though I could see she was strained.

I remained in the hospital for three months. I received good treatment, and gradually the swelling in my legs went down. For two of the months I was bedridden, but in the third I was able to walk cautiously around the room. After a while I felt almost well, but I continued to pretend I felt weak so I wouldn't have to go back to work. Had I not been helped by the kind doctor, I would have probably died. I've been told that if the water in your body reaches your heart, it is fatal.

When I returned to my cell, Tsering gave me news of my beloved Gyalsay Rinpoche.

"Rinpoche was imprisoned alone in a room in the monastery that had once been the room for the prayer wheel," she said, almost as soon as I sat down. "The prayer wheel had been destroyed by Chinese soldiers and the room was empty. The door was locked from the outside. The next day, Rinpoche was found outside the room. The door was locked but he managed to get out. Many people saw him, and were talking about it. When one of the guards arrived he said, 'Who has unlocked the door?'

"Later Rinpoche was transferred to another prison by yak with his hands cuffed. He was surrounded by guards and officers, all armed with rifles, and as he was riding his cuffs came unlocked. Each time they handcuffed him, the cuffs came off.

"That night, they stopped and put up a tent. The guards gathered wood for the fire, but the wood was no good and it was impossible to make the fire. 'Lama,' they called, 'we've heard about your great powers. We dare you to make this wood burn.' The guards gave him the wood and an ax and went inside their tent. When they came out a short while later, the wood was burning brightly.

"The next day, when they reached the prison, Rinpoche was put into a room with eight prisoners, including two other lamas. He told the lamas that there was no use for him to be alive anymore and that he would be leaving this life. 'If you die,' the other two told him, 'we will follow you.' That day, all three of them died.

"The other prisoners in the room didn't tell the guards. But three days later, the guards found out. When they found him he was sitting in an upright position. The guard kicked his body, and pulled out the mattress, but the body didn't move at all. It was as if he were floating in the air.

"The guards took the body down to a nearby river and threw him in. The body floated on the water in a sitting position and wouldn't sink. For a week after, there was a rainbow on the spot where he sat. Later there was a thunderstorm, at a time of year when there usually are none. A lama in another area saw the storm and said, 'Gyalsay Rinpoche has passed away.' All this has happened," Tsering said, "while you were away."

When I heard the story, I knew Gyalsay Rinpoche had attained the Rainbow Body. At the time of his true death, his body had dissolved into a state of rainbow light.

The story reminded me that this body is only a fleeting thing. There is something beyond it that endures. Whatever they do to my body, I thought, they cannot touch my essence. It is beyond the realm of physical existence.

Hearing the story, I felt hope.

"Mao is our father." A Chinese woman stood in front of us. Her name was Dolkar. She was one of the leaders of the women's division, and though her face was pretty it was known she couldn't be trusted.

"Repeat after me," she said, her long pale fingers fluttering in the air, "Chairman Mao is our father." I looked to see if a guard was watching, then spit on the ground. Tsering nudged my arm and gave me a sideways glance that meant, *Be careful!* Prisoners around me were moving their lips, but many were silent. I spit again, and looked defiantly at Dolkar.

"Mao Tse-tung is the greatest leader in the world," she continued. "Repeat after me."

"What does she know of greatness," I muttered to Tsering. I closed my eyes and imagined the face of His Holiness.

"Today Chairman Mao is encouraging honesty," Dolkar said, her voice filled with honey. "He wants each of you to express your doubts about the Communist Party and your criticisms of conditions in prison. If you confess," she said, "your treatment will be lenient."

When we returned to our cell we heard rumors that outside the prison young Chinese soldiers were running wild in the streets, wantonly destroying our religious statues and burning our sacred texts wherever they found them. The young soldiers were in a frenzy and couldn't be stopped, they even turned against their senior officers. That was the beginning of the Cultural Revolution. The year was 1966.

For the next few months, an officer gave us continual lectures. "Chairman Mao is eliminating the enemies of the Communist Party," he said. "You must eliminate your own backward thoughts." He announced new rules.

"It is forbidden to speak in Tibetan. It is forbidden to wear Tibetan clothing. It is forbidden to practice Tibetan customs. It is forbidden to hold old thoughts."

His words echoed the new Chinese policy of abandoning "The Four Olds": Culture, Customs, Habits, Thoughts.

The guards were ordered to go through the prison, collecting anything that was seen as Tibetan. They took clothing, shoes, quilts, even wooden bowls, and for days they piled them in the yard and lit them on fire.

The same thing was going on all over Tibet. For weeks smoke filled the air. We later heard that in Lhasa, the sacred texts had been taken out of the great monasteries of Sera, Ganden, and Drepung and burned. Those three great monasteries were built more than five hundred years ago by the great Lama Tsonkhapa; some of the texts that were burned were even older. Seeing the smoke rise up from the direction of Sera was more painful to me than being beaten. *"Blessed Dorjee Phurba,"* I prayed to my protector deity, *"come to the help of the teachings."*

During this time the struggle sessions increased. One of the prisoners had seen me read *Sheja,* the Tibetan magazine that had been smuggled into the prison, and reported me to Dolkar. I was accused of having "empty hope," hopes that the Dalai Lama would return to Tibet and Tibet would once again be free. I was also accused of not being a hard worker, not being an ideal prisoner, not criticizing other prisoners.

One day, before leaving for work, Tsering whispered that the guards had been told I had something Tibetan on my body. "They say it is a sacred amulet," she whispered, "and if it is found, you will be accused of holding on to 'blind beliefs.' You had better be careful."

After she passed by, I clutched at a seam in my clothing that ran between my legs, feeling for the small lump. It is still there, I thought with relief. It was a special turquoise bead that had been given to me by Terthong Sogyal Rinpoche, and I'd sewn it into the lining of my clothes. Rinpoche had taken it out of his treasury and given it to me when I was young, and I'd carried it with me ever since. I managed to hide it on my body whenever I was searched. I couldn't imagine who had seen the bead and reported me, and I was desperate to hide it. I didn't want the precious stone to get into the hands of the Chinese.

The morning was still dark, making it easier to move without being noticed. I got up and straightened my uniform, as if getting ready for work. I opened the door to my cell and looked down the hallway. It was empty, though I could hear footsteps on the walk coming in my direction.

I tiptoed quietly through the door and down the hall to the room with the toilet. Inside, the room was dark and damp. I reached along the wall for the wooden box that hung above the toilet hole. Behind the box was a space two fingers wide, and halfway up where it attached, a small ledge.

I looked around to see if anyone was nearby. I heard nothing, except for the sound of rain on the pavement outside. I bent over the hole, as if to urinate, and removed my stone. Bringing it close to my eyes, I could barely see its turquoise color in the dim light. The stone was shiny and smooth from years of my touching and holding it.

The day he gave the relic to me, Sogyal Rinpoche held it between his thumb and first finger. Rubbing the stone slowly, he reached over and handed it to me. I can still remember the way it felt in my hand. Warm. Almost alive.

In the dark, I put the stone against my cheek. It was still warm from my hand. Then quickly, without looking again, I put it on the ledge.

When the guard came to my room that night to get me, she was smiling. She looked smug as if she was about to catch me. She took me down the hall to a room where another guard held me down. She felt over my clothing. She felt over my body. She put her cold hand between my legs. A streak of pain shot up inside me. She could find nothing. She pushed back my head and put her hand in my mouth. I almost vomited. She boxed my ears.

When she took me back to my room, she was scowling. She seemed disappointed that she hadn't found me guilty of "blind belief" and had no good reason for torture.

They never found the stone, but neither did I. When I went back it was gone.

The days passed on into years without much notice. Every day after work we had "study sessions" to read Mao's "Little Red Book." We were shown films of Mao inspecting the troops. At least once a week there were special sessions of confessions and criticisms. The struggle sessions continued, though not as bad as in Chamdo. What was your crime? Have you improved? Have you given up empty hopes? Have you reformed? I was often singled out. Occasionally I received blows, but nothing like the beatings I'd received in Silthog Thang. "We are only helping you," Dolkar said smiling. "We are helping you to better yourself."

Every time soldiers marched up the path and instructed us to fall into line for a meeting, I trembled inside, never knowing if my name would be called. I always wondered, will I be killed? At the end of the meeting when nothing had happened, I relaxed until the next time I saw the soldiers.

But there was not even a single day when my mind was at ease. All the prisoners were like that.

~

One day toward the end of 1970, I came upon a woman outside the toilet. It was a late autumn day and the sun was filtered through a haze in the air. The light on the woman's face fell in such a way that all its marks stood out: wrinkles and scars on her forehead and cheeks. When she smiled, I could see she had no teeth.

As I reached her, she bent toward me. "Where are you from?" she whispered. "What is your name?"

"I am Pachen, a Gonjowa from Kham. And you?" I replied.

"I am Kundeling Kunsang." Hearing her name, I immediately bowed my head.

I had heard that Kundeling Kunsang had recently arrived in Drapchi, but because of the way we were restricted this was the first time I'd seen her. Everyone in prison knew of her. She was revered for organizing a large women's demonstration in Lhasa several days before the Dalai Lama fled to India, and admired for her bravery in standing up to the Chinese.

I looked at her face, still swollen and bruised. Who would have thought she came from one of the great aristocratic families of Lhasa? With her short-cropped hair and ragged Chinese clothes, she looked like a beggar.

"Buddha's blessings for all you've done," I said, bringing my hands together briefly in a gesture of respect. "You've given us hope."

She merely waved her hand. "We give each other hope," she said.

"What is the news?" I said. "Are we going to get freed? Are we going to die here?"

"No! No!" she said, taking my hands. "Don't talk like that." An expression of determination came into her face. "You are young. His Holiness is in India. Tibet will regain its independence some day. There are still good things happening, and people who are working for the cause of Tibet."

She looked into my eyes. Her face was disfigured, but her eyes were still clear and strong. Though it lasted only a moment, her look gave me hope.

"Never give up strength of mind!" she whispered. Squeezing my hand, she disappeared down the corridor.

From then on, we ran into each other often. Sometimes we spoke a few words outside the toilet. "Ah, Pachen!" she often said. "You and I are the same. We refuse to be broken."

At the hospital, waiting for treatment, we took turns bringing food for each other when no one was looking. "Here," she said one day, "I was able to get you some meat." And she gave me two small pieces, which I kept for days, taking a bite each night.

Sometimes when I was washing my hair she came up behind me and patted my back, showing her fondness. Though we cared for each other, we were never acquainted in the way that normal friends are. There was no possibility of that in prison.

Because of her fame, she suffered severe restrictions. No one was allowed to talk to her. If the guards ever saw us talking together, they questioned us for days. "What were you two talking about? What were you plotting?" We never answered, and luckily there was nothing they could do.

One day the soldiers came down the path as usual to take us to a meeting in the yard outside. It was an overcast day, raining off and on. I was tired of the meetings and the endless talk of the Communist Party, and I pushed roughly by the guards with my head down as I passed through the door.

We were crowded in front of the stage, and when I heard the officer step onto it, I refused to look up. But when I heard the prisoners being led out, I took a quick glance. There must have been twenty or thirty of them in a row. A wooden board was around each person's neck with writing I couldn't read, and a narrow piece of wood was on the back of some, indicating that they were to be executed. I shook my head in disgust, but I also felt despair.

The officer read their charges aloud, then signaled the prisoners to shout, "Protesters of the revolution must be put to death!" Cell leaders, Tibetans who were favored by the Chinese, led the cries. "Death to the enemies of the revolution!"

"Look!" a woman standing next to me whispered. I followed her eyes to a woman on stage. Her face was covered with fresh bruises, her eyes swollen shut. At the back of her neck was a narrow piece of wood.

"Kunsang!" I almost cried out, but the words turned into a moan in my throat before they came out.

An officer on the stage read names, announcing their crimes, passing verdicts. Death, life imprisonment, an extension of sentence. Kunsang's name was read.

"Kundeling Kunsang. Crime: Counterrevolutionary. Enemy of the Motherland. Reactionary leader. The verdict . . ."

I looked at Kundeling Kunsang. She raised her head.

"Death," the man said, and went on to the next.

Kunsang stood still; her swollen face wore an expression of calm. She didn't flinch when her hands were tied, nor when two soldiers came to drag her across the stage toward the waiting truck. She kept her head lifted, her expression defiant.

I watched as two young Chinese took either arm and pulled her across the platform. As she was being loaded into the truck, one of the soldiers kicked her, then pushed her inside. I watched as the truck backed up, then drove forward. Mud spattered up from its tires as it drove away. I heard the rattle of its metal doors, and the whir of its engine, getting dimmer and dimmer.

"Now that the criminals have left," the officer continued without changing his tone, "it is time for awards." He read off a list of names of those who had cooperated with the Chinese. They were awarded toothpaste and towels. Some received the "Little Red Book." Some who were particularly helpful were released early.

"Execution is for those who don't make positive change," the officer said impassionately. "Those who can't change, you see what will happen. Those who do"—he turned and gestured to the prisoners on the stage—"will receive an award."

That night, prisoners working at the brick kiln of Sera Monastery told us what they had seen that day. "Prisoners knelt at the edge of pits and were shot from behind. The force of the shots thrust them into the pits, and before their breath had stopped, the pits were filled in."

Later, as I was lying in bed unable to sleep, a face appeared before me in the dark. It was Padmasambhava. *"I am never far from those with faith . . ."* he said. *"My children will always be protected by my compassion."*

"Precious Guru Rinpoche," I said softly, *"guide Kunsang Kundeling on the path of clear light."*

Several nights later I had a dream. I saw a man standing at the door of a big assembly hall. He was making a statue of Mao out of porcelain or stiff earth. The statue was in an upright position, the hair combed back, true to life. Looking closely, I saw cracks at the base. *It is getting ready to crumble,* I thought, and woke up.

The next day I was stacking bricks with a woman who was a friend of sorts. She was considered a good person, from a respected family, and I had come to trust her. We often exchanged words when no one was looking, or during bathroom breaks.

"How are you?" she asked under her breath when we had stopped for a pause. "Have you had any dreams?"

I was surprised that she asked, as I'd had the one about Mao the night before. I told her the dream. "Maybe it means something will happen soon," I said. "Maybe the time for Mao to die is drawing near."

Several nights later at a "meeting," one of the leaders turned to me. "Pachen," she said, "we hear that you are predicting the death of Chairman Mao. This is a major offense. You will be punished."

A guard stepped forward and hit me across the face, three sharp blows. But the pain I felt was from betrayal, not beating. I had trusted, and the trust was broken.

Later I saw my friend carrying Mao's red book tied to her waist. "Aren't you ashamed of what you are doing?" I asked her. But I realized she was helpless, and must have reported me to the guards under great pressure, or in hopes of an early release. I didn't speak badly of her to others, but after that, I watched what I said.

One night as I was sitting on my bed saying my prayers in my mind, a guard appeared at the door. It was unusual to see them so late, and it made me apprehensive. She stood at the door and pointed. "Zayul Bumo, Drolma, Kalsang Dolma, Pachen—come!"

I quickly finished my prayer: *"I go to the Buddha for refuge, I go to the Dharma for refuge, I go to the Sangha for refuge,"* and pulled my jacket around me.

The night was cold and the sky was covered with stars. Two other guards climbed into the truck behind us and shut the door, and the truck started up. Are we being transferred? I wondered. Are we being taken to be killed? I felt compassion for all who'd died, and at the same time frightened at what might be about to happen. I wished the Americans would fly in and kill us all. That might help, I thought; if everyone was killed, then this nightmare would end.

Soon after we left, the truck stopped and we were taken into a large room. I could see from the nurses who passed by that it was some sort of hospital. We were given a sweet-tasting liquid to drink, and told to wait.

I noticed a crack on the wall, curling over and up like a conch shell. *"Like the right-turning shell of good fortune,"* Gonlha's voice came into my head, *"let blessings radiate."* For a moment I saw his large form walking back and forth in front of me, the long sleeves of his robe swinging against his knees. I heard his deep bellyful laugh.

"Gonlha," I whispered.

*   *   *

In front of me a Chinese doctor was standing with a tray full of bottles. He told me to hold out my arm and took a tube with a long, pointed needle out of his pocket. He wound a cloth around my arm, above my elbow. "Stay still," he said, and with a jab pushed the needle into a vein in the crook of my arm. A red liquid rushed into the tube, filling up one, two, three bottles. My blood, I thought without feeling, as if watching water pouring out of a pot. After many bottles had been filled, we were led back to the truck and driven back to our cell. Only then could we talk.

"What was that?" I asked.

"I have heard they take blood from the prisoners," Drolma said, "to give to their soldiers."

That night I couldn't sleep. Over and over I saw blood flowing out of me like a river, into the arm of a Chinese. I saw it spreading in his veins, running through his body. The thought of fluid from my body in somebody else haunted me. It made me feel like a traitor.

After several weeks, some of the women weakened. The loss of their blood was more than their bodies could handle.

One night I again dreamed of Chairman Mao. This time the dream was vivid and detailed.

I am in a huge prayer hall, filled with people. The ceiling is high and there is an unusual light coming in through the windows at the top. "Mao will be coming down the stairs," the woman next to me whispers.

"I must see what he looks like," I reply, and look up. All of us look toward the sky. We wait for some time, then we see him lowering down. A man is carrying his head, another his feet. When I look more closely, I see that he's dead and his corpse is a woman. His hair is red and dangling down, his body is black. He must have been a fearful witch in his previous life to look like that, I thought.

When he reaches the floor he is carried out through the big door at the end of the hall. The men who are carrying him announce, "This is Mao Tse-tung."

"It is the grace of Buddha," I say, "that he's dead."

*   *   *

At the time I wondered if my dream would come true, but said nothing about it. A few years later he died.

With his death, the Cultural Revolution ended and conditions gradually eased, but by then the Chinese had destroyed more than six thousand monasteries. Many of the great lamas were killed or imprisoned. Those not imprisoned were forced to go against their vows and marry. In the name of "Reform Through Labor" they were made to do the most degrading and menial tasks.

Under the movement "Destroy the Four Olds," they tried to eradicate our entire culture. But worst of all, the Chinese stole our priceless holy images from monasteries and homes, images collected over a thousand years. What they didn't take, they destroyed. Our holy Mani stones were used to pave roads, our holy scriptures were burned. The amount they burned was so great that for days the sky over Tibet was covered with smoke.

Shortly after Mao's death in 1976 I was told I was being transferred from Drapchi to join the fifth division of Tramo Dzong in Kongpo Nyingtri. Several days before I was to leave, a guard came to my cell with a letter. Unaccustomed to getting mail, I tucked it under my bedroll. All day I thought about it, wondering what might be inside. At night, before going to sleep, I pulled the envelope out.

The night was cold, the rain had just begun falling. I could hear drops tapping on the tin roof overhead. I sat cross-legged on my bed, gathering my bedding around me, and turned the envelope over in my hand. It was streaked with dirt, the ink partly smeared so I couldn't recognize the handwriting.

When I tore open the envelope I saw it was written by an acquaintance in Tramo Dzong.

> "Your mother fell ill and has died," the letter said. "In her last days, she was cared for by an old man who had once been a monk. He was exceptionally kind. She saved three

bags of barley, and a red shirt which is wrapped in a plastic bag, to give to you when you are released. She had wanted to give them to you herself. I have them here for safekeeping."

I read the letter over again to be sure I'd understood what was written. I read it several more times, then folded it and put it in a small bag by my bed. I sat staring at the wall, unable to grasp what I'd read. No matter how I tried, I couldn't connect the words on the page to my mother.

My mother took my breasts in her hand and kissed them. "I am going for some butter," she whispered. "It will keep you strong." I watched her small ragged shape disappear down the road.

Mama! I called.

Early one morning, a guard arrived at the door of our cell and escorted me to an open military truck. I had a little bag to carry on my back with two patched shirts, a very torn bedroll, and a small bag of tsampa that had been given to me by one of the friendlier guards.

The back of the truck was open, and I could see all around me. Beyond the low prison buildings, the hills in the distance were just becoming visible as the fog burned away. Their curving shapes stood out along the horizon, more like spirits than anything solid. The air was warm, and for the first time in many years, it smelled new.

As we drove over Birikuri bridge I caught a glimpse of the Potala. Its golden roof was lit by the sun. As I looked, it seemed as if the light were coming from inside, as if the sacred statues and teachings were emitting their own radiance, as if the spirit of His Holiness was still there. *"May the Buddha Dharma shine like the sun,"* I prayed. *"May His Holiness soon return to his rightful place on the golden throne. May there be a free Tibet."*

I was filled with a longing to remain in Lhasa. Even if I died, I thought, it would be better to be there, for my body would be taken to the funeral place at Sera Monastery.

The truck turned left and drove in the direction of Kongpo. The sweetness of the air on my face, the sadness at leaving Lhasa, the dread of returning to Kongpo with my mother not there, mixed into an indistinguishable lump of feeling. But there was nothing I could do.

Nyingtri was not far from Chundo Dzong, and as we drew near, the landscape began to look familiar. The fields with their new crops just beginning to rise up out of the soil reminded me of the fields I had cleared. Each brambly bush reminded me of my mother, and seeing them brought the words of the letter alive. Landscape enlivens memory, in a way that words on a page cannot. I began to cry.

The guard accompanying me thought I was crying from fear. "It's not so bad here," he said in an effort to comfort me. "This is a work camp. You will find it is much better than those you've been in before."

I was assigned to the women's division and issued a tin mug and a sack, which I later stuffed with straw to use as a mattress. There were several women I'd seen at a distance in other prisons, but no one I knew well.

On the third day I was sent with others in the fifth division to water the fields. Because of several famines, the Chinese were trying to cultivate land that was undeveloped. We were sent to dig up human waste from the toilet to use as manure. One woman was sent into the toilet tank to shovel the waste into a can, another lifted the can up. We formed a long line so the can could be passed from one hand to another, and the woman at the end poured it into the field. In the process of passing it, waste from the can often splashed on us.

The area in Kongpo was known for its rain, and though it rained night and day after I arrived, we never stopped working. We had nothing except the clothes on our backs, which were worn from heavy use. In the first few months I was there I often went to sleep in damp clothes.

Weakened by work in the fields, by the damp and the cold, I had difficulty keeping up my strength. The years without adequate food left me always hungry. My stomach, finding little to satisfy it, fed on itself. I felt it gnawing me bit by bit. My energy drained as if leaking through a hole at my center.

In order to gain strength and keep warm, I began to try a tantric practice called tum-mo. I'd heard stories of yogis dressed in thin white robes able to sit in the snow for days. This was the test of the power of tum-mo. I knew it took years of practice to reach a yogi's level of control, but I thought if I tried I might raise a small bit of heat.

At night, when I was left to myself, I lay in bed imagining my body filled with white light. With each breath I took, the light came in through my nose and moved to the center of my body, behind my navel. At the center, I imagined a small spark of a flame rising up through my stomach, my heart, my throat, to the crown of my head. It burned through all that was impure and weakening me, and radiated up through the crown of my head in a stream of nectar and light. As this sweet, pure light poured over my body, I imagined it washing away all my suffering and weakness, filling me with happiness.

Every night for several months I practiced like this. After some time, I began to feel stronger.

After several years, my division was sent to work in a forest miles from the prison. We had to leave before dawn and cross several hills and valleys to get there. As we neared the site, I noticed the hills were bare, the forests were gone. Trunks of trees had been stripped of their branches and lay strewn on the ground. Prisoners were already working at the site, chopping down trees. We were given axes and told to begin cutting branches off the smaller trees.

I took the ax in my hands and approached a small birch. In the morning light its rounded pale-green leaves fluttered in the breeze like hundreds of small wings. The sun filtering down through its branches reminded me of the forests near Gyalsay Rinpoche's monastery.

Shindruk is still wet from the crossing. In the cool air, steam rises up from his belly, filling my head with a pungent horse smell. It mixes with the fragrance of pine trees.

Above me the ancient trees stretch up toward the sky. Light from the sun drifts down through the branches. In places it catches the needles and turns them to silver, on the ground beneath it makes lace patterns of light. The wind makes a deep rushing sound as it blows through. They are ancient deities, living presences; I feel blessed to sit in their shade.

A wind started up and the branches of the birch began to sway, as if dancing. Leaves rustled like hundreds of silver moths in its gusts. I tightened my grip on the ax. *Om Mani Peme Hum,* I whispered under my breath as I approached. Forgive me, tree. I began to strike at the lowest branch. Chips of wood flew off. With each blow a tremble ran up the tree. With each blow I felt I was cutting my own arms and legs.

"The earth is a living creature," Gyalsay Rinpoche once said, *"you must treat it with reverence. All life is sacred."*

With each branch that fell, I asked its forgiveness.

Conditions continued to ease after the death of Mao, and in 1979 we heard that His Holiness was being allowed to send the first of three fact-finding delegations to Tibet to evaluate the changes that had taken place in the country since his departure twenty years before. The first delegation, which included his younger brother, Lobsang Samten, entered Amdo, then went on to Lhasa. On their way to Kham they were to come through Nyingtri, where our prison was.

Word spread through the prison like wildfire. "Lobsang Samten is coming," people whispered to each other. "In Amdo, it is said that thousands of Tibetans mobbed the delegation. In Lhasa the same." "They are here to deliver us from our torment," others reported. "They are coming our way." "It is the dawning of a new day."

The night I heard they were coming, I sat down to write them a letter. *"Keep working toward the independence of Tibet,"* I wrote. *"We who have suffered greatly support you. No matter how much we are tortured we never lose hope. Like the cuckoo waiting on the branch of a tree, we wait patiently for His Holiness's return."*

I gave the letter to the daughter of a prisoner who had come to visit him. She later said she was able to give it to them, but I never heard back. The delegation was only in Nyingtri for two days.

None of the prisoners were allowed to see them on their way through. We were gathered together into one area because the Chinese were suspicious that some of us might try to escape.

But one elderly monk, who lived in a small house on the edge of an apple field, saw them passing by. "There were three good-looking people among them," he said. "They looked very carefully and took photos of everything they saw." This was the only news we had.

Six months later two more delegations arrived from India. One was led by Jetsun Pema, the Dalai Lama's younger sister. A few days before they arrived in Nyingtri, we heard that the delegation would stay overnight and would be attending a performance of children's folk dancing that the Chinese were putting on in their honor at the camp.

One of the prisoners, a woman named Surkhang Dolkar, was notified that Jetsun Pema had asked especially to see her in order to deliver a letter from Dolkar's daughter, who was living in Switzerland. "Take off your dirty clothes," an officer told her. "Put on these clean ones and wash your face. We are taking you to meet the delegation."

Four of us decided to try to disguise ourselves and follow her. "Perhaps we will be able to meet Jetsun Pema-la," we said to each other. "We will tell her everything the Chinese have done."

That evening, we dressed in Chinese clothes one of the prisoners had been able to get. We wore straw hats and put on scarves to hide our faces. The door to our room wasn't locked, and we were able to go out without being seen, as many of the guards were attending the performance.

It was the middle of summer and the night was hot. The straw hat collected heat, and my brow began to get damp. We ran from one building to the next, stopping to hide in the shadows. Perspiration ran down my face. As I went to wipe it from my eyes, I noticed my hands were trembling. "It is worth it if we're caught," I thought. "I owe it to His Holiness to try."

Once a guard came toward us, and we lowered our heads and walked on as if nothing was wrong. He passed without a second look. The moon was full and cast shadows around us. A post looked like a soldier, the end of a building like a guard with a rifle pointed toward us. My heart was pounding, but I didn't stop.

When we reached the center of the camp, a crowd had formed around the auditorium. The building was already full and there were many people around the outside. We pushed our way through, but were stopped by the crush of the crowd before we could get in.

I was able to look through a small window. At the front of the auditorium I could just barely make out two women, sitting facing the stage. One of them had a chupa with an apron. I took that to be Jetsun Pema. The sight of her chupa and the thought that she might be His Holiness's sister brought tears to my eyes. *Om Mani Peme Hum,* I prayed, over and over.

I recognized several guards in the crowd. "There's no point in staying any longer," one of my companions whispered. "If they see us, it won't be good for us." She tugged at my sleeve and turned; with a heavy heart I followed. I wished I'd been able to feel Jetsun Pema-la's hand, it would have brought me that much closer to His Holiness.

The visit of the delegations from India had a tremendous effect in raising the hopes and morale of Tibetans, both inside and outside of prison. For weeks we heard news from other areas. Everyone felt their visits were a sign that independence was coming.

As a result of the visit and the international exposure it gained, the Chinese introduced small measures of liberalization. The old and infirm were released, the young and able-bodied who they could use were kept. As a small concession to the delegation, they allowed many of the prisoners home visits. I sent messages to the authorities repeatedly saying I had not seen my home for twenty years.

I was finally given permission to leave for two months. "Here are three hundred yuan," an officer said, "be back in two months."

10
Returning

I reached Chamdo in the late afternoon. The city had changed in the twenty years since I'd been there: There were high concrete buildings and many Chinese; the streets were crowded with trucks and carts, everywhere people sold wares at the side of the road; bodies of animals, stripped of their skin, hung on poles. Piles of turnips, cabbage, tomatoes, potatoes lay on blankets. Bags of grain, blocks of tea spread out on boxes. After so little food for so many years, I was overwhelmed at the sight. I'd seen nothing for so many years.

At the edge of the market, I recognized a woman who had been a friend of my family's. "Tashi Delek," I said running up to her, desperately hoping she'd recognize me. "Do you remember me? I'm Ashe Pachen."

The woman stepped back to look at me and her mouth opened in surprise. She threw her arms around me. "Your hair is so long," she said, "I can't believe my eyes!" She took my hand and, to my relief, she insisted I stay with her. I stayed several days, but the feeling of being alone outside prison was so disorienting that the first few days I was reluctant to venture out of her house.

After several days I felt an urge to visit the gorge behind the monastery where I'd first been imprisoned, the gorge where bodies of all the dead prisoners had been dumped.

It was late in the afternoon when I got there. Clouds lay on the horizon, and for moments the sun disappeared behind them. It broke through just before setting and cast a pale silver light over the ground. The tips of the grasses stood out like thousands of tiny flares, and I could hear the sound of doves calling each other in the distance.

I looked at the rocky cleft running between the monastery and the buildings beyond. There were still pieces of bone and skulls scattered in between the rocks. Seeing them, the memory of my years in Chamdo came flooding back.

I was reminded of the illusory nature of all worldly things, the impermanence of all we hold dear. Our loved ones and our wealth last only a fleeting moment. They disappear like lightning in the sky, like dewdrops on grass. The only changeless and steadfast truths one can hold on to are the teachings of Buddha.

I stood for an hour, watching the light dim on the rocks and the cracks below me. I thought of Dekyong. Her words flowed through my mind. *"I'm afraid of their torture . . . but I'm not afraid of death."*

I thought of the others who had died. I prayed, *"May all the unfortunate beings who died here be led on the path of ultimate freedom, may they attain the field of clear light."*

The next day I went across the river to Silthog Thang, the prison where I'd suffered so much. It was raining lightly, and prisoners were out in the field, clearing it of rocks. From their pitiable state it was obvious they had neither enough to eat or wear, and I stood for a long time watching them work, and wishing there was something I could do.

My mind went back to 1965, when Gyalwa Yungdrung was bound and dragged through the same spot. I could still hear his voice shout, "May His Holiness live for ten thousand years!"

It was in the prisons of Chamdo that my feet were bound for over a year, in the section of Silthog Thang that I was confined in a solitary cell. It was here that I endured struggle sessions so harsh that the ground was black with my hair. It was here that my spirit almost wore down.

Remembering all this, I was overcome with sadness. I thought of my fellow prisoners, and said all the prayers that I knew.

Blessed Lord Buddha, give me the suffering of all sentient beings. I will bear them as my own.

As I made my way toward Gonjo, the countryside seemed different. It was as though the land had lost its happiness. People were in rags, they appeared to be weak, emaciated, ashen. Each had a basket on his back, a broom or spade in his hands, and was driven to work in a drab-colored truck. The meadow on either side of the road was plowed under, and the soil had been readied for crops, but the earth looked barren. The soil was dry, and stretched row after row in long empty lines, as far as the eye could see. I covered my face with a scarf and went quietly on my way.

In Sheng, I was lent a horse by a young man visiting from Lemdha. Out of loyalty to the memory of my father, he offered to ride with me to our village. Along the way we passed a gang of people working on the road, supervised by soldiers. They all had the same ragged clothes, the same shuffled walk.

One of the men called out, "Ashe Pachen!" An old man with a flattened nose and a crooked smile, somehow he recognized me. He dropped his spade and limped toward me. "Ashe Pachen! Ashe Pachen!" Others around him took up the cry, and soon they'd surrounded me. Some held my horse, others tugged at my shoes, my sleeves, the hem of my chupa. Each had his hand outstretched, trying to reach me. All were calling my name. Tears ran down their leathery cheeks. Some were laughing with joy.

"I'm headed toward Lemdha," I called out over the commotion. "I must go, but I'll be back again some day soon."

"Don't lose heart," I whispered to those who were closest. "Remember His Holiness."

The night was still. The half moon, lowering in the western sky, cast a pale light as we rode. No matter where I turned the frost on the ground was shimmering, and at times I felt I was riding on water. Was there no place solid to rest, I wondered, no place to hide? No refuge, away from the unending sorrow? The landscape was drenched. Sorrow earth, sorrow hills, sorrow mountain. Wherever I looked, its hand had left a lingering print.

As I neared my home the feeling got stronger. I stopped on the hill above Lemdha and looked down into the town. The River Marchu, barely visible in the light of the fading moon, wound through the valley, its sound like a far away wind. For a moment I thought I saw women standing in the water, their hands moving, wringing, shaking, slapping clothes in its current. They were laughing and talking, while others were sitting on the rounded rocks at the river's edge. I took a deep breath as memories came over me.

We started down the thin rutted path toward the town. In places the grass on either side seemed taller, but the path itself was as thin as before. We passed several rock formations that were familiar and my heart sped up. I felt excited, sad, and filled with longing, all at once.

Farther down, the land leveled out in a small saddle before dropping more steeply to the river. The place curved in and was surrounded by rocks, as it used to be so many years ago. I remembered the warmth of Llamo's back leaning against mine, and her voice in my ear. *"Free as birds, but how long will it last?"* For a moment I saw her face, her eyes clouding over, and her body slumping to the ground. A sadness came over me, so heavy I felt I'd been hit. *Blessed Guru,* I prayed, *watch over all helpless beings.*

By the time we reached the river, the moon had set. We lit a torch and continued along the river's edge. When we got to the place where the path curved down to the crossing, my heart beat so fast I could barely breathe.

A thin layer of ice lay over the reeds. My horse stepped onto it, and his hooves made a sound like the breaking of glass. Just then my companion tugged at my sleeve and gestured to the other side of the river. There were silhouettes of people moving on the banks, hundreds of tiny fires wavering above ground, the sound of feet on pebbles.

Suddenly I was surrounded by people. "Ashe Pachen!" several cried. "Over here!" "Tashi Delek!" "Greetings!" From everywhere, calls and shouts. Everyone crying so loudly, it was like a roar around me.

"Let her pass!" someone called, but the crowd was so thick I couldn't move. I recognized many by the light of the flares, but was saddened to see how they'd changed. Each face bore some mark of sorrow, either a physical scar or subtler lines of grief. Their expressions of joy couldn't mask the anguish carved onto their faces. The combination was almost too painful to look at. I turned away, but wherever I turned they were in front of me, eyes filled with emotion, tears on their cheeks.

"Ashe Pachen, come to my house." "No, to mine." "To mine." Each pulled at the reins of my horse. As they were arguing over where I should stay, a man pushed through the crowd. It was Sheldu Tulku, the brother of Dorzong Rinpoche, one of my old teachers. He took the reins of my horse in his hand. "What are you doing?" he said to the people who were surrounding me. "Let her pass!" His voice was firm, and recognizing his previous status, people stepped back and let us pass through.

When we reached his house many were waiting for me, others came up behind. They pushed through the doors until the small house was so packed I could barely move.

"Tell us what happened," one called out as soon as I sat down. "Where did you get caught?" "What happened to Ani Rigzin, to your mother, to the elders?" One brought me a cup of tea and a small bowl of tsampa, and I began to talk. I told them my story, they told me theirs, our own suffering, the suffering of others we'd seen. We talked most of the night.

"Alog Rinpoche was suspended from the ceiling of his house," an old man said after I'd finished my story. "There was a heavily smoking plant burning beneath him. The soldiers kept the plant burning until he was almost dead. He suffered in silence."

"Sonam Paldon was the only survivor of the Gozetshang family," an old woman said in a wavering voice. "She had four children and all they had left between them was two adult sheepskin cloaks. The Chinese officials took these away, along with what little tsampa they had left. 'It is for others who are needy,' the official told her. 'You must share what you have. That is part of communal living.' And so they were left without clothing or food."

Their stories continued, one after another.

"Every day, we had to arise early in the morning, before the sun was up, and work until it was so dark we couldn't see," an elderly man said. "They told us the aged, the ill, and the young children were exempt. But I am old and infirm and I needed to eat, I had no choice. They took part of what I earned for a general fund, and though I worked all day, there was little money left."

"If the soldiers saw our mouths moving in prayer, they would condemn us for holding blind beliefs," another said. "If someone was found lighting incense, they were charged with arson and forced to wear tall pointed caps on their heads. They even sent children out in groups to hunt for birds."

Story after story, each wanted to speak.

"In autumn the fields are for the Tibetans, in the spring they are for the Chinese. That is a saying we have," an old man continued. "No matter how hard the people worked, their grain was taken away. I set my field on fire during the harvest, to keep it from going to the Chinese. Afterward, Chinese soldiers arrived fully armed to guard the rest of the fields. So you can see who actually benefited from their collectivization." He spat on the floor in disgust.

"In place of ox and yak, *we* were harnessed to the plow and made to plow without rest. The steel plow was so heavy, it injured my back and made my hands bleed. The work was more than anyone should have to bear," an old woman sobbed. "We treat our animals better than they treated us."

I was overwhelmed by the stories. They have suffered as much as those in prison, I thought. There is no place that hasn't been touched by the hand of the Chinese. Will we ever be free?

As the sky began to lighten outside, most of those crowded inside had gone home. Only Sheldu Tulku, his daughter, my old friend Goser Bumo, and several others were left.

With many gone, I could see the room for the first time. Stripped of all furniture, save the mattresses we were sitting on, it looked barren and cold. The altar, once at the back of the room, was gone. The water bowls and butter lamps, once on top, disappeared. But saddest of all, nowhere in the room was there a picture of His Holiness. A Tibetan home without a picture of His Holiness is not a home. Even worse is the home of a Tulku without one. But not wanting to make Sheldu suffer, I kept my thoughts to myself.

Sheldu Tulku moved to a space cleared beside me. His once rounded figure had thinned almost to bone. The long nails of his fingers were gone, replaced by stubs that were dirty and cracked. But his face, though creased with suffering, still glowed, his eyes even more compassionate than before. I hadn't known him well, but his presence beside me was comforting.

"I received word from Khaley Tulku of your mother's death," he said softly. "He was in Kongpo at the time and heard from the old monk who had cared for her."

I didn't answer immediately; I wasn't sure I wanted to know what had happened. Sheldu Tulku must have read my thoughts. "It wasn't bad," he said. "Would you like to hear?" Reluctantly, I nodded.

He shifted his weight and brought his legs closer together under him. He turned so he was looking into my eyes.

"One day," he began, "your mother sent for an old disrobed monk to visit her. She told him she was not feeling well as she had fallen ill just three days before. But after examining her, the monk could see nothing serious. 'I will not come out of this illness,' she told him, 'but I'm not afraid of death. Long ago, I went to Gyalsay Rinpoche's monastery with my daughter. When I came home, I wasn't able to continue the practice, but later, when my daughter was in prison, I was able to put what I learned to use. Now, I'm not afraid to die.'

"Her only concern," Sheldu Tulku said, "was to see you once again before she died. She wanted to leave you a will, but she had nothing to leave except three bags of barley she'd saved, and a red shirt." When he mentioned the barley, my eyes filled with tears.

He reached over and took my hand. He looked to see if I wanted to hear more. I nodded, and he continued on. "She told the old monk, 'If I die, my body must not be buried in the earth. Take it down to the river and throw it in.' That afternoon when he returned, she was dead. She was sitting in an upright position, her legs crossed beneath her, her left hand just above the navel, her right hand in her lap.

"He kept the body like that for the next three days, careful that no one alert the section leader, and three days later there was still warmth in her heart. The old monk found a man who reared cattle, and another who was kind; neither had committed any sins. He asked them to help him take her body to the river.

"They let the body into the river. Later, the cattleman went to the hills to tend his herd, and looking down spotted a rainbow on the place where her body had sunk.

"'She was a kind-hearted woman,' the monk later said. 'No

matter how mean someone else might be, she did her best to help them.'

"That is what the old monk told Khaley Rinpoche," Tulku said.

We sat together for a long time without speaking, Sheldu Tulku's hand on mine. I heard Khaley Rinpoche's voice. *When our time comes, each of us dies. There is nothing we can do.*"

Tears poured down my cheeks.

From the roof of Tulku's house the whole village was visible, and as the sun got brighter, I went up to it. The first thing that struck me was that all our holy temples and shrines had been destroyed. There used to be four monasteries. Now nothing was standing, only empty walls remained.

Then I looked toward the place where my house had been. Except for the northern portion of the ground floor, the rest was gone. I felt like the poet Milarepa returning to see his home in ruins. It bore no resemblance to what I once knew.

The wind was blowing and a slight mist hung in the air. For a moment I thought I saw Mama at the stove bending over a large pot, loose strands of hair fallen over her face. Her face was lit by the fire, glowing.

Up the darkened stairs, my father was waking from a nap. His features stood out like rocks on a hillside, his face glistened like clay from the earth. "Little Nyu," I heard him call. "Nyuuuuu"; the sound of the wind rose in my ear, and the mist blew on. I am here! I whispered.

When I looked again, only the walls at the north end were there. At that moment it struck me, I was truly alone.

They died before I could give them one good meal. I began to cry.

I stared at the town until the sun rose. I cried until I had no more tears.

Below me, people were beginning to go out, divided into work groups. Some had baskets on their backs, some carried shovels and packs. Many were getting into trucks to be driven to work. Everyone was covered with dust.

The wind picked up and I turned to go. Over its rush in my ears, I could hear Khaley Rinpoche's voice.

"The world is impermanent, like the clouds of autumn. The speed of human lives, like lightning in the sky passing swiftly as a stream down a mountain. Only by clearing your mind can permanent happiness be found. Only by following the path to freedom and liberation will you finally find peace."

For the next few weeks I went from home to home, starting out early in the morning and going until dusk each day. Some days I visited as many as fifty homes. I was worried that my presence would get people in trouble, but they would hear none of my concern. "We've already lived through hell and gone through every possible suffering," they said. "If you will visit, it would please us so much. Whatever happens, we'll have no regrets."

As I visited my neighbors' homes, rich and poor alike, I thought of the Chinese propaganda I'd heard in prison. "The Feudal Lords treat the people like animals," they said. But how is one to explain the open display of affection and loyalty to a chieftain like me? I wondered. Even after so much coercion and so many material incentives, their loyalty hasn't wavered. It heartened me that after years of oppression the people had not lost their faith in the leadership of His Holiness. They remained steadfast as ever in their loyalty to him, and to the cause of a free Tibet.

After having been gone for almost two months, I departed for Nyingtri. I was deeply saddened to leave, but had no other choice; the Chinese were waiting for me to return, and I knew if I didn't, they'd find me. "I'll be back some day," I called as I left.

On my way back I thought of the stories I'd heard. There was not a single family, high or low, rich or poor, who did not have a tale of woe.

There were very few old people left. Two generations, my parents and my own, had almost disappeared. Children who could barely walk when I left to join the resistance were now like old people, their faces covered with wrinkles. People who once had nice homes were living in barns with no windows. Families were living in fear and apprehension, not one complete family left.

I returned to Nyingtri in the late afternoon, two days late. I was searched and scolded. "Your lateness might affect a future leave," the officer said as he checked me in. But I was filled with emotion at having seen my village and friends, and his words didn't bother me.

I noticed that in my absence policies had been relaxed, and that our comings and goings inside the camp were not followed as closely as they had been before. It was rumored that one of the new Chinese leaders had visited Lhasa and had been so shocked at conditions there that he'd returned to China vowing to make sweeping changes.

Whether because of that, or because of the visit of His Holiness's delegations, things had changed and there was a feeling of hope in the air. Perhaps we would soon be released.

Most days, all I thought about was meeting His Holiness. I felt I couldn't die without seeing his face. I thought about him day after day. With my mind so focused I gathered two other friends, and in the darkness of night sneaked through the gates of the camp to make a pilgrimage to a holy lake near Bonri, the sacred mountain in Kongpo. The lake was said to hold visions for those who journeyed to its shore.

Because of the new policies, every Sunday we were freed from work so one Saturday night the three of us had a quick dinner, and after the others were asleep we headed toward the mountain. We walked the entire night under cover of darkness.

We reached a pass near the top of the mountain as the sun was rising and stopped to make tea and burn juniper leaves. We repeated several prayers and recitations, then circled the top of the mountain and walked down toward the lake.

On the path we came across a tree which was gnarled and old. Between the knots on its trunk I saw long strands of moss that were hairy and black. "Those are the hairs of one hundred thousand deities," one of my companions whispered. We tried to reach in with our fingers to pluck some out, but no matter how we tried, our nails weren't long enough to remove one; the hole seemed endless.

It was a clear morning, and as we came over the pass to the lake, the rays of the sun were beginning to strike the rocks on its distant shore. The lake was deep, its water clear and turquoise blue. It was sunk into the mountain like a hole scooped out with a spoon. Though there was a light wind blowing on my back, the lake's surface was still. The air was filled with silence, sky stretching in every direction, the lake radiant blue. The landscape existed so purely and without effort. For a moment I felt totally free.

We prostrated three times when we reached the mouth of the lake. A small cave sat just beyond it, at its edge. Inside, the cave was damp and dripping, the musky smell of an animal, or maybe a deity, close by. Near the back wall was a small body of water, more like a puddle. "They say that the bottom of that little lake touches the ocean," my companion whispered. "It is very deep." I looked, but all I saw was a small pool of water.

We settled down at the mouth of the cave, facing the turquoise lake. We burned juniper incense and prostrated, then sat down staring at the lake to wait. Will I have a chance to see His Holiness before I die? *Guru Rinpoche give me a vision,* I prayed.

The sun moved several hands across the sky, but the lake remained clear and empty of images. After some time the woman sitting closest to me said, "There is a blooming flower coming up from the center of the lake. Do you see it?" I looked, but the lake appeared no different than before. Its turquoise water was smooth and unruffled.

We continued to sit in silence. The sun moved even further toward the opposite shore. Just when I was convinced nothing would happen, I saw something dark rising up from the bottom of the lake. It rose up slowly.

At first all I could see was a curved shape. But as it got closer to the surface, I saw the face of His Holiness. He was young, with his teachers on either side of him. The image was so clear, I even saw his black rimmed glasses. His eyes were filled with light, and his smile kind. He was looking right at me. I gasped at the sight.

In front of him was a man in a khaki uniform, with a huge nose and deep-seated eyes. On his head was a hat with a feather, or a piece of fur; it was hard to see which. As I watched, His Holiness's mouth turned slightly up in a smile. Then his face began to fade and soon the water was clear, as before.

On the way down, I was so filled with happiness I didn't notice the sharp rocks under my feet, barely felt the downward pull on my knees. Halfway down, one of the women stopped. "I think that is the home of Chegya Lama," she said, gesturing to a small house off to one side. "He is a highly realized lama, and though he lives like a simple peasant now, his divinations are known to be accurate."

We went to the door and peered in. A woman came from the back of the room and asked what we wanted. She was a young woman, her hair pulled away from her face, and I noticed that her hands were unusually smooth, as if she'd been spared heavy work. "Come in," she said when we told her we wanted to see the great lama, and she led us into a smaller room. There was a small monk's bed in the corner, and on it Chegya Lama was sitting. At first I thought he was meditating, for his eyes were half open, his lips slightly parted. But when he opened his mouth to speak, I realized his eyes had been damaged and the lids permanently drooped. It was hard to tell his age, for I could see he had suffered. His body was frail, but his voice was strong.

"We are prisoners at Nyingtri," I said. "We have come for a divination."

Hearing that we were prisoners, he sighed, and seemed to relax. He asked how long we each had been imprisoned, then told us about his own misfortune.

"I was tied to the tail of a horse," he began slowly. "The horse was made to run, and I was dragged behind. I was dragged until the horse couldn't run anymore. The skin came off my face, and most of my body." He looked at us through his half-open eyes. "I, too, have suffered." He leaned forward, as if wanting to be sure we heard. "But it is possible to get beyond suffering, to a place of peace."

After he'd finished talking, he lifted his beads. Looking beyond us, he quietly said a prayer. Then, taking the beads between his fingers, he counted them off in pairs until one was left.

"There is no need to worry," he said, looking at me. "You will see His Holiness. I am so certain of it I will bet my neck on it. When you're released, go to Lhasa, not your homeland. Lhasa needs your help."

We returned to prison late that night. I could barely sleep, I was so happy at the favorable signs. It is certain, I thought. Someday soon, I will see His Holiness.

Several weeks later we were released.

It happened so quickly, I couldn't believe it was real. One day we were called into the courtyard outside the auditorium, at the center of the camp. Names were read out. So many came first I was worried mine wouldn't come.

But then I heard it. "Lemdha Pachen." The time has finally come! I thought. I will soon be free.

"What is the year?" I asked a man beside me. "Nineteen eighty-one," he said. "The first month."

I counted backward on my fingers. Twenty-one years.

Time moves slowly, each day endless, then one day without warning it suddenly speeds up. One day captured, the next released, just like that. I felt dizzy at the thought.

"You must each return to your hometowns," the officer announced. "Kham must go to Kham, Amdo to Amdo, Lhasa to Lhasa. Each district in charge will get the appropriate papers. You are to collect them from there."

I struggled to comprehend his words, but all I could think was, I will soon be released!

As people began to move around me, I felt panicked. Where would I go?

My place of collection was Chamdo, but remembering Chegya Lama's advice I felt I should go to Lhasa. "How will I get there?" I wondered out loud. "Tell them a lie," a woman from my room said. "I will help you write a false letter."

"A relative in Lhasa is sick," I told the officer sitting behind the desk. He was a sad-looking man and seemed overworked. "She has written to come and visit before she dies," I said. He scowled and took the false letter from my hand.

I held my breath as he read it. He looked up, studying my face. He hesitated, then opened his mouth as if about to say something, but instead turned back to the letter and read it again. He looked for someone to consult, but all were busy.

Suddenly, as if eager to move on to the next person, he stamped the letter and sent me off with papers to Lhasa, several food passes, and three hundred yuans. "You can visit Lhasa for a short time," he said as an afterthought, "but your papers are being sent to Chamdo."

I was in a daze when I climbed out of the truck in Lhasa.

There were soldiers, trucks, small military cars, police cars crammed into the streets. People were walking in every direction, Tibetan and Chinese. The air was filled with dust and smoke from the trucks, the streets were littered and the noise of motors, of people calling, coughing, spitting was almost deafening.

"Move on!" a soldier shouted at me.

The others from the truck had already disappeared into the crowd and I looked around for someone I recognized. Only strange faces, some slightly familiar, but none that I knew.

The sun was shining brightly overhead. Though cold, a bright glare glinted off the buildings, making it difficult for me to keep my eyes open. I felt dizzy from the noise, the dust, the brightness, and for a moment I had to lean against a post at the side of the road. I looked around, trying to get my bearings. I noticed that most of the shops were Chinese, and I suddenly felt lost. It was as if I were in a foreign city, not in the capital city of Tibet, and I felt angry that Tibetans had been pushed out of the shops, forced to sell their wares by the side of the road.

*   *   *

"Can I help you?" a young Tibetan man asked, noticing that I looked lost. With relief I bowed in greeting. "Can you tell me where the Jokhang Temple is?" I asked. He pointed beyond him and I hurried off in that direction, eager to find other Tibetans. There are bound to be people from Gonjo at Jokhang, I thought. People from all three provinces of Tibet come to circumambulate the greatest temple in Lhasa; I won't be alone for long.

Once I reached the Jokhang gate and saw there were many Tibetans but only a few Chinese, I began to breathe easier. I looked in awe at the temple. The great Jokhang Temple! After so many years I'm finally here! A chill ran down my back.

"Ashe Pachen." A young man came up to me. At first I didn't recognize him. "I am Jampa Tenzin," he said, "from Drapchi prison."

"Jampa Tenzin!" Though I hadn't known him well, at that moment I felt like throwing my arms around him as if he were a member of my family. "You have just been released?" he asked. He must have known by the look of bewilderment on my face that I had just arrived in Lhasa, and he told me I could stay with him until I found someone from Gonjo I knew. I moved into his little room. I was totally on my own, no longer under the authority of the prison, and it took me some time before I felt safe.

I hear footsteps coming down the walk. Clicking on the cement floor. Tat-tat. Tat-tat. I hear a knock on the door.

I woke with a start. In the dim light I saw a Tibetan curtain over the door. Not prison. I sank back with relief.

I am free, I said to myself over and over. I can go anywhere I want.

But it was such a new thought in those early days, I had difficulty really accepting it. Often I looked over my shoulder to see if a guard was nearby. I had difficulty talking freely in a regular voice. I stopped before going out the door, to see if someone was watching. Whenever I saw a Chinese person I ducked into a doorway, or behind a pillar out of sight.

In the first few weeks I went on a pilgrimage to Lho-nas and Tsang-nas. But my real desire was to go to India to see His Holiness.

I visited a lama from Pelbar who was living in Lhasa and told him my wish. "If I can just see His Holiness," I said, "then I can die."

"For the time being, that wouldn't be wise," Pelbar Tulku said, looking at his beads. He told me I should slow down, I had just been released from prison. "If the Chinese catch you trying to leave Tibet," he said, "they will do the worst possible thing. It is wise to delay."

"I have no family, my mother and father are dead. It is important I visit His Holiness."

Pelbar Tulku looked at me with compassion. "I understand," he said, his eyes filled with kindness. "But it is still wise to delay."

Every morning I said prayers on behalf of my mother and father. I included those who had died in prison, and the many more who were still not free. I prayed that all their karmic sins be washed away. I gave thanks for my good fortune.

I went to pay homage to the great monasteries of Sera, Drepung, and Ganden. All had been destroyed, but Ganden suffered the worst. There was nothing left except one small shrine, and I stayed for a week helping to rebuild the monastery. Hundreds of Tibetans were there, volunteering their time. We worked from sunrise to sunset moving earth and stones.

I was saddened to work there. It was as if a great hand had wiped across the monastery, crushing the buildings and breaking the holy statues. Pieces scattered over the ground, limbs, heads, torsos. The gold, silver, and coral, had all been taken to China.

I prayed as I worked throughout the day. *Let Buddha Dharma rise like a radiant sun. Let the teachings of Buddha spread over the entire universe. Let happiness return to Tibet.* I prayed that the work I was doing, stone by stone, would help all those still imprisoned become free.

I longed to devote all my waking hours to my spiritual life, and after I had been in Lhasa for several months, I set off on a year's pilgrimage. It was something I had dreamed of doing for many years. I first went to the monastery of Lhokha, then Shedra, Drolma Lhakhang, and Dhalakhampo.

When I reached Samye Monastery I stayed for eight months in the caves above the monastery. At the time, the outer structure of the main part of Samye was intact, and people were working to rebuild the rest. But the caves and shrines had been damaged, and the curtains to the caves torn down.

The area was especially revered, for it had been the place that Padmasambhava had meditated for many years. There were 108 caves scattered over the mountain, and the same number of springs.

The most sacred cave, that of Padmasambhava, had been filled in by the Chinese and was impossible to enter. During the Cultural Revolution, when the Chinese destroyed the rest of the monasteries that hadn't already been destroyed, the mountain had fallen into disuse. The paths leading up to it were blocked with thick bushes and small trees, making it difficult to reach the caves.

Some time after the end of the revolution, an elderly tulku visited the place and began to clear the paths to make it accessible to others. He searched for the caves and began to dig them out. But the task was slow, and during the time I was there only three caves were in use.

There was one near the top of the mountain named for the protective deity, Tamdrin Druphuk. It was believed that if the person meditating in that cave evoked the deity, he would actually hear the cry of a horse. I'd been told that the horse's voice was heard three times, and its cry reached around the world.

Below Tamdrin Druphuk's cave was a cave named after Martho Rinchen, one of Padmasambhava's great disciples. The cave was distinguished from the rest by an imprint made by Martho Rinchen's teeth as he was extracting "essence" from one of the boulders in the cave.

The third cave was called Metok Phug. I stayed in Tamdrin Druphuk's cave at the top.

Off to the side, quite a distance away, was a fourth cave so shallow it gave little protection to whoever was inside. It had a small red flag to mark its entrance; otherwise it would have been hard to find. At the time I was there, an eighty-four-year-old nun from Amdo lived in the cave. Amdo Jetsun became my teacher. She helped me retrieve many of the teachings that had faded from my mind while in prison.

During those months I existed in a state of abiding calm. No one to make me feel bothered, nothing to fear except the contents of my own mind. Food and drink were brought by those coming to Samye on pilgrimage. In the act of serving, both server and practitioner were blessed.

Later, Amdo Jetsun taught me Chud len, or Essence Extraction, the practice Martho Rinchen had performed many years ago, enabling one to live on the essence of things, a flower, a rock, a stick. She taught me to exist on a spoonful of finely ground rock boiled in water, twice a day. During those days my mind was unusually clear.

Each day, two hours before daybreak, I arose. I said my prayers and recitations and then observed two special practices: one in which I spontaneously dissolved my body and mind into radiant light, and one in which I destroyed self-grasping. In the afternoon I read texts given me by Amdo Jetsun and tried to stay focused on my practice. In the evening I said additional prayers and went to sleep shortly after sunset.

Staying to myself in this way, I was able to achieve a supreme focus of mind. I found that the focus created a lightness and expanse inside me. The more I stayed focused on meditation and prayer, the calmer and clearer I became. I realized that wherever I was, whether meditating or out in the world, if I maintained a strong focus on what I was doing, that same state of calm would continue. I didn't have to be dependent on anyone, I would be able to look after myself. It is the scattering of energy that makes one weak and dependent on others.

"What we call demons are not material individuals," Amdo Jetsun said. "A demon is anything which hinders us in our achievement of liberation. Consequently even kind and loving friends may become demons, as far as liberation is concerned. But there is no greater demon than ego clinging. All the demons will rear their ugly heads as long as one has not severed this clinging to ego."

We were sitting on the ledge outside my cave. It had rained the night before and the ground was still damp. A patch of moss at the side still held drops of water in its furry tendrils. It looked like a miniature forest with small moons caught in the branches of trees.

"Clinging must be cut," Amdo Jetsun said, "like this." She reached over and flicked the water off one of the tiny shoots.

"One of the best ways of cutting through is the Chod practice," she continued. "It involves making an offering of your body to demons and deities. You must be willing to give up all you have, even your body, in order to benefit all sentient beings. This," she said with emphasis, "is the perfection of generosity."

"Imagine Dorjee Phagmo before you. In her right hand is a hooked knife. With it she peels off your skin, and spreads it out, putting the rest of your body on top. The skin is the golden ground, the blood and lymph are lakes of sweet scented water. Fingers and toes form the mountains around the edge, the trunk is the mountain at its center. The four limbs are the four continents. The head is the residence of the gods. The eyes form the sun and the moon. The heart is the wish-fulfilling jewel."

Amdo Jetsun leaned toward me, trying to gauge my reaction to what she said. One of her eyes was milky white as if covered with frost. The other was black. I tried to keep my eyes steady, and returned her gaze.

"Deities and demons will feast on the ambrosia of your body and be satisfied," she said, seeming pleased at my concentration. "All living beings will benefit, and in the process you will sever your attachment to everything physical, and eliminate all mental impurities."

She looked at me, and suddenly stood up. "Continue your practice," she said, and turning, she walked unsteadily down the steep path toward her cave.

One day when she was in a talkative mood, Amdo Jetsun told me about the first time she practiced Chod in a graveyard, the preferred place to do the practice. She had been involved in practice and meditation since she was a young girl, but when her family decided to get her a husband, she ran away from home and never returned. She went on a pilgrimage to all the sacred places of Tibet and lived in the caves of sacred mountains. At that time she met a teacher who told her the time had come for her to perform Chod in the grounds of the dead. She was scared, but her teacher kept stressing its importance, and finally she agreed.

"One day I saddled my horse," Amdo Jetsun said, settling back to recount the story of her first experience in the charnel grounds, the grounds of the dead. "I went to a town which had a big cemetery. By the time I got there it was already late evening. Fear started to grip me as I realized I would be all alone.

"I built a small wall to protect me from the wind that was starting to blow, then sat behind the stones and began to perform a Chod visualization. I got to the middle of the practice and heard a dog barking in the distance. As the barking grew closer, it began to distract me, for I was worried I might be attacked. But I didn't want to anger the spirits by leaving the Chod unfinished, and so I continued.

"The dog was almost upon me, I could hear his bark only a short distance away. I picked up my ritual drum and beat it; to my surprise the dog ran away.

"When I finished the practice, I realized it had been a test. If I had lost myself to fear and run away in the middle of the Chod, I would have failed the test. From that, I learned to control my fear and hold my ground. I was never afraid again."

When she finished talking it was the late afternoon, and clouds had covered the sun. I was already chilled from the damp air, but her story chilled me more.

"Someday soon," she said as she rose to leave, "I will take you to do Chod in a place of the dead."

That night I couldn't sleep.

The ground stretches out in front of me. It is pale, like the color of bone. Ahead, I see a great ravine carved into the earth and hear otherworldly moans. Like the sound of wind, like the cry of an animal in pain. It gets louder. I am pulled, by a force I can't stop, toward its edge. Below there are bodies writhing in pain, some with their skin torn off, some with no heads, some pure bone. I try to hold on to a

rock at the edge, but it slips through my fingers. I fall slowly down.
A hand reaches toward me. The crying gets louder.

All day, my body was constricted in fear. I sat down to meditate and immediately broke into a sweat. At times I thought I heard a moan from the back of the cave. The rocks on its walls seemed to waver and twist, and once it looked like an arm reaching out.

I tried to pray, but in the silence I heard footsteps on the walk, coming closer. I tightened my stomach. *Om Mani Peme Hum. Help me cut through the fear in my mind,* I called out.

In time, the noise stopped, and my mind calmed. By then I was determined to go with Amdo Jetsun to a charnal ground. I will cut through my fear, I vowed.

Several months later, Amdo Jetsun and I left the caves and traveled to the cemetery at Sera Monastery. Sera Cemetery was the biggest cemetery in all of Tibet. There was a gigantic rock where corpses were brought, the bones beaten to pieces and left for the vultures. It was believed that no corpse brought to Sera would have its soul reborn in Hell.

Amdo Jetsun pitched a tent near the rock and, just before sunset, we performed a Chod practice, visualizing our bodies being cut and offered to the demons. When it was dark we crawled into the tent. In the distance I heard the voices of people leaving for the day, and nearby, the murmur of a stream.

Amdo Jetsun fell right to sleep. I closed my eyes, but as soon as I did I felt something pull at my feet. I opened my eyes; nothing was there. Each time I closed them I felt the same pull, as if something was trying pull me out of the tent. I moved myself closer to Amdo Jetsun. The warmth of her body calmed me for a moment, but soon the tugging came back. However I turned, I still felt the tug on my feet. *Dorjee Phurba,* I prayed.

As I lay praying, a loud clap of thunder broke overhead. The sky crashed, as if splitting in half, and flashes of light lit the top of the tent. The rain came in torrents, beating down on the walls. I called out, but Amdo Jetsun continued to sleep.

The sound of the stream nearby grew louder; I thought it might soon overflow. I remembered the time at Drapchi during a flood when we had to be evacuated. The same thing is happening again, I thought. We have to escape!

I shook Amdo Jetsun until she woke up. "There is water everywhere," I said. "We have to get out!"

The poles of the tent began to sag. Two came loose and one side of the tent began to flap in the wind. Amdo Jetsun and I crawled out. The rain was pouring down all around us. I trembled uncontrollably from fear and cold.

We began to gather our things. Suddenly Amdo Jetsun stopped. She turned to me. "We must not leave," she said, her clouded eye gleaming in the flashing light as she spoke.

"We will drown," I pleaded.

"Then so be it," she said. "We are not going to leave. Put the poles back in the notches of the tent."

I was shaking with fear, but did as she asked. Beside us, the stream had overflowed and was nearing the tent, but Amdo Jetsun went back inside and lay down. I went in and lay stiffly beside her. After a while the storm subsided, and the waters of the stream went down.

"Fear," Amdo Jetsun said the next morning, "is often an illusion formed by thoughts in our mind. Once you see its illusory nature you will learn that there is nothing to be fearful of. Obstructions may occur, in the form of natural calamities or in the form of thoughts, to distract a person from meditating. It is important not to give in to either."

Later, I realized that Amdo Jetsun had made the right choice. If we had run away, I would not have confronted my fear. Amdo Jetsun used a real life experience to convey her teaching. It made a deep impression. From that time on I never felt fear again in quite the same way.

11
Freedom

The September 27 demonstration of 1987 began as a non-violent protest. In the days before, handmade posters began appearing on the walls of Lhasa.

"We must all be prepared to die for our country," Tashi whispered. "That is what the monks of Drepung say on the declarations they have posted."

We stood in the hallway of a house I was visiting. Tashi spoke rapidly, looking over his shoulder to be sure no one was nearby. He thrust a bundle of papers into my hands. "Distribute these. There is a meeting at Yongdro's house tonight." He turned quickly and left.

That night, six of us gathered in Yongdro's small room to learn more about the demonstration planned by the monks of Drepung Monastery. Tashi gave us the background.

"His Holiness appeared before the United States Congress and asked that Tibet be a zone of peace, free of weapons," Tashi told us. "He asked China to abandon its policy transferring thousands of Chinese to Tibet. He asked that human rights and democratic freedoms in Tibet be respected, that Tibet's natural environment be restored and protected. He asked the Chinese to engage with him in serious discussions about the future of Tibet. He stressed that he was seeking a solution that was in the interest of world peace."

We all raised our hands in solidarity at the news.

"The Chinese response to the Dalai Lama's proposal," Tashi continued, "was to order fifteen thousand people to witness the sentencing of Tibetan dissidents. Eight sentenced to imprisonment, three to death. It is this that the monks of Drepung are protesting."

We were all horrified at the news. "What can we do?" someone whispered urgently.

"We must gather as many people as we can to join the protest," Tashi replied. "We must let the Chinese know that we support His Holiness's proposal." He raised his hand. "Free Tibet!"

"Free Tibet!" we whispered.

"Like a flowing river that won't stop flowing, the will and the determination of the Tibetan people cannot be stopped!"

"Be at Jokhang tomorrow morning," he added as we left.

*   *   *

As the sun was rising early the next day, I went to the Jokhang Temple. The morning was still quiet, and there was nothing to hint at the demonstration two hours later. A few people were out in the streets, a warm breeze blowing from the west, but nothing out of the ordinary. I circumambulated the temple with several others, performed an incense ceremony, then returned to the house I was sharing to recite my prayers. My usual routine; though I noticed while saying my prayers that my heart had sped up.

As I was having a cup of tea before setting out, my bench and the ground beneath my feet began to rumble. "What is it?" I called to my friend who was just getting up. "Are they bombing?" I leaped to my feet and started toward her. The walls of the house seemed to shake, the sound of a great wind in the trees filled the room. We stood holding each other, but in a moment it was still.

"An earthquake," she whispered.

"An omen," I said.

"May His Holiness the Dalai Lama live ten thousand years!" Two hundred people, led by thirty monks from Drepung, marched toward me, shouting and waving handmade Tibetan flags. "Tibet is an independent country," they chanted. "Chinese go home!"

I stepped into the group as they passed, and we went around the Jokhang Temple three times. After that we assembled in front of the temple by a willow tree believed to have been planted by the Chinese consort of Songtsen Gampo, Tibet's seventh-century king.

The leaves of the tree had turned yellow and were beginning to fall. The rising sun lit them in such a way that they looked like tears of gold falling to the ground. It reminded me of the many tears that had been shed all over Tibet. I am here for all who have died, I thought. One day I will see His Holiness. Until then, I will work for Tibet.

"The Dalai Lama is Tibet's true leader. Independence for Tibet!" the crowd continued to shout. We raised our hands in solidarity and set off toward the headquarters of the so-called People's Government of the Tibet Autonomous Region. We had just passed the shops in an area called Darpoling, but had not reached the TAR offices, when we heard the horns of vehicles coming toward us.

Suddenly, Chinese troops were upon us.

In Jeeps, in trucks, on motorbikes. They beat monks at the front of the procession with sticks and the ends of their guns. Soon they were beating everyone, monks and laymen alike. It happened so quickly I didn't have time to think.

In front of me, a young monk broke the pavement with a hammer. "Grab stones," someone cried. We scrambled to gather stones from under the slabs of pavement. A man near me pulled a decorative piece of cloth from a window. He made slingshots, and we took turns hurling stones at the soldiers. A few foreigners joined in, and we threw all the stones we could find.

Not far away, I saw a Chinese policewoman standing against a motorbike. Grabbing a handful of soil I ran up to her. "Free Tibet!" I cried, and threw the soil into her face.

I turned and ran down a side street with several others. At one point I tripped and fell, out of breath and dizzy, but I got up and continued to run. When I got to the home of a friend from Lemdha, they hid me inside.

That night the police went from door to door looking for people who had been in the demonstration. We were just getting ready to go to bed when there was a knock on the door. "It's the police," Tenzin said. He gestured to me. "Go hide." Everyone panicked, not knowing what to do with me; the house had only one room with no place to hide. Tenzin's wife grabbed my hand and pulled me into the toilet.

"Who is here?" we heard a man's voice in the room. "How many live here?"

Tat-tat. A knock on the toilet door.

"Who's inside?" the man called. Tat-tat. He banged on the door and started to open it. We looked at each other in panic. "We have no choice but to go out," I whispered.

A Chinese policeman was at the door, another looking over a list, checking the names of the people in the house.

"Where is your identity card?" he asked me.

"I don't have one." I hoped to look innocent.

"She is a friend who has come from Motogongka," Tenzin interrupted. "She couldn't return because of the commotion in the streets."

Just then five other police came into the room from outside. They saw their colleague questioning me and crowded around.

Om Mani Peme Hum, I said to myself; this is the end.

The one who had been questioning me shrugged to the others. "Take her home tomorrow morning," he said to Tenzin. "We'll check back . . ." his voice faded as they went through the door.

By the grace of Buddha, I thought, they didn't recognize me.

Four days later, on October 1, the monks of Sera circled the Jokhang, chanting proindependence slogans, waving Tibetan flags and demanding that those arrested be released.

"The monks have been arrested," a woman said, putting her head in the door of the house where I was staying. "They were beaten with clubs and rocks and shovels, and taken inside the police station across from Jokhang. Come! A group is forming."

I put on my shoes and ran after her. A huge crowd had assembled at the police station, maybe two or three thousand. They were angry and shouting for the release of the protesters held inside.

"They are beating the monks!" someone shouted. I thought I heard cries coming from inside the building.

The troops began to push in on us.

Several people in the crowd turned over Jeeps and motorcycles that were parked outside the station, then set them on fire.

Suddenly the police station was on fire. "Get the monks out." someone cried. "They are in danger of burning!"

"Stay back!" the police shouted over the noise.

People screamed. Flames shot up inside the station.

"There is a window at the back of the station," I said to a friend. "If we break it the monks can get out." I picked up an iron rod lying on the side of the street and ran to the back of the building. My friend followed.

I struck the boards covering the window ten, fifteen times, but couldn't get through. Two youths came from behind, took the rod, and broke through the wood. Others hurled rocks at the door beside it.

The fire was spreading further into the building. "They'll soon be burned." I cried.

"Everyone stop!" the police shouted. "Anyone who moves will be shot."

A monk inside the building came to the window. His eyes were wild with fear. Flames rose up right at his back. He put his leg through the window, but before he could get out, he was shot.

Seeing his body slump over and fall, I sat down on the ground and cried. It happened so quickly.

The police set a deadline for those demonstrating to turn themselves in. Two weeks later, they cracked down. Areas of Lhasa were sealed off. Houses were raided. Hundreds were taken away. Over a thousand were arrested.

The police had taken photographs from the roof of the station and had pictures of many participants. Those who weren't arrested went into hiding.

I went from house to house, staying with different people. Some I knew, some I didn't. One night I was having dinner with a family from Gonjo when we heard someone at the door. "The police are coming," someone whispered from outside, "they are going door to door."

There was a young girl in the house who lived across the courtyard. "I'll take you home," I said. Taking her hand, my heart pounding, we walked into the yard. The police had already been to her house, and we walked slowly toward it, as if we were mother and child. Step by step, I thought, keep the mind focused on one step, and then the next. Don't let it wander to fear. I heard Amdo Jetsun's voice: *Fear is an illusion, it is important not to give in to it.*

The police were busy inspecting and didn't see us. I was able to walk into her house without being stopped. The family was good and could be trusted. Once again, I escaped arrest.

For the next five months I went from house to house in hiding. During that period, two or three of us at a time got together to meet. We tried to remain as anonymous as possible, for it was important to maintain secrecy. Messages were delivered one to another, word of mouth, never in writing.

We had no way to print posters, so at times five or six people gathered and wrote them by hand. These would be distributed in areas such as Sera, Drepung, and Ganden and pasted on walls at night. I often took eight or nine people with me to post them, and we divided the sites to post them as we sneaked through the streets. At times I even took a chance and posted some during the day.

Foreigners were willing to take out letters we'd written to the United Nations or to the Tibetan Government in Exile. When we wanted to send one out, we went to the Potala and waited until we found a foreigner willing to do it. There were no leaders in an organized way, only Tibetans with dedication, like me.

On March 5, 1988, a third big demonstration took place. In the days leading up to it, I went from house to house trying to alert people and connect with others who were organizing. We had no cars and no telephones, so all the communication had to be conducted on foot.

The Great Prayer Festival of Monlam Chenmo began on March 3. Many monks were reluctant to celebrate the festival, fearing trouble from the Chinese. The Chinese, on the other hand, were eager to prove that they were tolerant of religious freedom, and forced the monks to attend.

"They call it religious freedom!" Tenzin scowled, as we were distributing posters one night. "What kind of freedom is it when monks are ordered to pray?"

The week before Monlam began there were thousands of police and military vehicles practicing maneuvers in front of Jokhang. There were roadblocks throughout the city and military Jeeps patrolling at night.

The first two days of Monlam were quiet. On the third, as monks entered Jokhang Temple carrying a statue of Maitriya, the future Buddha, monks of Ganden Monastery started to shout slogans. "Tibet is an independent country!" "Chinese out of Tibet!"

Soon the crowd was chanting, "Chinese out of Tibet!" At the same time they called for the release of all Tibetan prisoners, including Yulu Rinpoche, a lama arrested for giving a video interview to an Italian journalist in which he expressed support for Tibetan independence.

The crowd had just started around the Jokhang when thousands of armed Chinese soldiers appeared and surrounded them. They began to throw tear gas and dragged monks away, even some who were praying. They threw hand grenades at the Jokhang Temple, the ultimate sacrilege.

The demonstration spread all over Lhasa, and late into the middle of the night we still heard the shots of soldiers firing their guns. In the end, thirty monks died.

"Pachen!" A voice from a stall at the edge of the street. I looked over and saw an old man behind a pile of woolen scarves, someone I spoke to on my way to and from my daily round of Jokhang.

He gestured me over. "I've been watching you," he whispered, "Whenever you pass, there is a Chinese man following. Always the same one." He gestured toward a man who had stopped several stalls down.

I bowed, and walked quickly on.

I stopped at a stall several streets up. Pretending to look at a cabbage, I glanced to the side. The man had stopped two stalls away. He looked down. I quickly walked on.

I took a sharp turn down a narrow alley. I zigzagged in and out of alleys and streets without looking back. My heart was pounding; I was soon out of breath. I ducked into a doorway and looked back. The man was gone.

All the way back to the house where I was staying I looked over my shoulder, but he was nowhere in sight.

The next day, a friend who had been arrested by the Chinese twenty days before came to see me. He had just been released. "The Chinese are talking about you," he said. "They asked about you quite a few times. They are more interested in you than in me. Danger is building. You should leave Lhasa in the next ten days. Leave Tibet altogether. It isn't safe for you here."

I looked in disbelief.

"It's a miracle you haven't been arrested yet," he said. "The Chinese are watching you all the time. It would be crazy to stay beyond ten days."

"I don't want to leave," I said. I finally felt a sense of purpose, helping to speak out for Tibet. I knew Lhasa well, it was easy to participate in the political activities, my contribution would be more effective in Tibet. Besides, I thought, I don't know any other language. How could I possibly survive somewhere else?

But most of all, I didn't want to leave all the sacred places in Tibet. My prilgrimage had been interrupted out of necessity to help defend my country, but I still hoped one day to return to the caves for a life of quiet.

The next day I went to Lama Pelbar for a divination. Again he counted his beads. When he finished, he shook his head. "It is not favorable for you to remain in Tibet." Hearing his words, I knew I had no choice but to leave.

My one consolation: I would finally see His Holiness.

Before leaving Lhasa I went to the Jokhang Temple one last time to pray in front of the sacred image of Buddha. It was late in the afternoon, and the sun had already sunk behind the hills. Though the light inside the temple was dim, the statue of Buddha was surrounded by thousands of butter lamps and shone as if lit by the sun. I touched my head to his feet and offered a clean white scarf. I put a small butter lamp among the others.

For a long time I stood by the Buddha and prayed. I prayed that the minds of all beings be opened to the wisdom of his teachings. I prayed that they gain understanding of the nature of all things, and see the radiance and boundlessness at their core.

For the next few days I made arrangements to leave. It had to be done in total secrecy. I told three friends, but there was no possibility of telling anyone else. I didn't even tell the woman with whom I was staying.

I arranged to ride in a motor car to Mount Kailash, Tibet's most sacred mountain, and from there I planned to go by foot over the mountains down to Nepal, then on to India.

One night I met with my most trusted friend and told her I was leaving that night. "I won't stay long," I said. "Just long enough to have an audience with His Holiness."

I knew she was worried about my ability to make the trip. She was concerned that at my age, fifty-six, and after all I'd endured in prison, it might be difficult to get safely through. "I will write you if anything changes here," she said, trying not to show her concern, "but until then, it is better to stay in India."

"Take this," she said when we'd embraced, and pressed money into my hand. "You may need it." I touched my forehead to hers and I got into the car with three strangers who were going the same way.

We drove by several checkpoints. Twice the police put their head into the car and stared at each of us. I held my breath and looked down. They looked suspiciously at me, but said nothing and waved the car forward.

As the car drove on, I looked out the window at the land rushing past. I thought once again how quickly time passes. I was twenty-five when I gave my life to defend Tibet and preserve our spiritual teachings. I spent the better part of my life in prison. My youth passed without really living, but there was no use feeling regret.

Sometimes I felt such anger for the Chinese. Over a million people killed or dead from starvation. Forests stripped of their trees, precious metals mined from the mountains, animals slaughtered. My life, like so many others, passed in suffering.

His Holiness said that we must not hate the Chinese, that it was the policies of a few, not the people that had caused Tibet harm. He said we must forgive our enemies, and though I trusted his wisdom I found it was not so easy to do. Forgiveness comes from inside the heart, and though my body had been released from prison, my heart wasn't free. Even after my time in the caves, I still struggled with anger.

*　*　*

As we drove across the plains, Mount Kailash came into view. The great mountain rose up from the dusty plains into the sky, like a house of the gods. Clouds hung to either side as if in attendance. The broad rounded peak sparkled like a jewel in the light of the sun. So still, it felt like we were entering a timeless place, approaching the center of the universe.

As we drew closer, I could feel myself growing sadder. I thought that if all the sorrows we had suffered the last thirty years could be put one on top of another, that is how tall they would be. Sorrow as tall as a mountain.

Papa's voice came into my ear. I saw his long hair blowing behind him as he rode, his body flaming into the air. I saw Mama's hand reaching toward me, her head on my breast. I saw Dekyong walking away, a soldier behind her. Sorrow upon sorrow . . .

At Mount Kailash, I joined three others in making a round of the mountain. We started before daybreak and walked until two hours after dark. The path was rugged and steep. We passed pilgrims with aprons tied around their waists, shoes on their hands. Stretching out, standing up, stretching out, they prostrated the whole thirty-six miles.

As I walked, a lightness poured through me, my heart began to open. It was as if a special energy were radiating from the center of the great sacred rock, entering me with each step I took. Remembering that the mountain was said to be the abode of the mother and father of the earth and had the power to answer one's deepest prayers for the world, I prayed as I walked. *"Let all beings be free of suffering, let all beings find peace."*

By the time I got back to the place where we were staying, I was tired and sore. But the spell of the mountain stayed with me. My heart had expanded, and for moments I was filled with forgiveness.

The next day I took a bus to Purang and met a friend who was also escaping to Nepal. We started off on foot, joining a guide who knew the route.

"There will be three police checkpoints between Purang and Nepal," the guide told us as we started out. "We must walk under shelter of darkness. But first we must cross the high pass. That we can do by day."

The day was clear as we started to climb. I had canvas shoes, a jacket over my chupa, and was carrying a bag. I had emptied the bag of most of its contents in Purang, but still it was heavy.

When we reached the snow line, my friend took my bag and put it with his on his back. As he walked, I noticed he was holding his back in a peculiar way, and once when he bent over, I saw there was an open wound on his back. Without telling him I'd noticed, I took my bag back. "I'll feel better if I carry it myself," I said, not wanting to hurt his pride.

The snow got deeper, after a while it was up to our waist. We struggled with each step as if walking through water. We were further slowed by a shortness of breath, for the air was thin. As the sun began to go down, the wind picked up and whipped at the corners of my jacket. It spun up the snow in small icy stars which stung as they hit my face.

I stepped in the holes left by my friend; the next hole in front of me was all I could see. My mind was dull, my body ached. I felt myself fading until all that was left was the sound of my feet crunching through the snow. The words of Amdo Jetsun echoed in my head: "Obstructions may occur . . . it is important not to give in . . . ," and I kept walking.

That night we found cover behind an overhanging rock, and stopped to sleep. My legs below my knees were swollen, as if filled with water. I stayed awake shivering most of the night.

A faint streak of pink appeared on the horizon. I was still dazed from the day before, and at first barely noticed. But when the light became brighter, I sat up to look. The mountains were rippling in pale silver waves as far as I could see, and as the sun rose it turned them from pink to coral to red. At the sight of its beauty my heart turned over and I felt hopeful for the first time since leaving. Not a large hope, just a glimmer; but nonetheless it was there.

Nearby I noticed a small pile of stones with prayer flags dangling from sticks at its top, their faded cloth fluttering in the wind. Seeing them ragged, but still waving, I was overcome.

I stood up and, facing back toward Tibet, called on all gods, protectors, and deities of Tibet not to fail. "Stand firm," I said. "Do everything in your power to help His Holiness return. Help the people of Tibet become freed from oppression."

That morning as we started our descent, I had to be supported by my friend and the guide. My swollen legs trembled so much that when I stood by myself, they could barely hold me. My companion had been temporarily blinded by the glare of the snow the day before and couldn't see, so between the two of us our descent was slow.

"It is not uncommon," our guide said. "I have seen many worse." I knew he was right. I'd heard stories of Tibetans who had fled: Some lost toes and fingers, some lost feet. Many small children suffered such frostbite that they had to be nursed for months after reaching India. "But no matter how great the suffering," he said, "Tibetans keep fleeing."

After a long day of walking we came down into the valley and that night passed a police checkpost. It was dark, and though we couldn't be seen, a dog must have sensed us and started barking. A few moments later we saw torches. The guide and my friend took off. I ran to catch up. "Don't run so fast," I called quietly, "it is dark, we could lose each other." Though they promised to slow down, they were soon far ahead.

The moon was new, but not large enough to light the path, and several times I stumbled into the brush at the side. The path sloped down and I walked swiftly, trying to keep up. As I was crossing a stream I slipped on one of the rocks and fell into the water. The others weren't aware I had fallen, and when I got up I could no longer hear them.

A cloud passed over the sky and the path became darker. I looked ahead, but in the darkness I couldn't tell which direction they'd gone. Looking behind, I saw torches and heard the bark of a dog coming closer. I thought I heard someone walking on rocks not far away, and I started running. I ran away from the sound of the water into the woods. Once in the woods, it was even darker.

For a while it seemed I was off the path; the brush was high and there were trees everywhere. The trees rose above me, their twisting bare branches like coiling snakes, their trunks like spirits. At times I sensed someone watching me from behind a tree, and turning my head so as not to be recognized, I hurried on. The ground was uneven and several times I fell, and rose only to stumble and fall again.

I went up a steep hill, then down into a valley. For a while I thought I was walking through a field, for I felt stubbled grasses beneath my feet. But after a time, the ground evened out into a path. It was narrow, like a path for sheep or goats, and hoping it would lead me in the direction the others had gone I followed it.

Whenever I stopped to question where I was or whether I'd find my companions, I became frightened and lost my will to go on. But remembering my practices with Amdo Jetsun, I focused my mind on the path. I found that if I focused on one step at a time, my mind didn't have time to stray. In that way I was able to continue.

Walking on, I passed the light of a fire off to the side. My friends! I thought, and rushed toward it. But as I got closer, I saw more than two people huddled in front of the flames. They are villagers, I decided, but who knew what they would do? Lowering my head and bending my knees, I started to creep by.

Just then, I tripped over a rock and fell, crashing into a bush at the side of the road. Voices called out from the fire. My heart started racing, and I panicked. Oh no! I thought, they will find me. A torch was lit and I saw its flame flickering above the ground, coming in my direction. I flattened myself against the ground, and laid still, trying not to breathe. *Dorjee Phurba keep them away.*

My heart was pounding so loudly I was afraid someone would hear. I pressed my chest into the ground, trying to muffle the sound. Closer, closer the torch came until it was not more than an arm's length away. Then it passed. Before I had time to catch my breath, I saw the torch coming back. I held my breath—*Om Mani Peme Hum*—and tried not to move. The man with the torch passed again without seeing me and went back to the fire.

For the next four days I wandered, sometimes on the path, sometimes through meadows, fields, forests. Several times I made divinations with my Mani beads, counting them two by two, to determine which way to go. At one point I had to make a wide circle around a police checkpoint I saw in the distance. But whatever obstacles came, I continued to walk.

On the fourth day I came to a small village. I stopped at a house on its edge and asked where I was. I learned from the old woman who came to the door that it was the village of my guide. "He has been here with another," she said. "They left to look for their companion, but said they'd be back."

Ten days after we separated, they returned. I threw my arms around them when I saw them. "Lord Buddha has brought us back together!" I said. "From now on I have a feeling we'll be safe."

For the next twenty-five days we traveled; over steep passes, through lush valleys, and finally down into Nepal. At times it seemed like we would always be walking, at times I longed to stop. Just when I thought I could go no farther, we reached a small clearing nestled at the base of the mountains. "We're here!" the guide said, gesturing to the tiny green field.

"At last!" I whispered.

I looked up at the high mountains encircling us, and bowed.

The next day a speck appeared in the distance, silhouetted against the sky like a bird. It flew toward us, passing low over one of the nearby mountains. "It's the plane," my friend said, "coming to get us."

As I watched, the plane got larger. I could hear its engine, at first like the sound of an insect, then the familiar humming I had heard so many times in Shothalhosum. I looked up at the peaks soaring above, at the mountains all around us; how will it land? But before I had time to think more, the plane turned and dove abruptly down. Moments later it landed a few paces away in the tiny field.

A door opened and the pilot put his head out. He saw the three of us, and gestured for us to come. I had seen planes in the air, but never one on the ground and it was much bigger than I'd expected, like a huge gray dragonfly perched in the field. As I approached I felt a wave of apprehension sweep over me. Would it be able to carry all of us to safety? Would we be caught?

Reluctantly, I climbed in through its opening and sat down in a seat by a small window. I barely took notice of the plane's interior, I was so worried that the noise of the engine might alert the Chinese. I'd heard a story about a woman from Kham who was arrested as she was waiting for her plane to depart. The engines had already started, and a soldier climbed into the cabin and carried her off.

"Don't worry," my friend said. "We're safe." But it wasn't until the plane finally lifted into the air that I sank back in my seat. I was so relieved to have escaped, I didn't give a thought to the fact we were moving high above the ground. The ride was more comfortable than a bus, was all I could think.

But as I began to calm down, I looked out the small window at my side. "What is that?" I asked my companion, pointing to a small circle of blue in the distance. "A lake," he said. "A lake?" I said, shaking my head in disbelief. "It looks like a puddle."

For a long time I sat with my nose pressed to the glass. I couldn't believe what I saw beneath. "A miniature world!" I whispered.

After a while, I sat back and closed my eyes. For the rest of the trip I prayed. I thanked Lord Buddha for his mercy in letting us escape. I prayed that all those less fortunate than I be helped as I had been helped.

The bus clung to the side of the road. I closed my eyes and held tightly on to my Mani beads. Ahead, I could see that the road narrowed down to a path. "We're almost there," my friend called from the seat behind. The road was filled with so many different people. Women in bright-colored cloth wrapped around their bodies, bundles of straw on their heads. Men with trousers and shirts. Men and women in chupas turning prayer wheels in their hands. Children skipping hand in hand, small packs on their backs. Foreigners with unruly hair, bright-colored jackets.

But my heart turned over when I saw the long maroon robes of monks and nuns. I couldn't get over how many there were. They were walking together so openly, some talking, some saying their prayers out loud. It had been a long time since I'd seen such a sight, and I began to cry.

As we rounded a bend in the road my friend called out, "Dharamsala!" and pointed to some buildings ahead. We drove up a short hill and arrived in front of a cluster of shops. Everywhere I looked there were Tibetans. There were trucks, cars, people on motor bikes, dogs, cows, horns, voices, barking, all mixed together. But not one Chinese.

I got off the bus. Beyond me, the hill dropped down and a bright green valley spread out. Behind, the jagged white teeth of mountains rose up. The air was cold and clear. Each face that I looked at seemed to be smiling. I felt my eyes fill with tears again and had to look down. The home of His Holiness.

"Ani Pachen," a man's voice called through the door. He was standing outside the small room I was staying in, near His Holiness's monastery in Dharamsala.

"Ani Pachen." He knocked on its wooden frame. A young man with a pressed white shirt and trousers stood with a note in his hand. "I have come to take you to His Holiness," he said.

Ama, Ama, I thought, I haven't had time to prepare, and ran through the room gathering my things. I pulled a white silk scarf out of my bag, and a small coral bead.

Outside, the sun had just risen, and the air was fresh, like spring. I hurried after the young man down the road toward Thekchen Choling Temple. We walked past guards with deep-seated eyes and plumed hats, up a driveway to a building surrounded by gardens. At the top of a flight of stairs, a man in a gray chupa greeted us. It was His Holiness's personal secretary.

He took me to a room overlooking a rose garden. It was filled with windows and light. Tibetan benches ran around its edge, a cream-colored carpet with coral and green on the floor, sacred objects of gold, silver, and turquoise in cases on the wall. A man appeared with a cup of tea. "Only a few more minutes," he said.

It had all happened so quickly I felt stunned, and as I took the cup I could see my hands were trembling. The tea was fragrant and sweet, like nectar. As its warm liquid flowed down my throat, I felt as though my body were being purified and my mind began to clear. I sat for some time and looked out at the garden filled with flowers: pink, red, yellow, coral. The sun was filtering through the trees at its edge, touching the tips of the petals with light.

Pink, blue, yellow petals fall on my shoulders, into my lap. They catch the light as they fall. Anya sprinkles flowers over my head until I am covered. "The little Ashe Pachen is safe," she sings.

His Holiness's secretary returned. I smoothed the folds of my chupa, picked up my bag, and followed him. He escorted me down a walk into a large room hung with bright Thangka. As I crossed the entrance to the room, I began to prostrate. But before I could complete three full prostrations, I heard a deep voice: "Get up, get up."

I looked up and saw His Holiness standing in front of me not more than an arm's length away. He was taller than I imagined and his face was very big. He was smiling, and as I rose he reached out to help me up.

When his hands touched mine, I started to cry. I thrust my silk scarf and coral bead into his hands. I tried to speak but the words caught in my throat. Every time I opened my mouth, I broke into tears. His Holiness stood quietly, and after a time, I calmed.

I began to speak, and then couldn't stop. I talked for over an hour, telling him as much as I could. I said whatever came into my mind, not wanting to leave anything out. He asked me questions in great detail: Where was I from, where had I been imprisoned, and I was able to relate to him all that I'd seen and experienced.

At times I saw tears in his eyes as I spoke. At times I was overcome with emotion and had to stop speaking. At times the sorrow of what was happening to Tibetans was so strong that we both cried together.

After what must have been an hour and a half, a man came to get me. His Holiness took a white silk scarf and put it around my neck. He looked into my eyes. Gently taking my hands in his, he bowed his head toward mine.

It was as if a radiant sun had shone through the darkness. All the years I'd suffered had not been in vain. I was finally free.

 Epilogue

In 1989, the Year of the Water Horse, I settled in Dharam-sala. For the last seven years I have taken part in activities on behalf of Tibet. I've made friends and received people from around the world. But mostly, I've done my spiritual practice.

Every day I rise early. After changing the water in the bowls on the altar above my bed, I walk down the road to the sacred path that surrounds His Holiness's temple. There I join others making the daily round.

"What kept you going?" a foreign woman asked me one day. "How did you survive your time in prison?"

I didn't have to think, I knew the answer so well. "The wish to see His Holiness," I said immediately.

"And were there other things?"

"My lamas taught that praying day and night with steadfast and unquestioning faith, one will be rewarded with blessings. Every night, every day, I prayed to the Three Jewels to guide me, I prayed to Dorjee Phurba to protect me. I prayed to take on the suffering of others. Let me suffer so they won't have to, I prayed.

"And . . . I am stubborn. I didn't want to give the Chinese the satisfaction of seeing me fail."

When I finished speaking, she was silent, and though she didn't say anything more, I believe she understood.

The next day we sat down together, and once again I told my story.

"My name is Lemdha Pachen, chieftainess of Lemdha tribe of Gonjo. I was born in 1933, the Female Water-Bird Year. My childhood lama taught that nothing in this world is permanent, but at that time I only heard words. Now, I have seen them come true.

"I used to have wealth, cattle, horses, nomads, and servants. I had a precious family who loved me and gave me respect. But those times have passed. Now I'm alone.

"My generation is slowly dying. Your generation is coming up.

But your generation will age and die, and another will be born after them. That is how it is. Even the reincarnated lamas go through the same cycle.

"My father was known for his fierceness, courage, and cleverness. There was nobody in Gonjo who could challenge him or bring him defeat. But now, he is just a story of the past. When I die the Phomda Tsang line will end.

"As for me, the story will go like this: She led her people to fight against the Chinese. She was present at the protests in Lhasa. She worked to save the ancient spiritual teachings. When I die, just my story will be left."

Author's Note

My involvement in this project came about by chance. In a casual conversation over lunch, a friend told me about a remarkable nun living near the Dalai Lama in India. The next thing I knew I was standing in front of Ani Pachen in her room in Dharamsala.

Many small steps led to that initial meeting. In 1996 Richard Gere was in Dharamsala, and during a conversation with Tashi Tsering of the Amnye Machen Institute, he learned of Ani Pachen. Tashi, who had been compiling Ani Pachen's story, suggested her life as an inspiring subject for a book.

At the time, Danny and Tara Goleman, Sharon Salzberg, and Sunanda Marcus were also in Dharamsala, attending an international Buddhist Teachers' retreat with the Dalai Lama. When they heard how Ani-la had maintained her dignity and spiritual belief in the face of overwhelming obstacles, they resolved to help make the book a reality. A day after returning home, Sharon spoke to a mutual friend, the friend spoke to me, and soon Sharon and I were talking about the possibility of a book. Five months later, Sharon and Sunanda helped me to travel to Dharamsala to meet Ani Pachen.

I arrived at the end of the monsoon season, during a downpour. Lhasang Tsering from Amnye Machen met me and guided me through the flooded streets of Dharamsala to Ani Pachen's room. As I entered the room, Ani-la rose from her bed to greet me. She was slighter than I'd expected, more elfin, her body dwarfed by a long brown chupa, her rosy cheeks and dark hair highlighted by a bright yellow silk blouse. After having gazed at her picture on my wall for months, the sight of her walking toward me in person felt like a miracle. When she reached me, she took my hands in hers and bowed, then raised her head. Her eyes were so radiant and filled with compassion that I suddenly found myself in tears. There was an instant and mutual connection; she seemed as excited as I to be finally meeting.

Every morning for the next two months I climbed the steep hill from my guest house to meet with her in her room at the Gaden Choeling Nunnery. Her room was small, damp, crowded; two low beds lined the walls, plastic bags of belongings hung from hooks, a trunk at the end of one bed was piled high with blankets, duffels, colorful quilts, and in the closet there was a two-burner camping stove topped with various pots and pans.

Each day, after she had prepared butter tea and flat bread, we sat facing each other, cross-legged, on her bed, and with the help of Tenzin Sherab, a young Tibetan woman, Ani-la told me her life story. There were days when the rain beat so loudly we had to shout at each other in order to be heard over the din on the metal roof overhead, and as we talked we often sat wrapped in blankets to ward off the chill. But no matter what the weather, Ani-la was so eager to tell me the details of her story that she continued for hours.

When she spoke, her hands were always in motion, her body moving to the flow of words and to accentuate points. Her face was expressive, even playful, her voice, though insistent, was lilting and clear. Our rapport was so natural that I often forgot our lives had been dramatically different. But once or twice, when recounting particularly painful episodes, Ani-la burst into tears, and at those times I was reminded that the person sitting beside me had lost her entire family, had spent twenty-one years in prison, and had been severely tortured. The fact that she survived that terrible period is a testament to her courage and her faith.

I want to stress that the result of these joint efforts is a story *based* on Ani Pachen's life. It is as much narrative as strict biography. Since it was written with a Western audience in mind, I have "Westernized" traditional greetings and ways of speech, added elements to make it more accessible, and taken liberties to include outside stories and details where necessary in order to give a fuller picture of the tragedy that has occurred in Tibet. For those familiar with Tibetan Buddhism, I want to add that I have tried to remain true to the essence of the teachings rather than portray specific practices. Any inaccuracies are due to this overall approach, not to Ani Pachen's recollection or rendering of her story.

I have drawn background information and stories from many sources, among them: *In Exile from the Land of Snows,* by John Avedon; *Tears of Blood,* by Mary Craig; *Warrior of Tibet,* by Jamyang Norbu; *A History of Modern Tibet,* by Melvyn Goldstein; *Tibetan Nation,* by Warren Smith; *Penthouse of the Gods,* by Theos Bernard;

Resistance and Reform in Tibet, edited Robert Barnett, Shirin Akiner; *Four Rivers, Six Ranges,* by Gompo Tashi Andrutsang; *Tibet and Its History,* by H. E. Richardson; *My Land and My People* and *Freedom in Exile,* by the Dalai Lama; *Secret Tibet,* by Fosco Maraini; *Red Star Over Tibet,* by Dawa Norbu; *Saltmen of Tibet,* a film by Ulrike Koch.

Spiritual teachings, including those ascribed to Khaley Rinpoche and Gyalsay Rinpoche, have been taken from a wide variety of sources: the Dalai Lama, Sogyal Rinpoche, Dilgo Khyentse, Lama Thubten Zopa Rinpoche, Shantideva, Lama Tarchen, Tulku Thondup, Gomo Tulku, Lama Thubten Yeshe, Lama Surya Das, *Tibetan Buddhism,* by John Powers, and *The Tibetan Book of the Dead.*

Ani Pachen and I hope that this book serves as a portrait of the Tibetan people and the depth of their spiritual wisdom. It is our belief that the resilience of the Tibetan people and the wisdom of their teachings can serve as a compassionate model for the rest of the world.

Acknowledgments

Many people have contributed to the completion of this book. It would never have come into being without the initial group in Dharamsala—Richard Gere, Dan and Tara Goleman, Sharon Salzberg, and Sunanda Marcus. They have each, in their own way, provided encouragement, loving support, and invaluable assistance in making its publication a reality. In particular, Richard Gere not only conceived of the idea for the book but generously agreed to write its preface, Dan Goleman gave special help connecting us to an agent, and Sharon Salzberg stayed with the project each step of the way, lending her wisdom and great heart to every aspect, and earning the title "Mother of the Project."

His Holiness the Dalai Lama expressed belief in the importance of Ani-la's story from the beginning. It is typical of his generous spirit that no matter how busy he was, he met with Ani Pachen from time to time to ask how the book was progressing. We are honored to have his foreword and I want to thank him for his ongoing support.

Ngari Rinpoche and Rinchen Khando welcomed me into their guesthouse in Dharamsala and provided my initial education. Ngari Rinpoche arrived daily with books for me to read. He spent hours explaining the roots of the current Tibetan situation and subtle aspects of the Buddhist teachings, and was invaluable in helping me to understand what had happened in Tibet. Rinchen Khando spoke to me about her childhood in Kham, providing details of family life before the Chinese invasion. Their generosity and openheartedness was my first introduction to the spontaneous warmth of the Tibetan people.

In all my ensuing contacts with Tibetans, that same generosity of spirit has shone through. Lhasang Tsering and Tashi Tsering of the Amnye Machen Institute were tireless in their efforts to help. As my initial contacts in Dharamsala, they arranged for housing, provided me with translations of Ani Pachen's story, donated the services of one of their employees, Tensing Sherab, to translate. Though Lhasang was immersed in the work of the institute, which is dedicated to preserving and furthering Tibetan culture and facilitating its exchange with the West, he was never too busy to answer questions or provide help. Tashi Tsering generously offered to go over the manuscript for factual accuracy, and at a moment's notice he put his other work aside to read it through. The book would never have come into being without them.

The interviews that were started on my first trip to Dharamsala continued in California a year and a half later when Ani Pachen came to California to stay with me for six months. It was her first trip on a large airplane and her first trip outside India and Tibet into the "modern" world with all its conveniences and confusions. Pema Chogkha, Dhonyu and Samten Chinkarlaprang, and Nyaljor Samten helped to make her trip a success. Dhonyu made a valiant effort to teach me Tibetan before my first trip, and was in Dharamsala on a visit when I returned to escort Ani back to the United States. I arrived with an impacted tooth, and he effortlessly took over all the logistics of our departure. Pema began the transcribing/translating process after my first trip to India, explaining customs I didn't understand and giving generously of her time. She welcomed Ani-la and me with the traditional white scarves when we arrived at the San Francisco airport, helping Ani-la to feel comfortable in such a foreign city. When we reached my home in Berkeley, Samten, Dhonyu's wife and owner of the wonderful Cafe Tibet in Berkeley, greeted us with freshly cooked Tibetan meals to help ease Ani-la's transition.

Nyaljor, Samten's cousin, was indispensable as my assistant, researcher, translator, transcriber. His patience, his quiet intelligence, his humor, and his generosity with time were remarkable. He has been the single most important person in helping me write the book.

Rinchen Dharlo of the Tibet Fund graciously agreed to represent Ani Pachen's interests. Tenzin Geyche, Ven. Lhakdor La, Jampal Chosing, and Lobsang Jimpa, each were of great help in facilitating His Holiness's foreword. In addition, two of Ani-la's relatives, Palljor Phupatsang and Tsering Topgyal Phupatsang, thoughtfully taped reminiscences of life before the invasion and during the early resistance movement.

If Sharon is the "Mother of the Project," Chris Desser is its "God-mother." She was the "mutual friend" who provided the initial spark, connecting me to Sharon. I relied heavily on her wisdom at the beginning, and later she helped make Ani-la's trip a reality. My longtime friend James Howard also contributed generously to Ani-la's trip, as did Lee Swenson and Vijaya Nagarajan of the Institute for the Study of Natural and Cultural Resources, and many other friends. Before my initial trip to Dharamsala, Canyon Sam, Ellen Bruno, and Barbara Green provided invaluable insights into Tibet which helped inform my writing.

In the writing process, I was given sanctuary by my friends at Occidental Arts and Ecology, and by Roger and Suzanne Adams. Their warmth and generosity of spirit created perfect writing environments.

The book would not have reached its present shape without the insightful guidance of Shoshona Alexander. Her loving support for every aspect of the project has been unending. My good friend Kathleen Fraser responded to the first few chapters with her usual poetic sensibility. Nina Wise provided laserlike critique.

Many friends listened patiently to my thoughts and read over the manuscript, offering suggestions. My writing group—Susan Griffin, Bokara Legendre, Nina Wise, Don Johnson, Pamela Westfall-Bochte—gave encouragement and help with early chapters. In addition, Susan Griffin, who was part of the project since the beginning, offered indispensable advice throughout. As always, I relied on her mastery and refined sensibility. Bo Legendre sustained me during the writing process with daily phone calls and responded to the manuscript with astute observations. Her unfailing loyalty, her great heart, her deep-ranging mind, have been my mainstays. Barbara Sonnenburg and Ron Greenberg generously took time out of their busy schedules, giving their usual insightful comments, which deepened the manuscript. My brother Rick Matteson, and my friend Ruth Zaporah, each played important parts in crafting the title. In addition, Ruth's unerring instinct for what is "real" and "alive" challenged me to make needed changes in early chapters. Barbara Green's long association with Tibet and Tibetan Buddhism was helpful in the chapter containing Buddhist teachings, her sensitive eye caught subtle misrepresentations and righted them. Judy Oliver, as usual one of my most valued critics, gave encouragement and advice on design from the beginning. Jeff Masson gave tirelessly of himself as always, and I turned to him frequently for advice. Linda Blachmun and Pat and Dan Ellsberg were careful readers and supportive friends. Henry Meyer and Benina Gould gave thoughful assistance in the research phase. In early drafts, my brother Sumner Matteson gave valuable comments, along with Barbara Gates, Bill Broder, and Arden Jones. Later, my brothers Rick and Sumner poured tirelessly over the manuscript catching many small errors. Throughout the project, Jennifer Greenfield was an indispensable presence, generously giving advice and helping to facilitate preface, foreword and publicity, despite the fact she was in the midst of coordinating the Dalai Lama's visit to New York (in itself a full time job).

In addition to help with the manuscript, each friend spent time with Ani-la when she was in California, bringing her gifts of welcome and taking her with them on outings. Mary Hitchcock was especially kind to her, and Ani-la always looked forward to their time together. Mary was equally kind to me and whenever I needed help she was there; without her I would never have finished the book.

During her visit, Ani-la felt a particular bond with my mother and continually asked me to call "Ama-la Jonie" to see how she was doing. She delighted in meeting my "Aunt Mimi" Burke, whom she immediately recognized as a remarkable woman. She was fascinated by my close friendship with my ex-husband David Donnelley, whose unique enthusiasm and generous heart touched her as it does me. But her favorites were my children, Elliott and Owen. To her delight, they demonstrated the "Lindy Hop," taught her to play Frisbee, and kept her laughing. They do the same for me; their indomitable spirit is a constant inspiration; their loving support has sustained me.

My agent Eileen Cope championed the book from the beginning. Her enthusiasm was contagious and resulted in international contracts, allowing Ani's story to be told around the world. My editor, Nancy Cooperman Su, was everybody's dream editor: supportive, calm, patient throughout, and wise in her editorial choices. She never imposed her point of view, but instead guided me to a clearer understanding of my own. I also want to thank Deborah Baker who masterfully took over as editor in the final phase of the book, Nicki Britton and Jodie Hayes, the book's publicists for their patience and their skillful help with publication, and all others at Kodansha whose hard work helped bring this book to fruition.

Lastly, I want to thank Ani Pachen herself for sharing her story and opening her life to me. Though the interview process was long and sometimes difficult, she never faltered in her desire to have me understand what she and other Tibetans had been through. Her courageous spirit has been a model of strength and inspiration for me; knowing her has changed my life. I believe, as she so often said, "It is karma that we met."